THUNDER ON BATAAN

The First American Tank Battles of World War II

DONALD L. CALDWELL

STACKPOLE
BOOKS
Guilford, Connecticut

STACKPOLE BOOKS

Published by Stackpole Books
An imprint of The Rowman & Littlefield Publishing Group, Inc.
4501 Forbes Blvd., Ste. 200
Lanham, MD 20706
www.rowman.com

Distributed by NATIONAL BOOK NETWORK
800-462-6420

Copyright © 2019 Donald L. Caldwell
Maps created by Leslie Sawyer

British Library Cataloguing in Publication Information available

Library of Congress Cataloging-in-Publication Data available

ISBN 978-0-8117-3771-5 (hardcover)
ISBN 978-0-8117-6741-5 (e-book)

♾™ The paper used in this publication meets the minimum requirements of American National Standard for Information Sciences—Permanence of Paper for Printed Library Materials, ANSI/NISO Z39.48-1992.

Printed in the United States of America

CONTENTS

MAP SYMBOLS

Military Units - Identification

Armored Command.. ▭

Cavalry, Horse... ◫

Cavalry, Mechanized.. ◪

Infantry.. ⊠

Size Symbols

Platoon... •••

Company.. I

Battalion.. II

Regiment or Group... III

Division... XX

EXAMPLE

The letter or number to the left of the symbol indicates the unit description; that to the right, the designation of the parent unit to which it belongs.

Company C, 192nd Tank Battalion... C▭192

Preface

Six American towns sent many of their young men off to an unknown destination when their National Guard tank companies were federalized in the winter of 1940–41. In the autumn of 1941 the men and their new M3 light tanks were sent to the Philippines, where they formed the fighting components of the newly activated Provisional Tank Group. The Japanese attacked the Philippines on December 8 and landed in force on December 22. The tankers fought bravely and skillfully but were surrendered with the Bataan defenders four months after the initial attack. The six towns thereby lost a greater percentage of their male population in a single day of war than any other U.S. city. The men had to endure three and a half years of torture and abuse until Allied victory released the starving survivors, reduced in numbers by half, to return to their celebrating hometowns in an America that was otherwise indifferent to them. This is the story of these men and these towns.

CHAPTER I

The Heartland Mobilizes

IN THE LATE 1930S THE UNITED STATES WAS STRUGGLING TO RECOVER from the Great Depression. Principal occupations of its 130 million people were in manufacturing; steel, copper, and coal extraction and processing; and agriculture (a quarter of the population lived on farms). The agricultural economy had bottomed out in the early 1930s and had been hit again in the mid-1930s by the Dust Bowl. Franklin D. Roosevelt's New Deal programs had helped industry and the unemployed. The military, spurred by events in Europe, increased dramatically in size. There were 334,473 men on active duty in the military in 1939; 458,365 in 1940, and 1,801,101 in 1941. The sudden surge came from the Selective Service Act (the draft) in 1940 and the federalization of state National Guard units. The states either commanded or shared infantry divisions; eighteen of these divisions had a tank company headquartered in a single town or small city in the state. Tank companies represented armor, the newest and most technical arm of the U.S. Army's ground forces, and were popular among small-town politicians and youth. Six of these companies found themselves in the Philippine Islands in December 1941 and were taken prisoner by the Japanese the next April. This is the story of the men of these six companies.

JANESVILLE, WISCONSIN

White settlers began moving into the fertile Rock River valley in southern Wisconsin in 1830, as soon as the Indian Removal Act authorized the expulsion of the native inhabitants. The town of Janesville was established in 1835 and soon became the county seat of Rock County. The first dam was built on the Rock River in 1844, and waterpower led to the establishment of flour and lumber mills along the river. The area grew quickly and prospered. The abolitionist movement and the new Republican Party were popular during the 1850s. During the Civil War Rock County sent more men to the army than most Wisconsin counties; many went directly into the Iron Brigade of the West, one of the best units in the Grand Army of the Republic.

After the Civil War several foundries and farm implement companies were established in Janesville, followed by several manufacturing firms of international significance. George Parker founded the Parker Pen Company in 1892 to manufacture fountain pens of his design and built the largest writing instrument plant in the world, with more than 2,000 employees in Janesville. The pens were sold worldwide and were especially popular in Japan, later becoming favored loot for Japanese soldiers in the Philippines. Parker pens were used both by General Eisenhower to sign the armistice with Germany and by General MacArthur to end the war in the Pacific. By the 1980s the company had fallen victim to cheap imported ballpoint pens and disappeared in a leveraged buyout.

Another major manufacturing facility in Janesville was a General Motors (GM) plant. When the market for its original product, tractors, dwindled, the plant switched to light trucks and automobiles, and operated from 1919 until 2008.

In World War I Janesville's contribution to U.S. military forces was strong. Its National Guard infantry company served with distinction. This disbanded after the armistice, but by the summer of 1919 former Guard officers and Janesville businessmen were expressing interest in reestablishing the unit or something similar. The officer they elected to head the organizational effort was a former captain in the now-defunct U.S. Army Tank Corps, and the "something similar" he came up with was a tank company, which received federal recognition on May 5, 1920, as Tank Company I of the Wisconsin National Guard. This was the first unit of its kind in the entire National Guard, which Janesville always considered a special distinction. It was in fact established before the infantry division to which it would be attached; a few years later it would become the 32nd Tank Company of the re-formed 32nd Division, Wisconsin's major National Guard unit.

The company received its first tanks in March 1921, four six-ton M1917s, American versions of the French World War I Renault FT. It received four more two years later. Of the eight tanks, six were armed with machine guns, one had a 37mm cannon, and one was an unarmed signals tank. Additional vehicles included a traveling machine shop, a kitchen trailer, a water truck trailer, two tank carriers, an ambulance, and several utility trucks. The tanks and most of the support vehicles were put into dead storage in 1934, and the company served as a transportation unit until the first tanks of post–World War I design were received in the late 1930s.

Duties were light and typical of the National Guard between the wars. Drill was held every Monday night and comprised close-order drill followed by technical training. On Wednesdays additional training was conducted for noncommissioned officers. Several buildings were used until an attractive armory was built downtown and dedicated in 1929. Summer camp lasted two weeks and was usually held with the entire 32nd Division at a nearby army base in late July or early August. Guard training became more serious as war neared and, for the 32nd Tank Company, included winter training in late 1939 and participation in war games with the entire Second Army in the summer of 1940.

Personnel strength of the company varied over the years, but was close to its authorized strength, which varied with the national budget. It began with 110 men and dropped to as low as 46 before the country began to rearm in 1939. It reached 126 enlisted men and five officers in 1940 before dropping slightly; its strength at the time of federal induction in late 1940 was 126 enlisted men and six officers.

One early enlistee was Walter "Peewee" Write, who joined in 1926, stayed with the unit, became a sergeant in 1928, was commissioned in 1934, and was in position to take command of the unit when it was federalized in late 1940. Fred "Fatty" Bruni, an assembler at the GM plant, was another man who joined early and was commissioned before the war.

Turnover was high; it is estimated that as many as 2,000 Wisconsin men put in at least one tour with the unit. The Guard could be called up by the governor to aid with natural disasters, which was fine with the men, and also to curb labor unrest, which was much more distasteful to the working-class enlisted men of the 32nd Tank Company.

Men joined for a variety of reasons. Many were at loose ends once the Depression started in 1929. Guard pay, although low, was important, as was companionship, and some men just liked tanks. One of these men was Forrest "Knocky" Knox, a small, stringy, weak-eyed town boy who expected little from life. After graduating from high school in 1935, he tried roofing and rough carpentry without much luck and joined the company on impulse in January 1938 after seeing one of the unit's new M2A2 tanks. In later life he was quick to put down the peacetime Guard as a social club that was mostly interested in dances, saying that promotions were automatic after taking a few courses. He did take advantage of these himself, however, quickly rising to sergeant and becoming a tank commander. Despite his caustic personality men were eager to serve in his crew because of his wit and curiosity; he was always able to make quick sense of what was going on around him, saving his tank and crew when lesser commanders stumbled. He never hesitated to express his opinion of the officer class and was fated to remain a sergeant when many men around him were being commissioned. One of these men was his older brother Henry, who joined the company in August 1940, shortly before it was called to active duty, after working as a salesman for a roofing company (whether this was the same company as Forrest's is not known). Henry was commissioned in October 1941, just before the unit left for the Philippines, and remained a second lieutenant until the surrender.

By the summer of 1940 it was apparent that the nation was heading for war. The Selective Service Act of September 1940 obligated all able-bodied young men to one year's active duty in the United States. Simultaneously the National Guard decreased its service obligation from three years to one. Although there were strong rumors that the Guard was to be federalized soon, active service was to be within the boundaries of the United States, and the Guard immediately became an attractive alternative to the draft. The 32nd Tank Company filled the vacancies it had with men from the Janesville area and prepared for active service. It was to split from the 32nd Division to become A Company of the 192nd GHQ Reserve Tank Battalion (Light). Capt. Lester W. Schuler, who had commanded the unit for two years, turned it over to 1st Lt. Walter Write and took command of a quartermaster unit that shared the armory with the tank company. The company was called to active duty on November 25, 1940; 108 enlisted men and five officers left Janesville on November 28. They took the train to Chicago, where they joined B Company and proceeded to Fort Knox, Kentucky, headquarters of the new U.S. Army's Armored Force.

MAYWOOD, ILLINOIS

Maywood was an early example of a planned city, established in 1869 with features that distinguished it from other towns in the area. The developer chose prairie land along the Des Plaines River ten miles west of Chicago and laid the town out in a grid pattern with a large city park in the central block. The park featured a lagoon, an ice cream stand, a band shell, benches for 2,000 people, an open-air dance floor, and a 124-foot-high observatory. The village had only four houses per block, one on each corner. Maywood was named after the 20,000 trees the developer planted and his deceased daughter. This "railroad village" had excellent railroad service, guaranteeing the town's success as a Chicago suburb; in the early twentieth century the fare to the Chicago loop was only ten cents.

By 1930 Maywood's population had reached nearly 26,000, and it was surrounded by other residential developments. It benefited greatly from the presence of an American Can Company factory, which made the Maywood area one of the major can manufacturing centers in the world. In 1938 the factory employed over 2,500 workers and pumped money into the town's economy after the failure of its largest bank wiped out the savings of many. Another important manufacturer was the Electric Motor Corporation, which built electric locomotives.

The town was now solidly lower-middle class, its men a mixture of white-collar workers who commuted by train to Chicago and blue-collar laborers who worked in the local factories. Maywood's only high school, Proviso Township High, grew rapidly in the 1930s, to 4,000 students. Dropout rates were low. Pupils tended to stay in school as long as they could because jobs were scarce. Post-secondary education was out of the question.

Of the eighty-nine officers and enlisted men who went to war from the town's National Guard company, only one, Donald Hanes, had a college degree, and he was working as a machinist. A few enlisted men had skilled professions such as mechanic, machinist, punch press operator, or power shear operator. Some were still in high school; the rest were working anywhere they could, as shopkeepers, meter readers, caddies, or groundskeepers. The officers were all former enlisted men who had been commissioned from the ranks. Most were employed as clerks in various offices. 1st Lt. Theodore F. Wickord, who as senior platoon leader became company commander when the Maywood Company was federalized in 1940, was a former power company lineman who had been promoted to supervisor.

Benjamin Ryan Morin was a boy of the Depression and a 1938 Proviso High graduate. He was born on August 18, 1919, the second-oldest child of a French Canadian father and an Irish mother. His family moved from Rhode Island to Chicago in 1923 and to the Roman Catholic section of Maywood in 1925. The Morins moved five times during the next decade. According to Ben they did not have financial difficulties but were always looking for more space; there were eventually nine children. Ben's father was a self-taught accountant and apparently never had trouble finding work in Chicago. There was always food on the table.

The Morins were observant Roman Catholics. Attendance at Sunday mass was obligatory. Madonna, Ben's oldest sister, became a nun. Ben himself had religious feelings from his youth; as a young man he avoided sharing his friends' worst vices and drank nothing stronger than beer. His POW experience led him to act on these feelings, as will be seen later.

Ben's childhood was happy. Maywood's large backyards, many parks, and the Des Plaines River made ideal playgrounds. Baseball was the most popular team sport. The players organized their own games; there were no adult-sponsored leagues. Although there were no gangs as such, Maywood's ethnically divided neighborhoods had definite boundaries, and boys risked catcalls and fistfights when passing through certain areas. Ben took pride in yelling at the larger Italian kids and then outrunning them. Spending money became a concern when Ben reached high school, and he began looking for odd jobs. One of his first was driving a small delivery truck for a produce store on Saturdays. His helper was a big Italian boy, the son of the owner.

Ben began developing his leadership skills. He had no career plans while in high school but had always been interested in the military. His father, a former battleship sailor, had been invalided out of the U.S. Navy after contracting a severe case of smallpox while on a Vera Cruz shore party in 1915. All the Morin boys eventually joined the service. In the summer of 1937 Ben signed up for the Citizens Military Training Corps (CMTC) at Fort Sheridan, Illinois—an unusual move for a Maywood youth. Authorized by the U.S. National Defense Act of 1920, the CMTC provided young volunteers with four weeks of military training in summer camps each year from 1921 to 1941. Its goal was to get American youth to look favorably on the military, but it was derisively called "Boy Scouts with Guns." The full course lasted four summers and ended with the offer of a reserve army commission, but Ben spent only one term in the Corps, primarily learning close-order drill.

In October 1937, while Ben was a senior at Proviso Township High, a classmate came to school with a belt of .30 caliber machine gun ammunition draped around his neck. Ben asked him where he had gotten it. The boy had picked it up at a nearby army camp on the shore of Lake Michigan, where the local National Guard tank company had gone to train. Intrigued, Ben quickly looked into joining the National Guard. He now remembered his excitement as a young boy when the company's two six-ton M1917 tanks had rumbled down the street several times a year, but they had been mothballed for several years, and Ben had forgotten all about them.

Ben made inquiries at the town armory, which was only two blocks from the high school; passed his physical exam at a doctor's office in neighboring Melrose Park; and was sworn in for a three-year tour in the Guard, all in the same month that an ammunition belt had aroused his curiosity. For $1 per week he was obligated to attend one weekly meeting—from 8 to 10 p.m. on Friday—and spend two summer weeks at Camp Grant, Illinois, seventy miles northwest of Chicago.

The imposing all-brick Maywood armory had been built at 50 Madison Street, two blocks east of First Avenue, and opened on May 3, 1929.

Its first floor was a wooden-floored open gymnasium for calisthenics and close-order drill. The basement contained a two-lane bowling alley, a cafeteria, and quarters for a live-in maintenance sergeant. Down the street was a garage housing the two light tanks and five supply trucks of the 33rd Tank Company, the one-hundred-man unit Ben had joined. The tanks were M2A2 "Mae Wests," nicknamed for their twin turrets. They were armed with one .50 caliber and three or four .30 caliber machine guns, and in 1937 were the best equipment the army had to offer. The company was in the special troops battalion of Illinois's 33rd Infantry Division and was the division's only armored unit.

In 1937 the National Guard was very much a young men's club, and the tank company old-timers, who called themselves a "syndicate," saw to it that new recruits were properly initiated. Ben remembers being stripped naked and having his genitalia coated with Cosmoline, a thick corrosion-preventive grease. The recruits had to clean themselves off. The secret, which the new men didn't know, is that Cosmoline is very soluble in boiling water, and only slightly less so in very hot, and thus tolerable, water.

The weekly meetings comprised close-order drill followed by training classes. The Guard had nothing comparable to the Regular army's basic training or service schools. All training was carried out within the units. Ben already knew close-order drill from the CMTC, and classroom work came easy, so the best parts of Friday evenings were the after-drill bull sessions, playing pool, and card games in the basement.

The men spent some of their drill nights in the garage with the tanks and mastered the mechanical aspects of their equipment. Summer camp was the place to fire their guns and conduct drills to develop maneuvers and tactics, but with the entire 33rd Infantry Division in the crowded camp, there were not enough tanks for joint maneuvers, and there were far too many crewmen for the tanks that were available. As a junior man, Ben was given a lot of kitchen police duty.

His friends took the opportunity after hours to raise hell in the nearby towns. Here their status as special troops proved useful. The division's MPs were in the 33rd Military Police Company, and like the 33rd Tank Company were in the division's special troops battalion. These "special" units stuck together. The two companies bivouacked together with the division staff and considered themselves part of the same team. When the tankers got into a brawl with artillerymen, the MPs would bring the tankers back to their unit, while the gunners went to the guardhouse. The tankers wore special uniforms, indicating their high esprit de corps. Tankers received government-issue coveralls to wear on duty. The men of the 33rd felt these were inadequate and purchased civilian coveralls with "33rd Tank Company" and a tank emblem embroidered on the back.

After he graduated from high school in the spring of 1938, finding a job became Ben's top priority. No one was hiring. A tour in the Civilian Conservation Corps didn't appeal to him, so he returned to a job with which he had experience—deliveryman. This time he would be his own boss. He borrowed $35 from his father and bought a 1931 Chevy truck. It ran well, but the bed was just a platform. He reinstalled the cabin's top, which was lying on the platform, and built a proper bed from lumberyard 2x4s. He then advertised for business. He would move anything he could fit on the bed, including pianos. When he needed help he would hire large men, mostly married men several years older than he. His workload varied with the season, but on summer days he would often have five or six jobs and work from early morning to late at night. He kept his crew together and would always buy their lunch—fried chicken, fifty cents a plate. His work ethic and leadership skills impressed his Guard officers, and he quickly rose through the ranks to sergeant. Ben did not find the 1938 and 1939 Camp Grant summer camps especially noteworthy, but when Germany invaded Poland in September 1939, a special one-week camp was ordered, and this was when Ben finally got to drive a tank.

Drills at the armory became more serious in mid-1940 when Germany's Blitzkrieg ("lightning war") overran Western Europe in a few weeks. Few Americans believed that their country would become embroiled in another foreign war—and Franklin D. Roosevelt won a third term in November on that very issue—but prudence dictated rearmament, and on September 16, 1940, the first peacetime draft in the nation's history was signed into law by President Roosevelt. All able-bodied men would be required to serve for one year in the armed forces. The government assured everyone that this term would be fixed, and service would be restricted to the continental United States. A popular song was titled, "Goodbye Dear, I'll Be Back in a Year." At this time the National Guard dropped its service requirement to one year and immediately experienced a large upsurge in recruits. Young, unmarried men with no critical skills knew that they would be among the first to be drafted, and many preferred to choose their own service branch and begin their one-year tour at a time of their choosing. Small-town units were popular, and the 33rd Tank Company attracted men from several neighboring towns and states.

James P. "Jim" Bashleben was one of those men. He was born on December 20, 1917, and grew up an only child in Park Ridge, Illinois. He graduated from Maine Township High School in 1936. He eventually found a good job with a utility company and spent most evenings playing baseball with two friends. When the Selective Service Act was passed, the three realized that they would all be classified 1A and would be called up soon. They decided to enlist together. One of the men saw an article in a Chicago newspaper saying that two local National Guard units would soon be inducted into federal service. One was the Chicago Black Horse Troop, a cavalry outfit; the other was the 33rd Tank Company in Maywood. Jim argued with his friends, "Cavalry means horses, horses mean stables, sables mean horse shit, and I have no intention of spending my year of active duty shoveling horse shit. Tanks are mechanized, and that means we would ride in an iron horse, with no walking."

They decided to go to Maywood on the next drill evening. Sitting outside, they agreed before entering the armory that they would not sign up, but would just go in and look around. One of the company's M2A2 tanks was on display nearby, and the men were duly impressed. Once inside they were split up among three officers and went in different directions. Jim wound up outside the office of the company commander, Capt. H. W. Cathcart. Also standing outside was another potential recruit, who said, "Hi. I'm Bud Bardowski from Gary." Jim replied, "Hi. I'm Jim Bashleben from Park Ridge." The two men bonded immediately and became best friends. Inside his office Cathcart turned on the charm and told the men what a terrific outfit the 33rd was. "Only the best and the toughest men will be accepted into this elite outfit." His sales pitch was effective—both

Jim and Bud signed up on the spot. When Jim later confessed to his friends, both sheepishly admitted that they had volunteered as well.

Zenon Roland "Bud" Bardowski joined the 33rd Tank Company for only one reason—he wanted to drive a tank. The Gary, Indiana, native had done pretty much whatever he wanted for his entire life. At six feet tall, 230 pounds, and strikingly handsome, the voluble son of Lithuanian and Czech immigrants always stood out in a crowd. He was born on October 17, 1914, and was thus six to eight years older than the average recruit. He had crammed more experiences into his life than the rest of the men put together. His larger-than-life persona was well established by high school, where he starred on both the football team and in the band. His father, a successful grocer, had donated the band's instruments and uniforms, guaranteeing Bud a place in the band, but his playing was so bad that his cornet's mouthpiece was taken away before any public appearance—this did not diminish Bud's enthusiasm in the slightest. During high school Bud and a few friends adopted new middle names to honor King Arthur's Knights of the Round Table. Bud changed his middle name, Kospur, to Roland, in an unofficial and inadvertent homage to one of Charlemagne's knights rather than Arthur's. He used Roland for the rest of his life.

After high school Bud spent some time in his father's grocery store but lost interest in the grocery business after he was awakened by a burglar one night in the store and killed him with a single shot from his bedside pistol. He played semi-pro football, in which expenses were met by passing a hat in the stands. But his greatest love was automobiles. He received a car at high school graduation, making him one of the youngest automobile owners in Gary, but this wasn't enough. In 1935, at age twenty, he was arrested with two other young men for car theft. They had stolen a car, filed off the serial number, and then built a composite jalopy with parts from two other cars. Bud's father knew the judge and told him he'd take care of his son. Charges were dropped after Bud was chained in the grocery store for several days and nights. Bud's police record stayed clean.

Bud Bardowski was soon racing on dirt tracks throughout the Midwest. He apparently signed with a promoter and followed a regular circuit. He was involved in at least one major accident that left him in a full body cast for six months. According to family lore, the day before he was to be discharged, he goosed a nurse who was bending over beside his bed. Startled, she fell on the bed and knocked him to the floor, re-breaking several bones and extending his hospital stay.

Bud also spent several months riding the rails as a hobo, not because he was destitute (although it was the depths of the Depression, his family could be considered well-to-do) but for the experience, and because there was someone in California he wanted to meet. Other adventures are lost to history. The 1940 passage of the Selective Service Act convinced Bud that the best way to maintain control of his own future was to join the National Guard. The Gary company was an engineering unit, Chicago had its cavalry, and Maywood had tanks. The choice was obvious. He had a girlfriend drive him to Maywood where he met Jim Bashleben, listened to Captain Cathcart's spiel, and signed up. As he recalled, his physical examination was an examination of his hands for evidence of manual labor.

Lester I. "Les" Tenenberg found his way to Maywood after a more thorough search. The Chicago native was the youngest child in a Jewish family of seven. He was born on July 1, 1920, two years after his two sisters died within a week of each other, one from an exploding stove and the other from pneumonia contracted during the resulting exposure. Les was obviously a spoiled child. In his senior year he dropped out of his private high school, where he was studying aeronautical engineering, because the father of his current girlfriend wanted her to marry a successful business-man. He got a job selling knickknacks made by a friend's firm to department stores and, according to his memoir, made enough money in a year to open his own little factory producing goods that he designed himself. (However, a newspaper article written when he went on active duty said that he went to work for Liquid Carbonic after he dropped out of school. This is the first of many discrepancies between his memoir and more objective documentation.) At age twenty he was on his way to becoming successful in business in his own mind, but passage of the Selective Service Act caused him to change his plans. He knew he would be classified 1A but did not want to be drafted and "thrown into a group of strangers." His primary concern was anti-Semitism, which was common throughout the armed forces and especially prevalent in Chicago. One of his brothers had wrestled in the mid-1930s under the name "Wild Bill Tenney," and although Lester felt that he did not look Jewish himself, he used the name Tenney to minimize problems, not dropping Tenenberg officially until 1947. Joining the National Guard seemed like a good idea, and he began a systematic evaluation of the units in the Chicago area. He would go in, meet the men, stay for the day, and leave. He visited three or four that did not seem adequately welcoming—not necessarily hostile, just clannish—and then he went to Maywood, where he was impressed by the men, the bowling lane, and the pool table, and decided that was where he wanted to spend his time in the military.

Les had to stretch his age by a year on the enlistment form—the Guard's minimum age was still twenty-one—but his family was proud of his decision to serve. Jim, Bud, and Les had only attended a handful of drill nights when all states received word that their National Guard units would be federalized for a year's active service. In the case of the 33rd Tank Company, the call-up date was November 25, 1940, and under a new designation—Company B, 192nd GHQ Reserve Tank Battalion (Light). The company would leave the 33rd Division and join a pure tank organization just forming at Fort Knox.

Maywood had time to plan an elaborate sendoff party for its tankers. An open house with refreshments and dancing was held at the armory for the men, their wives and sweethearts, and the public. The Proviso Fellowship for Servicemen sponsored the party with the aid of twenty-two civic organizations. Entertainment featured the Winfield Scott Jr. Band, the Sons of the American Legion Drum and Bugle Corps, the Georgine Reay Dancers, and the Maywood Players, a light comedy troupe. After a day and a half to recover from the party, the men mustered at the armory in clean uniforms and carrying full packs and pistols. Captain Wickord had just been promoted from senior platoon leader to company commander; Major Cathcart had left to take command of the 33rd Division Special Troops Battalion. Wickord inspected the men and led Company B from the armory to the Northwestern station, past hundreds of townspeople standing in the nighttime snow to wave them goodbye. One hundred and twenty-one officers and men boarded the train for Chicago, where they joined Janesville's Company A and transferred to a train that was scheduled to arrive at Fort Knox, Kentucky, at seven-thirty the next morning, November 29. The next stage in their lives had begun.

PORT CLINTON, OHIO

Port Clinton was established in 1828 on the shore of Lake Erie. It has a good harbor, but the shallow Sandusky Bay isolates it from the rest of Ohio and fated the town to remain a small fishing port and vacation destination. Its motto, "The Walleye Capital of the World," summarizes the town's view of itself. Today its population has stabilized at about 6,000. It is the only incorporated city in Ottawa County and is the county seat.

In the late nineteenth and early twentieth century the town's industry was restricted to a sawmill and small shipbuilders. Limestone was mined nearby for a while, and gypsum mines and plants for producing plaster and wallboard from gypsum remained profitable for decades. U.S. Gypsum was formed here in 1902 by the amalgamation of several smaller firms and was the area's largest single employer. During the Depression many men dropped out of school to work in the gypsum mines and plants. Another major influence was Camp Perry, which the Ohio National Guard established west of town in 1906. (Today this is the site of the world's largest outdoor rifle range, which has hosted the NRA's National Rifle and Pistol Matches since 1909.)

The Ohio National Guard infantry regiments saw distinguished service in World War I as the 37th Infantry Division. The unit was demobilized quickly after the war, but only a year later Ohio and many other states began to set up Guard divisions, most under the designations they had had during the war. The citizens of Port Clinton lobbied for a tank company. These were new; each Guard infantry division was to have only one, which was a real prestige item for the town that got it. Port Clinton won, and Company H, Tank Corps, was established there on June 21, 1920, the second such organization in the National Guard. The 37th Division itself was reconstituted a little later, and the tank company became the 37th Tank Company of the 37th Division Special Troops.

The tank company moved into an impressive multistory brick armory that Port Clinton built for it. Its history for the next twenty years paralleled those of the tank companies in neighboring states. Its establishment strength of about one hundred officers and men was filled with men from northern Ohio. Drill was one night a week at the armory; a two-week summer camp was held at Camp Perry; Fort Knox, Kentucky; or Fort George G. Meade, Maryland. Its armor comprised seven six-ton M1917 tanks that were placed in dead storage in 1936. The unit was without tanks until new equipment, two M2A2 tanks, arrived in 1938. Like every National Guard unit, the 37th Tank Company could be called into emergency service by the governor, but this happened only once: The unit was sent to Sandusky Bay in 1924 for relief work after a destructive tornado swept the shore.

Men enlisted in the tank company for many reasons, including financial; during the Depression the dollar the men received for each meeting was more than just beer money. Training, moderate adventure, friendship, and family relationships were all important. As in the Regular army and National Guard as a whole, many members of the company had less than a high school education. However, two men who went to war with the 37th Tank Company had college degrees, an unusually high number. The best-known member of the unit in the town, Arthur Burholt, had an education degree from Michigan State Normal College and was the athletic director of Port Clinton High School. Robert Sorensen, the senior platoon leader, was a graduate of Ohio State University who kept the books for his father's grocery store. He had been with the unit since shortly after its formation and went to war at age thirty-eight, its oldest man.

The United States began to rearm in 1939, and to increase its number of men under arms in 1940. In September of that year, the Selective Service Act obligated all able-bodied young men to one year's active duty in the United States. Many draftable men chose to sign up with nearby National Guard units to give them some control over their future and serve with friends. The 37th Tank Company filled some of its vacancies and prepared for active service. It was to split from the 37th Division and become C Company of the 192nd GHQ Reserve Tank Battalion (Light). The company was called to active duty on November 25, and after a banquet at the United Brethren Church and three days at the armory, five officers and seventy-four enlisted men under the command of Lieutenant

Sorensen left for Fort Knox, Kentucky. The men and their two tanks took the train; their two wheeled vehicles, one truck, and one command car, drove.

HARRODSBURG, KENTUCKY

Harrodsburg was laid out in 1774 and is generally considered the oldest city in Kentucky and the oldest permanent settlement west of the Appalachians. It was abandoned at least once due to Native American attacks, but was well established by 1785, when it became the county seat of Mercer County. For the next fifty years it served as an important stopping point on the road west. It has seen continuous, slow population growth, from 4,000 in the 1930s to 8,000 today. Several manufacturing plants have come and gone. The largest was probably Bohon's Bluegrass Buggies, which started in the 1880s as a carriage dealer and survived until 1935, before becoming a victim of the automobile and the Depression.

Harrodsburg is in the heart of bluegrass country and has always been a farming community; early crops included wheat, hemp, tobacco, and corn. Many of the men who joined the local Guard unit in the 1930s were members of large farm families who were in great need of the dollar-a-drill pay, as well as a little excitement off the farm. The unit was more closely knit than most; nearly all of the men were friends off-duty, and six sets of brothers went to war with it.

The lineage of the unit itself differed from that of the other tank companies discussed in this book. It owed nothing to Kentucky's National Guard Division, the 38th Division, but originated as Company D of the Kentucky State Guard, which was formed in Covington while the 38th Division was in France in World War I. More than most states, Kentucky needed its own military force for internal emergencies. Company D was called up several times, most notably to quell riots in Lexington in February 1920, in which six persons were killed and twenty injured. Company D became the 38th Tank Company in March 1921 under the new National Guard organization, and was called upon repeatedly for active service, especially for coal mine strikes, until it was disbanded in March 1932.

The 38th Tank Company was reconstituted in Harrodsburg in June 1932 and extended federal recognition in July 1932. Its first commander was Captain Bacon R. Moore; he and the company's other four officers were all World War I veterans. Men joining the unit during this period included Archie Rue and his brother Edwin "Skip," Bill Gentry, and Arnold Lawson. The company and its two six-ton M1917 tanks performed all its military duties satisfactorily, continuing to be called up for parades and Kentucky Derby security duty as well as for real emergencies such as the Harlan County coal strike and the great flood of January 1937. After the latter the men had to guard and move prisoners from the state prison in Frankfort, feed 3,000 evacuees, and maintain quarantine guard duty on the roads around Frankfort. Fourteen men stayed on prison guard duty until June.

The 38th Tank Company was handicapped in its weekly drills, the military duty in common with all Guard units, by the absence of a dedicated armory. Meetings were held Monday nights in three rooms above a restaurant. There was no outside lighted area for drills or tank maintenance. After the company received two new M2A2 tanks to replace its six-ton M1917s, they were kept either in an old building several blocks from the restaurant or on Bill Gentry's family tobacco farm. Gentry and his brother could take advantage of daylight to service the tanks. Gentry logged in the time spent driving to drills and became a "1st Class Maintenance Specialist," which gave him a private first class stripe and added to his pay. Summer drills were usually held at nearby Fort Knox, which helped the Harrodsburg company's training because Fort Knox was the home of the 1st Armored Division and, when it was established in 1940, the U.S. Army's Armored Force.

Passage of the Selective Service Act in September 1940 was convincing evidence that the country was getting ready for war. Draft-eligible Mercer County men were nudged to serve their one year of active duty in the 38th Tank Company. Although there were rumors that farmers would be exempt from the draft, avoiding military service was considered shirking, and most farm families quickly thinned out the young men in their ranks and sent them off to military service. The company filled its vacancies and prepared to be called up. On November 20 Secretary of War

Henry L. Stimson ordered the Kentucky governor to call the 38th Tank Company to active duty. Captain Bacon Moore was promoted to major and ordered to take command of the new 192nd GHQ Reserve Tank Battalion (Light), which would contain four tank companies including the 38th, now to be D Company of the 192nd. The older platoon leaders had had too much time in grade for active duty and were released from service. Command of D Company was given to the senior remaining officer, 2nd Lt. Edwin "Skip" Rue. The company hit the road to Fort Knox on November 25 with five officers, seventy-one enlisted men, two M2A2 tanks, and a handful of trucks.

BRAINERD, MINNESOTA

In February 1870 surveyors for the Northern Pacific Railroad identified a site for a bridge to span the Mississippi River several miles north of its confluence with the Crow Wing River in central Minnesota. The town of Brainerd grew up around this crossing and became a railroad town, the home of Northern Pacific shops and a number of ancillary facilities. The legacy of the railroad lives on today at a former railroad tie creosoting plant, which is now a U.S. Environmental Protection Agency Superfund site. Lumber was an important early commodity, replaced by agriculture as the forests were depleted. The town, the seat of Crow Wing County and one of the largest in central Minnesota, remained relatively prosperous during the Depression. Its population rose from 10,000 to 12,000 in the 1930s and has stabilized at 13,000 to 14,000 today.

The 34th Tank Company was established in Brainerd as part of the special troops battalion in the Minnesota National Guard's 34th Division. In 1935 the town used WPA funds to build a nice armory. In common with other National Guard tank units, the 34th Company's first tanks were probably put into storage in the early 1930s, and they had none until two new M2A2s were received in 1937, along with one 1½-ton Chevrolet truck. Duties were standard for the period: a drill every Monday night and a two-week encampment at nearby Camp Ripley in June or July.

The company commander was Capt. Ernest Miller, who in 1912 had enlisted in the Minnesota National Guard at age fourteen as a bugler and had seen service in France in World War I. He became a civil engineer after the war and is credited with laying out Camp Ripley. He remained in the Guard in Brainerd and quickly rose to command the company. He was one of a very few war veterans young enough to remain in the Guard when it was called up in 1941, and his experience was invaluable.

His officers, including John Muir and Edward Burke, were typical of those produced by the Guard between the wars. None was educated beyond high school. They were typically working as salesmen or mechanics and joined the Guard to better themselves. They kept their records clean, passed the required courses, and were commissioned within a few years.

The enlisted men joined for the money, the comradeship, and the prestige of belonging to an organization that was highly respected by its hometown, which hosted an annual New Year's Eve ball for the Guardsmen. Kenneth Porwall's motives for joining included this dance:

You had to be dressed in a tux if you weren't a military man. The women wore long formal dresses, and it cost twenty-five bucks a person. This was Depression times, and that's a lot of money. And us young fellows that wanted to be a part of that, we says, "Why don't we join the Guard, and then we get new clothes, we get new boots, we get the whole bit, and you go as a shined-up soldier and you get in free?" And there must have been ten, twelve of us that signed up at that time to get in there and go to that New Year's dance.

In 1939 America began to rearm as Europe slid into war, and passage of the Selective Service Act in September 1940 led to the swelling of the ranks of all Guard units, including Brainerd's 34th Tank Company. One Brainerd native who joined during this period was Glenn Oliver, who wanted to get into the radio field and recalled that he needed a recommendation from the communications sergeant.

The company became Company A of a new 194th GHQ Reserve Tank Battalion (Light), which was to be commanded by the newly promoted Major Miller, whose place as company commander was taken by the senior platoon leader, First Lieutenant Burke. The company was not called up immediately, as were those for the 192nd GHQ Reserve

Tank Battalion (Light), possibly due to the lack of space on the army bases. Orders eventually arrived for the company to leave for Fort Lewis, Washington.

Eighty-two officers and men assembled at the Northern Pacific station at about midnight on February 20, 1941. It was -20 degrees F and snowing lightly, and the khaki-clad men raced for the station shelter and their families as soon as they were dismissed. According to the newspaper, much of the town was there in the cold to see their men off, stamping their feet to keep up the circulation as a local band played patriotic music. The mood of the crowd was upbeat—everyone expected the men to be back in a year. When the train arrived, the men re-formed, the band played the national anthem, and the nascent soldiers boarded, squeezing themselves into the windows to wave goodbye as the train pulled away into the night.

SALINAS, CALIFORNIA

Salinas was the most prosperous of the six towns that sent its National Guard tank companies off to an unknown fate in the winter of 1940–41. The fertile Salinas Valley in central California had been the home to Native Americans for 2,000 years when the land fell to Spain. The Spaniards built missions but otherwise left the land unchanged; the Mexicans who replaced them rewrote the land titles and brought in settlers who split the area up into small ranches. After two years of struggle centered in the Monterey Bay–Salinas Valley area, California broke free from Mexico and joined the United States in 1850. In 1856 the town of Salinas was established as a crossroads rest stop. It was incorporated in 1874, and its future was ensured when it was named the seat of Monterey County and the railroad arrived.

The Salinas Valley's ranching heritage lives on in the Salinas Rodeo, which has been held annually since 1911, except for the World War II break, and is considered one of the "big Four" rodeos in the United States and Canada. However, since the turn of the nineteenth century, tilled agriculture has been the area's major industry.

Claus Spreckels saw a potential for sugar beets and began digging irrigation canals, contracting with farmers, and building private narrow-gauge railroads to connect their farms with his sugar mills. The Spreckels Sugar Company soon dominated the national market. In 1922 three Japanese American farmers planted thirty-five acres of lettuce, taking advantage of the Spreckels irrigation system, and by 1930 the Salinas Valley farmland was dominated by vegetables. The year-round mild weather and water from accessible aquifers were ideal for higher-value row crops, which were tended by low-cost migrant labor coming from different areas at different times—China, Japan, the Philippines, Mexico, and America's own Dust Bowl. In 1924 Salinas had the highest per capita income of any city in the United States. The Depression lowered this average income, especially as the population swelled with poor migrants from the southern and southwestern United States. The plight of these migrants was documented in the novels of Salinas's native son John Steinbeck. Labor unrest kept the area in turmoil through the 1930s, but World War II brought sustained prosperity to the area. Population grew from 10,000 in 1930 to 150,000 in 2010. The city's motto is still "The Salad Bowl of the World," and it is the heart of a $2 billion agricultural industry.

Salinas has a long connection with the National Guard. The lineage of its most famous unit, Company C of the 194th GHQ Reserve Tank Battalion (Light), can be traced to Troop C, Cavalry, National Guard of California, which was established in August 1895 and headquartered in a brick armory in town. This was the first Guard unit formed in California's central coast region. Given the town's equestrian history, cavalry was a popular choice as the service arm of the local unit. It was first called up for active duty in April 1906, when it was sent to San Francisco to aid in maintaining law and order after its disastrous earthquake. Its next extraordinary duty was in June 1916, when President Wilson called 75,000 National Guard troops into federal service to secure the southern border against the depredations of Pancho Villa. Troop C did not cross the border but fulfilled the arduous role of patrolling the U.S. side until November.

The next mobilization of Troop C was its last. On April 6, 1917, the United States declared war on Germany. Troop C was inducted into the army on August 12 and sent to Camp Kearny with its horses, where it gave them up and became Company B, 145th Machine Gun Battalion of the 40th Division. The division did not get to France in time to see any combat, and Company B was released from federal service in May 1919 and returned to Salinas to be deactivated.

The National Guard units of the various states were reestablished in 1920 with a new, standardized organization. Eighteen states or groupings were to have infantry divisions, each containing one tank company. Salinas was awarded California's company, and the 40th Tank Company was authorized in June 1924. It received eight six-ton M1917 tanks and outgrew the town's old armory and two that succeeded it. After lobbying by various civic organizations, the town and the federal government put together $250,000 to build the last armory that the town would see. The tank company occupied it in November 1932. The company contained sixty-five officers and men; two lieutenants, Lyman "Eddie" Johnson and Fred Moffitt, would take it to war. Johnson had been commissioned in 1925 and gained a reputation as one of the top junior officers in the California National Guard. In 1933 he completed the three-month National Guard and reserve officers' tank course at Fort Benning, Georgia, with superior marks, and on his return was lauded in the Salinas newspaper as "unsurpassed in the U.S."

The 40th Tank Company was called to active duty once prior to its ultimate call-up. This was for a typical National Guard job between the wars—curbing domestic violence. In July 1934 a longshoreman's strike on the San Francisco waterfront turned ugly, and the governor sent in the 40th Tank Company. The company spent eight days in San Francisco and then reported to San Luis Obispo for its annual two-week camp.

The company had no difficulty keeping its ranks filled during the Depression. The men seemed to have little trouble finding work, but salaries were extremely low. The most common occupation listed for the company's enlisted men was farmhand, and the dollar-a-drill pay was welcome. Ero "Ben" Saccone was born in San Francisco of Italian immigrants and moved to Salinas in 1929 with his new wife. The best job he could find was at a service station, and he joined the tank company that same year. His leadership skills were apparent; he was promoted to staff sergeant and eventually became first sergeant, the top enlisted position in the company.

In common with the rest of the National Guard during this period, the educational level of its members was low. Most of the officers lacked college degrees—Fred Moffitt was a postal carrier—and many of the enlisted men did not finish high school. As one example, Roy Diaz had to drop out of school to help full-time on his family's ranch and joined the Guard in 1936 for the money.

In 1937 the Salinas company received new M2A2 light tanks in place of its old six-ton M1917s. It continued drilling as small wars erupted in both Europe and Asia. The future looked increasingly grim, and the country began to remilitarize. Capt. Eddie Johnson replaced longtime company commander Capt. Frank Heple. The fall of 1940 brought the Selective Service Act and word that the National Guard would soon be called up for one year's active duty. The orders came on January 20, 1941. The 40th Tank Company would become Company C of the new 194th GHQ Reserve Tank Battalion (Light). Johnson was nearly forty, too old for field command, and Captain Moffitt replaced him as company commander. The army recognized Johnson's abilities, however, and he was given a job on the staff of the new battalion. He became S-3, in charge of operations and training. On February 10 five officers and ninety-eight men of the Salinas tank company marched from the armory to the train station to entrain for Fort Lewis, Washington, which would be their base for what was believed to be a year's training.

CHAPTER 2

The National Guard Tank Companies and the U.S. Armored Force

ARMOR FIRST ENTERED THE U.S. ARMY IN FRANCE IN 1917. GEN. JOHN J. Pershing established an independent Tank Corps within the American Expeditionary Force (AEF) to speed up the entry of this brand-new technology into the U.S. Armed Forces. American tank units went into action in 1918 using borrowed British and French equipment. When the war ended, armor officers urged that the Tank Corps be given formal status as an independent arm of service, but Pershing, the new Army Chief of Staff, disagreed, arguing that the only future of tanks was in direct support of the foot soldier, and the Tank Corps was disbanded.

The National Defense Act of 1920 established this limited role for tanks as law and restricted their development and use to the infantry. This Act also strengthened the National Guard, declaring it to be the principal reserve force for the army while retaining its traditional role in handling state emergencies under the state governors. Eighteen states were to maintain divisions having the same organization as those of the regular army: Called "square" divisions, these were essentially infantry units but contained one special troops battalion with one tank company, one military police company, one signals company, and one quartermaster company. The tank units were very popular and had no trouble maintaining their establishment strength in men, although their tank strength varied from zero to eight.

The Guard kept armor alive in the penurious 1920s and early 1930s while the Regular army withered to a shameful degree: In 1930 the U.S.

Army contained 12,000 officers and 130,000 men, half of its authorized strength and sixteenth largest in the world, behind Greece and Portugal. All of the armor units were short of equipment, and those of the Regular army were also short of personnel, but the units themselves were intended to provide nuclei for expansion. There were almost twice as many tank companies in the Guard (eighteen) as there were in the Regular army (ten).

U.S. law may have confined armor to the infantry, but experiments with mechanized forces in Germany in the 1920s and in England in the 1930s convinced some U.S. Army officers that the inherent speed and mobility of armor were too great to shackle it to foot soldiers. Most of these officers were in the cavalry, which was itself undergoing an internal struggle over mechanization. In 1937 the army contained seventeen active horse cavalry regiments; two were mechanized in that year as the 7th Cavalry Brigade (Mechanized). Its commander, Lt. Col. Adna R. Chaffee Jr., was an outspoken proponent of mechanization, but he was limited to following developments in armor tactics abroad—especially in the Spanish Civil War—while a lack of funding limited changes in the U.S. Army. Chaffee promoted an offensive doctrine for mechanized units, highlighting their maneuverability and speed and using long movements, night attacks, and combined arms. His doctrine owed little to the tank-heavy British maneuvers in the early 1930s, but was very similar to that adopted by the German Wehrmacht.

Germany's Blitzkrieg in Poland in September 1939 and in France and Flanders in May 1940 opened the eyes of Congress and the budgetary floodgates. On July 10, 1940, the U.S. Armored Force was established under General Chaffee. It contained the 7th Cavalry Brigade (Mechanized) and the Provisional Tank Brigade (containing all but one of the infantry tank units), which were to be transformed as quickly as possible into two armored divisions and an armored corps and prepared for offensive warfare. The role for tanks mandated by the National Defense Act of 1920, infantry support, was apparently neglected, but only briefly.

A major reorganization of the army took place before the end of July. The army had always been run by a mass of independent bureaus. This was a major reason for the disorganization and tardiness that characterized the

U.S. mobilization for World War I. Things would have to be different this time. The organization of the army would be more vertical, with strong direction from the top. The General Headquarters, U.S. Army (GHQ) was established, commanded by the U.S. Army Chief of Staff, General Marshall. Initially it was intended to be a field command, but instead took on the responsibility of organizing, raising, and training a mass army. It was also the home of units that were outside the normal chain of command. Important for this story were the "GHQ Reserve Tank Battalions," which were to be prepared quickly for any required foreign service. Their table of organization specified only a headquarters company, four tank companies, and a medical detachment. Their size made it clear that they were intended to be attached to other units—especially infantry. They were part of the Armored Force for administration, but were not in the Armored Corps, which was to be maintained intact for its offensive mission and not split up into small attachments for other units—welcome news to General Chaffee.

On September 1, 1940, four GHQ Reserve Tank Battalions were ordered to be established from existing National Guard companies. Prior to federalization, this was by no means simple, as Guard officers were forbidden to command men from other states, and thus there was no built-in mechanism for filling battalion headquarters staffs and companies. There was also long-standing resistance within the army to Guard officers being allowed to command units larger than companies. But Gen. George Marshall's GHQ overruled such prejudices, and by the following autumn two battalions, the 192nd and 194th, were judged suitable for foreign service and were ordered to the Philippines, fulfilling the mission intended for them.

The Guard has often had to make do with hand-me-downs from the Regular army, but that was never true of the tank companies. Their equipment—personal, mechanical, weaponry—was identical to that of the regular army. Until the late 1930s all equipment was of World War I vintage. The Rock Island Arsenal designed and built experimental tanks that advanced the technology but did not go into production. The infantry and cavalry tested models that differed only slightly. By law the cavalry could not operate tanks, so their armored vehicles were called "combat cars." The standard U.S. Army pontoon bridge limited all armor to seven tons in weight and seven feet wide. The army bought an example of the most popular export tank of the interwar period, the Vickers six-ton light tank, for comparative purposes. U.S. tanks matched the British in armament (machine guns) and armor (light), and evolved to become greatly superior mechanically.

In 1932 the rubber-bushed tank track was invented. Replacement of the dry metal pins that had been used first for agricultural tractors increased track life immediately from 500 to 5,000 miles; this technology is still used today. The same year saw the invention of the vertical volute spring suspension, featuring the most compact spring possible, which was much sturdier and easier to maintain than the Vickers's leaf spring suspension, and took up no room beneath or inside the tank, very important given the American tanks' size restrictions.

In 1934 the experimental T2E1 Light Tank and the T5 Combat Car had features giving U.S. armor the best mechanical performance and reliability in the world: rear-mounted air-cooled radial aircraft engines, front drive, vertical volute spring suspensions, and rubber-bushed tracks. These vehicles had a weight of 6.5 tons and a highway speed of forty-five miles per hour. Both models were upgunned and uparmored over the next two years. The T2E1 received one .50 caliber and one .30 caliber machine gun in twin turrets, which immediately gained the tank the moniker "Mae West," and was earmarked for infantry (and National Guard) units as the M2A2. The T5 was standardized as the M1 Combat Car and was redesignated an M1A2 Light Tank when the combat car fiction was discarded with the formation of the Armored Force. It bequeathed some of its features to the M2A3 light tank, which was uparmored and featured a newly designed turret containing a 37mm cannon. This went into production as the M2A4 Light Tank.

The 37mm gun was installed in American tanks as a result of the Spanish Civil War. The Republicans' Russian T-26, with a 45mm gun, handily defeated the Nationalists' machine gun–armed German PzKpfw I and Italian CV.3/35 light tanks. Since the T-26 was built on a Vickers six-ton chassis, American generals mistakenly concluded that cannon-armed light tanks would be the tanks of the future. But the major continental nations—France, Germany, and the Soviet Union—saw the ease with which T-26s had been destroyed by Nationalist antitank weapons and even machine guns and drew a different conclusion. Their next generation of tanks would be much larger and heavily armed and armored than those that fought in Spain. Unfortunately for the United States, its closest ally, the British, produced tank designs that were catastrophically bad, and remained so for most of the coming war. America's next-generation tank, the M3 Light Tank, was outdated for European combat before it was built, but that was all that the United States had to fight with and offer its Allies for nearly two years.

The M2A4 finished its trials in September 1939 and became the first tank mass-produced in the United States. The mobilization plan called for tanks to be produced by locomotive and heavy equipment manufacturers. American Car & Foundry of Berwick, Pennsylvania, received a contract for 329 M2A4s, with delivery to begin in six months. In one of the first miracles of World War II production, deliveries began in May 1940, and the plant completed 365 M2A4s before smoothly transitioning to the production of M3s in March 1941. All M3s were produced by American Car & Foundry; most were delivered to the U.K. and other Allies under the Lend-Lease Program.

THE 192ND GHQ RESERVE TANK BATTALION (LIGHT) AT FORT KNOX

The trains carrying the men of the newly formed 192nd GHQ Reserve Tank Battalion (Light)'s four companies reached Fort Knox in the last days of November 1940. The men disembarked into a sea of red mud. Fort Knox had the prerequisites for a major army base—south of Louisville on the Ohio River, it had 60,000 acres of varied terrain—but saw little activity until it was chosen as an armor base and became the headquarters of the new Armored Force and the 1st Armored Division. The facilities on the base were being expanded as rapidly as possible, but the battalion's quarters were not finished, and the men moved into pyramidal five- to six-man wooden-framed tents. Mess halls and latrines were ready, one for each company, and their barracks, nice green-trimmed white wooden buildings, were occupied the following spring.

The group's immediate priority was organization. Capt. Bacon Moore was the commander. He was promoted to major and replaced as D Company commander by Lt. Edwin "Skip" Rue. Capt. Ted Wickord became executive officer, was promoted to major, and replaced as B Company commander by Lt. Don Hanes. A functioning headquarters company was needed as quickly as possible to handle supply and administration. Capt. Havelock Nelson, a reservist from Kansas, was named its first commander; its ranks were filled with skilled personnel from the tank companies.

Senior enlisted men were encouraged to complete the required courses and apply for commissions. When received, the young second lieutenants were typically transferred to other companies so they wouldn't have to give orders to their old buddies. Ben Morin was one of these and transferred briefly from B Company to D Company. When commissioned, Bill Gentry moved from D Company to Headquarters Company, where he became the 192nd Battalion Communications Officer—electronics had been a childhood hobby, and he had built crystal sets and superheterodyne radios.

The large holes in the tank company rosters were filled with reserve officers (mostly recent ROTC graduates) and early draftees and volunteers, some of whom arrived at Fort Knox without training, for lack of anywhere more suitable to send them. Someone, probably the base commander, made the unprecedented decision to give the tank company commanders freedom to choose men from any of the casuals on base. After reviewing their service records, the commanders hand-picked suitable men from their own state: A Company from Wisconsin, B Company from Illinois, C Company from Ohio, and D Company from Kentucky. This kept morale high and maintained the Guardsmen's "small-town" bonds.

Albert Allen Jr. was one of these early fillers. He had dropped out of Wooster College after two years for lack of money, and on January 29 volunteered for the army with seven other Mansfield, Ohio, men. Two failed their physicals, but the other six were sent to Fort Knox for basic training, where Lt. Robert Sorensen scooped them up for C Company (which will be known in this book as C/192TB).

John Rowland was drafted on January 20, one of the first from Westerville, Ohio. He had attended Wheeling Business College and Ohio State University and was working in the classified department of the *Westerville Dispatch* when Uncle Sam called. He was sent to Fort Knox, but unlike Al Allen he did not join C Company but was assigned to the new Headquarters Company, where he was trained for reconnaissance in scout cars and motorcycles.

Another draftee, Frank "Goldy" Goldstein of Chicago, had a special skill that the army was able to use. While a student at Roosevelt High School, his math and shop teachers encouraged his interest in electronics, and while working for a lamp company he became a ham radio operator with government aid and equipment. Frank's father, a tailor, had lost his job and the family home in the Depression, and the family had moved into a one-bedroom apartment. Frank's bed folded up into the living room closet, and his radio equipment covered a table set against the living room wall. At full power his equipment dimmed the lights in the building, and his Morse code signals interfered with nearby radio reception, but the government offered advice on how to get along with the neighbors. When Frank got his draft notice and reported to the Maywood armory for processing, he and another radio buff were pulled from the line and ordered to report directly to the 192nd Tank Battalion at Fort Knox. There they were immediately assigned to the tiny B/192TB radio crew, where Frank was given the option of teaching classes or working on equipment; he chose the latter.

Second Lieutenant Gentry was ordered to run the Fort Knox radio school, where he was able to pick the best-qualified of the draftees for the battalion. He got ham radio operators and design engineers from both Philco and Stewart-Warner, who redesigned old tank radios with new components, and from salvage he built up a large inventory of spare parts, which he was ultimately able to take to the Philippines.

The battalion had to build a medical detachment from scratch. Alvin C. Poweleit, MD, an army reservist, was practicing medicine in Newport, Kentucky, when he was called up for a year's active duty and ordered to report to the 192nd Battalion at Fort Knox. Here he was told he was the second doctor in the detachment and advised to become familiar with all of the battalion's military equipment. The senior doctor transferred out and Poweleit became commanding officer (CO) of the detachment, eventually leading one more doctor and eighteen enlisted men to the Philippines.

The battalion's pathetic inventory of equipment arrived at Fort Knox in due course. Most companies had a full supply of small arms from their armories, but only two M2A2 "Mae West" tanks and a few trucks and automobiles. The only way to get enough tanks for realistic training was to build them from scrap. The men of the 192nd made frequent visits to the salvage yard and pulled junk into a three-pole circus tent (Army General Purpose Large Tent) in their area. The men completely disassembled the scraps and, by drawing replacement parts from base ordnance, reassembled enough tanks for the Louisiana maneuvers in the autumn. Other motor vehicles were assigned to the battalion, some of them brand new, including 2½-ton trucks; the first peeps, as the Armored Force called jeeps; one half-track; and two motorcycles. Machine guns were adequate in number, but to prevent pilferage Cpl. Carl Maggio slept with his guns (there were 105 in B Company) after he was named company armorer.

The tankers understood that they had been called up for a year of training, but the lack of tanks restricted training in their specialty. They spent time on the firing range and took whatever courses were available, especially radio school and motorcycle school, and for officers and prospective officers, Fort Knox's Armor School, but their enthusiasm, tightness, and lack of interest in military discipline annoyed the Regular army enlisted men, many of whom were lifers who were putting their time in and were not interested in field exercises, and there were confrontations both on the base and off. These confirmed the prejudices of regular officers against the guard officers, most of whom owed their commissions to correspondence courses and their ranks to time in grade. The new ROTC officers increased the number in the tank battalion with university degrees; these men were probably cultured enough for acceptability in the Fort Knox officers' clubs, but problems with underqualified, undisciplined ex-Guard officers persisted to the Philippines.

The ex-Guard enlisted men, on the other hand, tended to be fully qualified for service in an armored unit, no matter how obstreperous their behavior off-duty. Most had very good mechanical ability; many of them were mechanics in civilian life, working in garages. Others had experience operating heavy equipment such as bulldozers and tractors. Nearly all were skilled motor vehicle operators, a trait not shared with many draftees. Within the barracks the men's unit loyalty showed itself in innocent pranks such as dying the hair of all members of a tank platoon a uniform color and fights between the "smart alecs" of Companies A, B, and C and the "shit kickers" of Company D. The MPs had to be called to the barracks several times to break them up, and on at least one occasion the men were locked outside overnight.

Off base the Guardsmen banded together against the Regulars. Liquor and women provided nonviolent entertainment and could be found in Louisville, the nearest city, and Elizabethtown ("E-town"), the nearest town. One veteran fondly recalled "Dirty Nell." Men restricted to base found refuge in Mint Springs, a bourbon sold in the PX.

The battalion received much classroom training, but little field training during its nine months at Fort Knox, and what they got was either self-administered, as a few men recalled, or supervised by the 1st Armored Division's 69th Armored Regiment, as others remember—and which is more likely. In either case the men felt their time was being wasted and were more than ready for the next step in their year's adventure, which came at the end of August with an announcement that they were leaving for Camp Polk, Louisiana, to participate in the largest field exercise the country had seen, known to history as the Louisiana Maneuvers.

THE 194TH GHQ RESERVE TANK BATTALION (LIGHT) AT FORT LEWIS, WASHINGTON

Maj. Ernest Miller reached Fort Lewis, Washington, on February 22, 1941, with the three lettered companies A, B, and C of his 194th GHQ Reserve Tank Battalion (Light). The 194th Battalion never had a fourth tank company, as was specified in the early tables of organization for GHQ reserve tank battalions. B Company was from St. Joseph, Missouri. It was the former 35th Tank Company of the 35th Division of the Missouri National Guard and had a similar history to A and C Company, but was fated not to go to war with them.

Fort Lewis was a spit-and-polish base. The 194th Battalion was its first Guard unit and its first armored unit, and the base personnel had little use for it. Major Miller presented himself to the base commander, M/Gen. Kenyon "God Almighty" Joyce, as was customary, and was berated for being out of uniform—he was wearing a new regulation OD uniform unfamiliar to Joyce. Miller struggled from that day forward to create an operational unit despite a minimum of cooperation from the base staff. He designed and built training aids to maximize the value of his eight M2A2 "Mae West" tanks. In July the 194th received a few M2A4 tanks: these were the same age as the others, but contained 37mm cannon, so some of the men picked up experience with cannon-armed tanks before receiving M3s on the San Francisco docks.

Miller's energy and can-do spirit pervaded the ranks. The men didn't mind that their unit was putting in more time on the exercise fields than any other on the base and delighted in showing up the "lifers." In April the battalion received a sudden influx of Minnesota draftees; seventy-seven of them, including Bernard FitzPatrick of Brainerd, were inducted in Minneapolis, put on buses, and sent directly to the 194th. This was seen as evidence of the unit commander's ability to get things done, even if he had nothing to do with it, and morale soared.

The battalion was short fourteen officers, and requisitions for them were being processed, but Miller wanted to give the positions to his best noncommissioned officers. Receiving no cooperation from the base, he had a copy of the qualification courses necessary for commissioning from the ranks, known as the "10 Series," pilfered from the reserve office in Seattle. He then had twenty-five of his men take the courses and requested a promotion board come up from San Francisco to evaluate the top fourteen. The board knew nothing of the controversy and, after being briefed by Miller and examining the men individually, recommended all fourteen for commissions. Of course, the fourteen Miller had requested through channels showed up shortly thereafter. Some of them were assigned to the Headquarters Company. Miller had arrived without one and had had no ready means of establishing one.

In August 1941 he was given the opportunity to pick up some experienced tankers from a source he would never have chosen—B Company, which was to be taken away from the 194th and shipped to Alaska. Miller protested all the way up to the Armored Force headquarters at Fort Knox, without success. He was told that his battalion was to prepare for immediate overseas shipment, and that he would receive a replacement company in theater. Returning to Fort Lewis and pulling the battalion from the Pacific Maneuvers, the West Coast's first armor-infantry exercise, he transferred all of the battalion's old tanks as well as some of his men to B Company in exchange for some of their best men. He picked up B Company's commanding officer as his executive officer. The forty-seven-year-old Capt. Charles Canby had fought in France and was one of the battalion's two World War I veterans, Miller being the other.

Before the end of August Major Miller had his orders giving his destination ("tropical service"), his POE (San Francisco), his ship (the liner SS *President Coolidge*), and his departure date (September 8). He drove the 770 miles to San Francisco nonstop to see what he was getting into. He would be bringing thirty-four officers, 390 enlisted men, thirty-seven M3 light tanks, nineteen half-tracks, and other vehicles onto a transport that was still rated as a passenger liner and had a small cargo capacity. The ship was taking other units to "the tropics," notably half of the 200th Coast Artillery Regiment (AA) with seventy-six officers, 1,681 enlisted men, twelve 3-inch guns, and twenty-four 37mm guns from the New Mexico National Guard; and the 17th Ordnance Company (Armored) with 155 men and its equipment.

Documentation is lacking, but at some point in mid-1941 it had been decided that the independent tank group that was being formed in secret to send to the Philippines would need more maintenance capabilities than were available in the tank companies' maintenance platoons, and an ordnance company was established to join it. Company A of the 19th Ordnance Battalion, 1st Armored Division, Fort Knox, was deactivated and reactivated as the 17th Ordnance Company (Armored). A full complement of six officers and 142 enlisted men was selected from the battalion to bring the new company up to full strength. Its mission was to perform heavy (4th echelon) maintenance on a light tank group's armored vehicles—it had supplies, spare parts, maintenance facilities, and wreckers to retrieve and tow wrecked vehicles to field shops. It was equipped to service all mechanical, electrical, ordnance, and communications systems. It would be under the command of Richard Kadel for its entire existence. A civil engineer, Kadel had managed the Civilian Conservation Corps (CCC) camp at Mammoth Cave from 1933 to 1935 and had joined the Army Reserves in 1940. He had quickly been called up, commissioned, and assigned to the 19th Ordnance Battalion. The vehicles and men of the 17th Ordnance Company were put on a troop train on September 1 and headed for the San Francisco Port of Embarkation for foreign service. It sustained one loss when a canvas truck top was ignited by engine sparks but arrived in time to help the 194th Tank Battalion load its gear on the SS *President Coolidge*.

Equipment stowage was a problem. The Army Transport Service's loading orders mentioned only "men and tanks"; Miller argued that these were useless without their equipment, and that he had been told to expect to "come off the ship fighting." Room was eventually found for everything except the gasoline and ammunition that arrived in the tanks, which the ship's captain refused to take and had to be left on the dock. One hold intended for nineteen tanks was too low to fit them without removing the turrets. Miller's men had never seen an M3, but Kadel's men were experienced with M3s and would be serving with the 194th in the Philippines (in the Provisional Tank Group, although this was unknown to all these men). The tanks arrived in time (without their radios, which were packaged separately). Kadel took responsibility for dismantling the tanks and loading them. The road convoy with the rest of the vehicles got there in time for the men to receive a quick physical exam and round of shots at Fort McDowell on Angel Island. The *President Coolidge* got underway on September 8, on schedule.

THE 192ND GHQ RESERVE TANK BATTALION (LIGHT) IN THE LOUISIANA MANEUVERS

Major Moore put his battalion and all of its wheeled vehicles on the road from Fort Knox on September 2 and established a bivouac near Fort Polk, Louisiana, on the 6th. Their M2A2 tanks, followed by train and trailer, and the battalion was reported 100 percent ready for operations by September 15, the beginning of the Louisiana Maneuvers. In late 1939 there had been no functioning corps or army headquarters in the U.S. Army. The army had comprised only 190,000 men in three half-strength infantry divisions, six skeleton cadre divisions, two horse cavalry divisions, a mechanized brigade with a handful of tanks, and a tiny air arm. Now, two years later, B/Gen. Leslie McNair, GHQ Chief of Staff, was able to assemble 400,000 men—twenty-seven divisions, nine corps, three armies, and nine air groups—to test the ability of the U.S. Army to fight a war. Evaluation of tactics was of secondary importance. What Generals Marshall and McNair wanted to see was how well high-level commanders and staffs—most of them unfamiliar with units larger than a regiment—could handle armies and corps under realistic restrictions of space and time. Not only did the performance of the combat arms exceed expectations, but the supply arm was able to transport and supply 400,000 men over the back roads of Louisiana with few glitches, a pleasant surprise to the GHQ, which was facing the greatest logistical challenge in history, supplying World War II's European campaign.

The 192nd Tank Battalion survivors remembered only the nighttime movements, with "21 bivouacs in 21 days"; some complained that they never practiced operating with the infantry, their ostensible specialization, and that the exercise rules were arbitrary and unrealistic. But their training in quick nighttime transfers and the smooth erection of base camps turned out to be exactly what they would need in the Philippines, and their performance in that regard was flawless. Major Wickord, their executive officer, read them the preliminary official report on the maneuvers, commending the unit for carrying out all orders in a timely fashion while not losing a single man or vehicle.

During the war the word spread within the unit that General Patton had "personally" chosen the battalion for foreign service as the "best tank unit in the maneuvers." I consider this story apocryphal because Patton was a division commander in Louisiana and would not have had an official role in such a decision, although the 192nd served under him for a while in the maneuvers, and the outspoken Patton's opinion of the unit would have been listened to. The other tank battalions in the maneuvers, with one exception, were in armored regiments in the two armored divisions, from which they would not have been separated. The exception was the 191st GHQ Reserve Tank Battalion (Light), which was obviously beaten out for the Philippines assignment by the 192nd, but which served adequately later in the war.

The 192nd returned to camp at Fort Polk to await further orders. They were expected to entrain shortly for the Carolina Maneuvers, but on October 4 they received orders to prepare for foreign service. They were to replace their M2A2s with "new" M3s, but these were new only in the sense that they were the latest U.S. design. The tanks themselves were clapped-out examples from the 753rd Tank Battalion and the 3rd Armored Division on the base. Some had ninety-six running hours and were due an overhaul at one hundred hours. Ordnance was stingy with ancillary parts. They supplied a set of blank firing attachments for each tank—useless, of course, in a combat environment—but only one rammer staff for the entire battalion. The unit did receive a full quota of auxiliary vehicles, some new: M2 and M3 half-tracks to replace their M3 combat cars, jeeps (still "peeps" to the Armored Force), motorcycles, and trucks.

The TO&E (Table of Organization and Equipment) was stretched to authorize 2nd Lt. Bill Gentry, the 192nd Battalion Communications Officer, a large amount of new equipment plus the men and spares he had had since Fort Knox. He did not find out until he reached the Philippines that he was to set up a school to train 10,000 Filipinos.

None of the radios in the M3 light tanks worked, and Frank Goldstein's choice to become an equipment specialist gained him a reputation in the battalion as a fixer. It turned out that all of the radios had the same problem. Small neon tubes had been installed to protect a sticking relay, apparently by the manufacturer, but these were not vibration (i.e., "tank") proof and had shorted out, burning out the coils. Frank fixed all the radios in short order and was promoted to private first class and specialist third class. He applied for a radio instructor's job at Fort Monmouth but heard nothing; he learned much later that Captain Hanes had trashed the application, apparently to keep Goldstein in the unit. He was fated to remain a B/192TB radioman for the duration.

Some men—those over twenty-nine years old, had dependents, or were sole sons—were allowed to resign from the Guard and return home. Some age restrictions were mandatory. Major Moore was ruled too old for overseas service and had to give up the battalion to Major Wickord. Moore went all the way to Washington, D.C., to protest, to no avail. The battalion brought its personnel roster up to establishment strength by soliciting skilled enlisted volunteers from the 753rd Tank Battalion. Junior officers were found among reservists (recent college graduates fulfilling ROTC obligations) on the base. One of the last orders from Major Moore gave every man who could be spared a week's leave. Goldy Goldstein borrowed enough money to go home and pack up his radio equipment for the government to retrieve.

Everyone else worked full-time to get the battalion ready for a sea voyage: updating records, packing, and waterproofing all metal equipment. Guns were coated in Cosmoline, a grease that could be removed at their destination with boiling water. The men were given a new mailing address: "c/o APO PLUM," which some companies decoded in minutes to mean "Philippines-LUzon-Manila," but some men did not realize their destination until formal orders were read to them at sea. On October 20 the equipment and vehicles from Headquarters Company and Company A were lashed onto flatcars on a waiting train; the men boarded passenger cars; and the train departed for Fort McDowell, Angel Island, San Francisco Bay, California. Three trains followed, each carrying a lettered company and its equipment and vehicles. The four trains took different routes, possibly for security but possibly also to reduce stress on the tracks and bridges in an excess of prewar caution; all reached Fort McDowell by October 24. Their ship, the transport USAT *Hugh L. Scott* (the former passenger liner *President Pierce*) was commodious but betrayed its origin with weak cargo gear. Harbor barges had to be used to load the tanks, but the process went smoothly, and by the 27th seventy-one M3 light tanks and thirty half-tracks and other vehicles were aboard. The 598 men of the 192nd stood for roll call on the San Francisco dock and boarded ship, which steamed under the Golden Gate on October 28, 1941, headed for PLUM.

THE LIGHT TANK M3

The Light Tank M3 was the standard light tank and the most numerous armored vehicle in the U.S. Army when it went to war. The tank was a progressive improvement on the cannon-armed M2A4. Its glacis armor was increased to a maximum of 1.5 inches, and more protection was given the engine. To better distribute the added weight and decrease ground pressure, the trailing idler wheel was hinged and dropped to ground level, lengthening the track footprint and the overall length. This balanced the tank and improved the ride; it was a distinguishing feature of all M3 and follow-up M5 tanks. It was never used elsewhere, possibly because, as crewmen complained, the complicated idler mechanism made it difficult to tension the tracks properly, and the M3 was notorious for throwing its tracks. Other changes from the M2A4 were a reduction in size of the vision slits and a new gun mount modified to bring the recoil mechanism inside the armored mantlet; that mechanism's position along the M2A4 gun barrel was very vulnerable. The weight of the M3 increased to 13.5 tons, but with no loss of performance. Sources list various top speeds; the average was probably thirty-six miles per hour on roads and twenty miles per hour cross-country.

The M3 light tank first saw combat in the spring of 1941 with the British Army in North Africa. The British crewmen complained about the rough ride and asked for some padding for the interior, which was later provided. The Guardsmen are not known to have commented on the ride, possibly because they had never known any better. The M3 was far superior to the Crusader, the British tank it supplemented in the desert, and it was nicknamed "Honey" for its reliability. The British also gave it a formal name, the Stuart, by which it is still known today, although the U.S. Army never assigned official names to its tanks in World War II. The men headed for the Philippines never heard the name "Stuart," and it is not used in this book.

In late 1941 the M3 light tank was state of the art in U.S. tank design. Its 37mm gun fired a two-pound fixed charge that could penetrate any Axis armor known to be in service and could also fire canister and high explosive, a round not available to the otherwise-comparable British two-pounder and which added greatly to the tank's versatility. It was also armed with five .30 caliber air-cooled machine guns, more than any other light tank. Its armor thickness exceeded that of the foreign light tanks to which it was compared, but it was vulnerable to Axis tank and antitank guns already in service. It was powered by a Continental 250-horsepower, air-cooled radial gasoline engine that was lightweight, reliable, serviceable, and in full production for aircraft trainers. Veterans recalled hot-rodding their lighter M2A2s on the highways around Fort Knox at eighty miles per hour; whether or not this was true, M3 engines were given governors to prolong their life, and the M3's maximum speed was less than forty miles per hour. The vertical engine mounting resulted in the high silhouette that characterized all U.S. tanks of this generation. The tank got two miles per gallon of 100-octane gasoline, and its limited tankage restricted its range to seventy miles, a real burden to the British in the desert, who needed the tank for British armor's self-defined "cruiser" mission.

The hulls of the M3s that the Guardsmen received were fabricated by riveting flat armor plates to an internal framework. The turrets of the first one hundred M3s built were also riveted, but the model that went to the Philippines had turrets welded from seven flat armor plates. The defects of rivets were well known, and it was always the U.S. goal to weld all of its armored vehicles, but it was somewhat tardy—in 1937 the Russian T-26 in Spain, often held up as a model of light tank design, was of all-welded construction.

The M3's manual transmission was standard for the period, as were its radios—receivers for all tanks, transmitters for platoon commanders and above. There was no intercom, and communications inside the tank were by hand and foot signals. Vision devices were crude—six- by one-half-inch armored glass slits for drivers and commander and a simple sighting telescope for the gunner—and visibility from a buttoned-up tank was very poor.

The crew of four had well-defined tasks, although these shifted quite a bit with combat experience. The Guardsmen were all well cross-trained on their M2A2s, but not on the M3s they took into combat. The driver operated the two fixed sponson .30 caliber machine guns. The codriver operated the machine gun in the flexible bow mount. His duties were the lightest, and he was usually the junior member of the crew. The radioman was stationed in the turret and loaded the cannon. The tank commander, who was a sergeant, or if a platoon leader, a commissioned officer, had to aim and fire the cannon, the coaxial machine gun, and the antiaircraft machine gun, as well as direct the tank. The turrets of the Guardsmen's M3s were trained manually and had no baskets, which were introduced later in the production run. The two men in the turret stood on the tank floor and scrambled around in its confined space as the turret turned, hopping over the drive shaft tunnel that passed through the fighting compartment. The cannon could be moved slightly in its mantlet, and turret rotation was kept to a minimum. The early M3 models lacked a gyroscopic gun sight, and firing on the move was out of the question. The tank was usually fought by pointing the hull directly at the target, stopping, firing a round, and then racing off.

CHAPTER 3

The Philippines

THE PHILIPPINE ISLANDS STRETCH 1,150 MILES ACROSS THE WESTERN Pacific Ocean, in the geographic heart of the Far East. The United States wrested them from Spain in 1898, intending them to be jewels in its new imperialist crown. The 7,100 islands of the Philippine Archipelago lack the natural resources of a Malaya or a Java, and where inhabited are primarily agricultural. The islands are largely mountainous, with elevations rising to 10,000 feet. Beaches are narrow, rivers are many and swift, and the foliage covering uncultivated areas is typical tropical jungle. The Philippine climate is tropical, with an average temperature of 78 to 80 degrees F and wet and dry seasons that come at different times on the eastern and western sides of the islands. Annual rainfall in different areas ranges from 38 to 160 inches. Almost 12,000 species of native plants have been identified, including 3,800 species of hardwoods, bamboo, coconut and nipa palms, ferns, jasmine, and 1,000 kinds of orchids. Rice is the main agricultural crop and the staple of the Filipino diet; copra, hemp, sugar, and tropical fruits such as pineapples and bananas are important cash crops. The 1941 population was 17 million, primarily of Malayan extraction; indigenous tribes such as Igorots and Negritos had fled to the mountainous interiors. The islands' largest city was Manila, Luzon, with 684,000 inhabitants.

In 1521 the Philippines were caught up in Europe's Age of Exploration when Magellan claimed the islands for Spain. Magellan himself was killed in the islands, but his sole returning ship brought back enough cloves to pay for the voyage, and it was only a matter of time before Spain returned with troops and priests to take over the archipelago. They were never entirely successful, and the ninth rebellion ended in 1897 when a Philippine Republic was formed. This lasted only a few months; the Spanish regained control just in time for their decisive defeat by Commodore George Dewey. The rebels assisted the United States, declared another republic and introduced another constitution, only to see Spain cede the Philippines to the United States in the treaty ending the war. The rebellion broke out again, this time against the United States, and it ended only when the United States agreed to allow the establishment of a National Assembly.

The United States was never comfortable in its role as a colonial power, especially after it found that the occupation of the Philippines was not profitable. By the 1930s the Philippines was financially dependent on the United States. There was little manufacturing; most inhabitants worked in home industries, in agriculture, or in the processing of agricultural products. The major civic institution was the Catholic Church. The islands themselves had little money for infrastructure such as roads and schools. There were periodic rebellions by the Moros, the Muslim inhabitants of the southern islands. The United States assumed the obligation for defending the islands against the only credible external threat, Japan. For decades it maintained a garrison of about 10,000 men.

In 1913 the garrison became the Philippine Department, a regular U.S. Army organization headed by a general officer. Half of the garrison were Philippine Scouts, U.S. Army units in which the enlisted men were predominately Filipino and the officers were nearly all American. There were two Scout infantry regiments and one cavalry regiment. The U.S. Army's Philippine Division contained the two Scout infantry regiments and one all-white infantry regiment. A career in the Scouts was one of the most prestigious to which a Filipino could aspire; many enlistees served a full twenty years in one unit, and the Scouts were considered, within the U.S. Army at least, to be among the best infantrymen in the world. The American officers and enlisted men present on the Philippine Department staff, in the Scouts, and in the few all-white units were not as well thought of. The army tended to send the Philippine Department its underperforming officers and men with good military skills but an inability to hold their liquor—the all-white 31st Infantry Regiment was known as the "Thirsty-First." The Philippines was a tropical paradise noted for its golf, polo, liquor, and low cost of living, and a tour of duty in the islands was much sought after prior to retirement. The men's duties were light. A houseboy could be hired for fifty cents per day to handle the men's cleanup chores, and work during the week stopped at noon for a three-hour siesta.

The military mission of the Philippine Department was restricted to the defense of Manila Bay and the port of Manila, the best port in the western Pacific and the only strategic target in the Philippines. Its putative opponent, Japan, was growing in strength. Manila was 7,000 miles from San Francisco and only 1,800 miles from Tokyo. The approach to the Philippines from the east was blocked by the formerly German-mandated islands that the Japanese occupied after the First World War. The Philippines were thus very vulnerable to attack, but not until 1941 was the threat taken seriously, as the United States treated the Japanese as it did all Asian races—with contempt.

From the beginning of the twentieth century, the Joint Army and Navy Board prepared color-coded plans pitting America's armed forces alone against all conceivable enemies—Japan was "orange." It was agreed that the Philippine Department and later, the small U.S. Asiatic Fleet, were present in the islands as deterrents, and if deterrence failed and the Japanese invaded, the navy would attempt to repel the landings and then depart for safer waters; the army would withdraw to the Bataan Peninsula and to Corregidor and the other fortified islands in the mouth of Manila Bay to seal off that important port. The army was expected to hold out for six months, at which time the navy would come to its rescue. In 1935 the navy withdrew this commitment, believing that intermediate bases in the Marianas would be needed and that no timetable could be guaranteed. MacArthur, who was then Army Chief of Staff, agreed to this "minor" change in the wording, and thus, in the words of the War Plan Orange historian, "signed the death warrant of Bataan and Corregidor." The last version of the document, WPO-3, removed any suggestion of a six-month siege and directed the garrison to fight on Bataan and Corregidor to the "last extremity" without promise of reinforcement or relief, words that were never passed on to the men on the ground.

During the 1920s and 1930s the United States gradually loosened its grip on Philippine institutions. In 1933 the U.S. Congress passed legislation establishing the Philippine Commonwealth, promising complete independence in 1946. By that time the Philippines was to have fully functioning armed forces. In 1935 the closest thing the Commonwealth had to an army unit was the Constabulary, a militarized national police force. President Manuel Quezon needed a strong military leader to organize a national army from scratch, and asked an old friend, Gen. Douglas MacArthur, to take the job. He accepted, with President Roosevelt's consent. MacArthur was given the title of Military Advisor to the Commonwealth Government and the rank of field marshal. His office was to function independently of, but in cooperation with, the Philippine Department. He brought two of the army's brightest staff officers, Maj. Dwight Eisenhower and Maj. James Ord, to Manila and set to work. In December 1935 their plan was presented to the first session of the Philippine National Assembly and passed as the National Defense Act. It called for the formation of a small professional army of 10,000 men, a conscription system, a ten-year training program of two classes per year to build up a reserve force of 400,000 men, a small air force, and a fleet of small torpedo boats. Infantry divisions would be small, 7,500 men, and armament and equipment, nearly all of which would be imported, was to be simple and suited for tropical service. The program proceeded slowly owing to lack of funds and infrastructure. By 1941 the Philippine Army had one regular and ten reserve divisions, most as cadres, and approximately 100,000 reservists, most with a bare minimum of training. There were not enough officers to man staffs and training camps, and these men had to be drawn from the Scouts and the United States. Heavy weapons were almost nonexistent, and the infantrymen were lucky if they had an Enfield or Springfield rifle, which were longer than they were tall, and a single uniform comprising a coconut-husk helmet, denims, and rubber-soled sandals.

By June 1941 a future war between Japan and the United States seemed inevitable. Defense of the Philippines was the responsibility of two weak, independent entities: the U.S. Army's Philippine Department and Field Marshal MacArthur's Philippine Army. MacArthur believed that the two should be combined in a Fil-American Army, and wrote General Marshall proposing that he, MacArthur, should be recalled to active duty in the U.S. Army; the Philippine Army should be mobilized; and that it and the Philippine Department should be placed in a new command, U.S. Army Forces, Far East (USAFFE) under MacArthur himself. Marshall and President Roosevelt agreed, MacArthur was restored to his U.S. rank of major general, and the USAFFE was established on July 26. MacArthur immediately denounced WPO-3 and its global equivalent, Rainbow 5, as defeatist, and pledged to defend the archipelago's entire 22,500-mile coastline "on the beaches" if given some reinforcements and material—primarily supplies for his beloved Filipino troops, but also American artillery, tank, and aviation units. The only reinforcements en route were 400 reserve officers to assist in training the Philippine Army. Defense of all of the 7,100 Philippine islands had never been considered remotely possible, but within days MacArthur was told he would receive substantial reinforcements, primarily aircraft groups, and Marshall told his staff, "It [is] the policy of the United States to defend the Philippines." In the words of the army's official historian, "The reasons for this change in policy are nowhere explicitly stated." In this author's opinion the main reason was an overconfidence in the U.S.'s premier offensive weapon, the B-17 Flying Fortress, coupled with an endemic underestimation of Japanese capabilities. The versions of the B-17 in service lacked the armor, armament, and high-altitude performance necessary for survival in combat, but the War Department relied on misleading combat reports from the Royal Air Force to conclude that these would be an effective deterrent to the Japanese and committed to send USAFFE four heavy bomber groups by April 1942, the earliest Japanese invasion date that American intelligence believed possible.

The rapidly expanding air forces warranted a new command, the Far East Air Force (FEAF), and a new commander. MacArthur was given his choice of three and picked M/Gen. Lewis H. Brereton, a noted facility and supply specialist. That this command was given to a two-star demonstrates the importance that Generals Marshall and Arnold attached to it. When Brereton reached Manila on November 3, he informed MacArthur that Marshall agreed to MacArthur's revision of the Rainbow 5 Plan.

Any invasion would be met on the beaches by MacArthur's army and Brereton's air force.

One B-17 group with thirty-five planes was operational in the Philippines by December; this was the largest concentration of these bombers outside the continental United States. Only one airfield, Luzon's Clark Field, could operate B-17s, and it lacked revetments and adequate anti-aircraft protection. Pursuit aircraft were also reaching the theater, and by December there were seventy-seven operational late-model P-40Es. These aircraft were doomed to early destruction. MacArthur had also requested a group of dive-bombers. The men of this unit, the 27th Bomb Group (Light), arrived on Thanksgiving, but without their A-24 attack planes, which were in a later convoy that was diverted to Australia. There was only one functioning early-warning radar unit; this had been cobbled into the existing air warning service that until then had been based on poorly trained ground observers.

To better manage his new forward-oriented defenses, MacArthur divided the Philippines into five tactical commands:

- Northern Luzon Force (M/Gen. Jonathan Wainwright), the most critical sector, including Lingayen Gulf, the central Luzon plain, the Zambales coast, and Bataan
- Southern Luzon Force (B/Gen. George M. Parker Jr.)
- Visayan-Mindanao Force (B/Gen. William F. Sharp)
- Reserve Force (USAFFE HQ), which included the Philippine Division
- Harbor Defenses (M/Gen. George F. Moore)

MacArthur's requests for ground units and equipment brought mixed results. The first unit to arrive was the 1st Battalion of the 200th Coast Artillery Regiment (AA) (ex–New Mexico National Guard), which reached Manila on September 16 on the SS *Franklin Pierce*. The SS *President Coolidge* left San Francisco on September 8 with three units aboard: the 194th GHQ Reserve Tank Battalion (Light), the 2nd Battalion of the 200th Coast Artillery Regiment (AA), and the 17th Ordnance Company (Armored). Thanksgiving brought the 192nd GHQ Reserve Tank

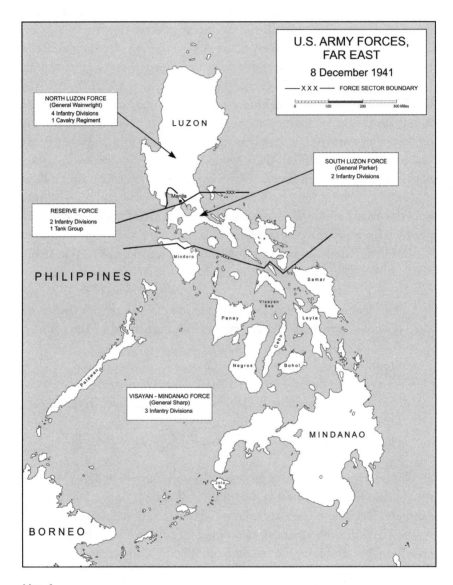

U.S. ARMY FORCES, FAR EAST

8 December 1941

—— X X X —— FORCE SECTOR BOUNDARY

0   100   200   300 Miles

NORTH LUZON FORCE
(General Wainwright)
4 Infantry Divisions
1 Cavalry Regiment

LUZON

SOUTH LUZON FORCE
(General Parker)
2 Infantry Divisions

Manila

RESERVE FORCE
2 Infantry Divisions
1 Tank Group

Mindoro

PHILIPPINES

Samar

Visayan
Sea

Panay

Leyte

Cebu

Palawan

Negros

Bohol

VISAYAN - MINDANAO FORCE
(General Sharp)
3 Infantry Divisions

MINDANAO

Jolo
Is.

BORNEO

Map 1

Battalion (Light) and the headquarters of the Provisional Tank Group (PTG), which was to command the tank battalions and the ordnance company. No American field artillery units reached the Philippines. The 2nd Battalion of the 131st Field Artillery, which was ex–Texas National Guard, was diverted to Java where it was captured by the Japanese and became the "Lost Battalion"; word of the men's survival did not reach the United States for three years.

The small amount of equipment MacArthur got for his Philippine Army units was primarily shaken out from the Hawaiian Department, but one brand-new piece of equipment came as a great surprise to USAFFE. The first M3 75mm self-propelled mounts (SPM) off the Autocar assembly line, plus a few T12 prototypes converted from White half-tracks, made it to the San Francisco docks in time to be loaded aboard the *Hugh L. Scott*. These were M3 half-tracks carrying forward-firing M1897A4 75mm guns behind small shields. They were intended to be self-propelled antitank weapons and saw such service in North Africa as M3 75mm Gun Motor Carriages (GMC). The fifty that arrived in the Philippines without crews were welcomed as the most modern artillery in the islands. The Provisional Field Artillery Regiment of three four-battery battalions was quickly organized to put them to use. Gun commanders were American; drivers, Philippine Scouts; gun crews, Philippine Army soldiers; ammo truck drivers, Guardsmen from the 200th Coast Artillery Regiment. The SPMs gained an admirable record in the next few months both as conventional artillery and in ambushes in cooperation with the PTG light tanks.

The SS *President Coolidge* reached Honolulu from San Francisco on September 13 and, after less than a day for refueling and a brief liberty, set sail for Manila. Security precautions made it clear that war was expected in the near future: A heavy cruiser escorted the liner; blackout was enforced; and the small convoy's course was to the south of the shortest, Great Circle route, in a weak attempt to avoid detection. When the transport left the South China Sea and entered Manila Bay, the soldiers on deck rushed to the port side to see the fortified island of Corregidor, and beyond it an alien landscape—a misty, dark-green jungle penetrated by jagged, vertical-sided, bare mountaintops. The fragrances of jasmine, frangipani, and hibiscus wafted over the water, adding to the exotic atmosphere. They were passing the Bataan Peninsula, a name none of the men knew then, but which they would curse for the rest of their lives. As they crossed the bay and approached the Manila docks, the odors became more complex and pungent—flowers mixed with burning incense, garbage, and sewage. This characteristic smell of a tropical Asian city would stay with the men only until they reached the countryside, where the new smell assaulting their noses was that of carabao wallows—fetid, slimy cooling ponds used by the local beasts of burden. Those men who survived prison camp would long remember still other odors from the camps—those of human excrement and decaying corpses.

The ship docked at Manila's Pier 7 on September 26, 1941. The men began debarking at 3 p.m. The M3 light tanks of the 194th needed to be reassembled and made ready for road travel, which looked like it would take at least a day, so Major Miller assigned a maintenance detail and Captain Kadel's 17th Ordnance Company to that task and raced ahead by car to Fort Stotsenburg in central Luzon, which was to be the unit's base. B/Gen. Edward King, the fort's commander, apologized that permanent barracks were not available; the tankers were put up in framed, screened, and floored tents. The 1st Battalion of the 200th Coast Artillery Regiment had arrived the previous week, and that regiment claimed possession of a satellite cantonment under construction—large sawali mat barracks raised off the ground, open windows all around with broad eaves and shutters to hold out the typhoon rains. The fort could have been a tropical post out of a Hollywood movie—it had a permanent stucco headquarters complex and dispensary, but most buildings were constructed of woven bamboo mats, called *sawali*, with grass roofs. There were several large drill grounds that doubled as polo fields. The fort's property abutted that of Clark Field, the largest air base on the islands, on two sides.

Major Miller's tanks did get on the road to Fort Stotsenburg the next evening, a task made more complicated by the men's complete unfamiliarity with the M3 light tank and the Philippine law placing vehicles on the left side of the road. The 194th's problems did not stop once they reached their base. Four of Miller's new jeeps were appropriated by USAFFE, leaving him short of staff cars. The 92-octane gasoline that USAFFE G-4

(Supply) had assured Miller was readily available for the tanks had to be begged from the air force—this was aviation gasoline, and the rest of the army had none. Their 37mm cannons lacked rammer staffs, recuperating oil, and high-explosive ammunition. There were no mechanical loaders for the machine gun ammunition belts. The radios were not designed for the M3 and could only be fit in the tank by removing the right sponson gun, leaving a large hole in the sponson that Miller could not get welded shut without authorization from the Ordnance Department in Washington. A large shipment of tank repair parts arrived on a later ship, but since they were classed as "supplies," they were stored in the Manila warehouses rather than being released to the unit.

Major Miller's problems with supply officers and Regular army officers in general were a continuation of those he had experienced at Fort Lewis, exacerbated by the languid pace of men who had spent years in the tropics and whose workdays broke at noon for their siesta. His sense of impending crisis met an unbending bureaucratic wall. He could not get enough high-octane gasoline to operate his tanks. He could get no ammunition at all—this was considered "ordnance reserve," not to be disbursed to combat units in peacetime. M/Gen. Jonathan Wainwright, commander of the forces in northern Luzon, did schedule several maneuvers, all of which would split the 194th into small packets over Major Miller's objections, but all were canceled, and the tanks did not move far from Fort Stotsenburg and Clark Field except for one quick road march to Lingayen Gulf and back, for which Miller took weeks wrangling permission from the USAFFE staff. Miller and his own staff did reconnoiter the neighboring territory in their staff cars and half-tracks, checking bridge capacities and road conditions and making rough maps. Miller sent his intelligence officer to give these to USAFFE G-2 (Intelligence), only to be told that the 194th had wasted its time: "It would be absolutely impossible for the Japanese to attack the Philippines successfully."

MacArthur had requested a full armored division for the USAFFE, of which the 194th was the first installment, but no one but MacArthur seemed to know why, beyond impressing the Filipinos and the Japanese. The Philippines was not conventional tank country, and the tankers would have to establish doctrine as they went along. Brigadier General

King did order Miller to work up an Alert Plan with the commanders of Clark Field and the 200th Coast Artillery Regiment. In case of war the 194th was to be stationed on and around Clark Field to repel the paratroopers that USAFFE Intelligence was certain would be dropped in any Japanese invasion (since the Wehrmacht's invasions of Holland and Crete, these were the new bogeymen in the minds of staid military planners). Miller's men now had a mission—an unsatisfactory one, but a mission nonetheless.

On October 28 the 192nd GHQ Reserve Tank Battalion (Light) sailed from San Francisco on the transport USAT *Hugh L. Scott*, the former liner SS *President Pierce*. The 588 men included many who had joined at Camp Polk to replace overage Guardsmen. Maj. Theodore Wickord, himself new in the job, assigned the newcomers to his headquarters and Headquarters Company, the four tank companies, and the medical detachment. His own replacement as executive officer was Maj. Havelock Nelson, a forty-three-year-old World War I veteran who was not a tanker but was a Guardsman and a banker with administrative experience.

Every military unit has at least one operator, a man who can turn any situation to his advantage. Pvt. Lester Tenney of B Company certainly qualified for the title. According to his memoir, Tenney heard on his first day at sea that the ship's chaplain was looking for an assistant—someone to oversee the ship's entertainment for the men. Tenney, one of about six Jews in the battalion, volunteered and was selected. He was now exempt from drills and other shipboard duties such as KP. He was moved from his three-deep bunk in the hold and given a two-room cabin, one room for an office and one for sleeping quarters. His official role was to check out game equipment, but before the voyage was over he was printing a daily paper and running a ten-piece band in addition to loaning out individual games and running group games.

On their first day at sea, the men of the 192nd were surprised to learn that they were traveling with a full colonel who was not only the senior officer on board but also would be their superior officer when they reached their still-secret destination. Col. James R. N. Weaver was born in Ohio in 1888 and after one year at Oberlin College received an appointment to West Point. He graduated in 1911 in the middle of his class and joined the infantry arm. After his first tour, ironically in the Philippines, he was sent to West Point to teach English and missed going to Europe in World War I. His early postings after the war were fairly typical for a promising infantry officer, but in 1937 he joined the tiny Tank School at Fort Benning. He remained in armor, rising to colonel and commanding the 68th Armored Regiment of the 2nd Armored Division during the Louisiana Maneuvers. He led the division temporarily in the absence of its commanding officer, General Patton, and was probably on the short list to take over one of the new armored divisions when on October 9 he received a top secret letter ordering him to report to Camp Polk. He was told that he was to leave for the Philippines immediately to command a new unit, the Provisional Tank Group (PTG), which had a table of organization betraying its provisional nature: It would comprise two light tank battalions, one medium tank battalion, and an ordnance company for heavy maintenance, but would lack many of the subordinate units found in an armored division. There were no organic infantry, artillery, or antitank units, and the headquarters staff was very small. Weaver was taken aback when told that the tank battalions were 100 percent National Guard. He asked for a West Pointer as his executive officer and was promised a specific lieutenant colonel who was attending the War College and would not be available until January or February. He was given three reserve captains as the nucleus of his staff. He met them for the first time in San Francisco, and they traveled with him on the *Hugh L. Scott*.

The transport's first port of call was Honolulu, which it reached on November 1. It remained for a few days while a convoy was being formed, giving all men of the 192nd ample opportunity to sample the delights of Oahu. Private Tenney was given a wallet full of money to spend on games for the rest of the trip and stayed out of trouble. The island was not yet overrun with servicemen and was eager to service those who came through, and the tankers fondly remembered Honolulu's bars and "two dollars a throw" cathouses. It was easy to strike up bar conversations with sailors who were eager to know where the men were going. Their official destination was still a secret, but they knew that they would be facing off against the Japanese. This tickled the sailors, who joked about Japanese capabilities. Sgt. James Bashleben of B Company recalled being told that the Japanese flew only wooden-propeller biplanes. Sgt. Al Allen and some men of C Company were given a tour of the USS *Arizona*'s Turret #2 by some inebriated sailors. The group was caught, and one man had to surrender his camera's film for immediate development in the *Arizona*'s darkroom. The man's protest that he had not photographed any of the ship's secret equipment was true, but the last chance to document the battleship's primary weapon had been missed. The magazine of Turret #2 was blown up on December 7 by a Japanese deep-penetration bomb, taking the *Arizona* to the bottom of Pearl Harbor, where it rests today.

One tanker's behavior was a little more outrageous than the usual hijinks. Capt. Don Hanes, the B Company CO, robbed the company's recreation fund and rented an airplane to visit a former girlfriend who lived on Oahu. He bragged about his exploit in the wardroom, the word spread to the company's enlisted men, whose money it was, and he was never able to regain their respect.

The convoy that left Honolulu consisted of the *Hugh L. Scott*, its traveling companion *President Coolidge*, the heavy cruiser *Louisville*, and a couple of destroyers. They were very much on a war footing, and it was interesting to watch the *Louisville* and the destroyers chase down every freighter that was visible as a smudge of smoke on the horizon. A zigzag course was added to the blackouts of previous convoys, and Sergeant Bashleben was nearly put on report for throwing an apple core overboard rather than putting it in an approved garbage can to be sunk after dark. Major Wickord announced their destination, which was greeted enthusiastically by the men. Duties were light—KP, cleaning the ship, and attending a few impromptu lectures on the Japanese and the Philippines. There was little military training. In San Francisco Major Wickord had tried without success to obtain a practice 37mm cannon and some machine guns for firing drills. Most of the men considered the Japanese to be a laughable enemy. Capt. Alvin Poweleit, the battalion's senior medical officer, was an exception. He had bought a Japanese grammar book in San Francisco and studied it on deck with the aid of a Japanese crewman; he told anyone who would listen that they were all doomed to be either killed or taken prisoner by the Japanese, and if the latter, he wanted to be able to converse with them. B Company's Cpl. Frank Goldstein stayed busy in the cargo hold for the entire voyage. As the company's senior radioman, it was his job to install and tune the radios in his seventeen tanks. No one in the other three companies seemed to want to install theirs, so Goldstein volunteered for that job as well. It was quiet in the hold, and Goldy Goldstein enjoyed being his own boss.

The *Louisville* convoy stopped at Guam for a few hours and then proceeded to Manila Bay, where the *Hugh L. Scott* dropped anchor on the morning of November 20, "Roosevelt Thanksgiving." Major Miller attached himself to the landing party, met Colonel Weaver and Major Wickord, and apparently warned them of the situation in the islands as he saw it. The ship tied up and the men filed off, past the first Filipinos they'd seen—primarily boys peddling Cokes, pesos, and their sisters—and boarded buses for the train station. The original plan to travel to Fort Stotsenburg by bus had been changed, and in the resulting confusion—the reception committee was at the wrong place—the men of the 194th were ordered to leave their eagerly anticipated Thanksgiving dinners to help the newcomers. The 192nd had lost its chance at a good dinner when it left the ship, and the enlisted men were served either slumgullion stew or hot dogs slung into mess kits—only the officers were invited to share the 194th's late turkey dinner.

The men of the 192nd then had to erect their own camp on a Fort Stotsenburg drill field one mile from Clark Field. This comprised two rows of pyramidal tents for the tank companies, two supply trucks and a kitchen truck for each company at the end of its row, and tents for the headquarters and headquarters company. The sleeping tents were equipped with cots and mosquito bars. These were the plushest accommodations the battalion saw in the Philippines; their bamboo barracks were under construction but never completed.

Second Lieutenants Gentry and Bush returned to Manila to oversee the unloading of the *Hugh L. Scott*. It took about three days to get the tanks and other vehicles and supplies to Fort Stotsenburg. All had survived the voyage well—seventy-one M3 light tanks, twenty-four M2 and M3 half-tracks, and a full allotment of trucks, trailers, command cars, jeeps ("peeps"), and motorcycles. Sgt. Al Allen, the C Company reconnaissance sergeant, lost his beloved peep to the recon corporal in the latest

Table of Organization and Equipment (TO&E) and had to learn to ride a Harley-Davidson motorcycle. The tankers had to install the Basic Items of Issue (BII)—radio antennas, ammunition, spare parts, tools—in their M3s after cleaning the Cosmoline from all their weapons. Ammunition was a problem even after USAFFE G-4 unlocked their warehouses—there was none of the promised high-explosive 37mm cannon ammunition. In common with the 194th, they were unable to get permission to fire their cannons until war began. Their .30 caliber machine gun ammunition had to be belted by hand; the battalion had been able to obtain only one automatic loader in San Francisco and was unable to borrow any on Luzon.

Bill Gentry quickly got the 192nd Tank Battalion radio shack set up and established radio contact with the United States using the Headquarters Company ham radio operators and the extra equipment he had brought. The 192nd now had the best communications in the Philippines. Within a few days his unit was sending personal messages to the United States from the men of the battalion. When the USAFFE communications staff traced the large amount of new radio traffic to Gentry's radio shack, Col. James Weaver was delighted at Gentry's initiative and planned to set up a radio room for the entire group under Gentry's command, but he was outranked by B/Gen. King, who summoned Gentry and offered him command of a new communications school with the rank of lieutenant colonel. Gentry would be allowed to staff the school with his own noncommissioned officers. It is possible that buildings for the school were already under construction, but events intervened, and the school never opened.

The men of the 192nd had little time to savor the pleasures of their new theater of operations. The plants and animals were all new to them. The weather was hot and damp, but better than that of "Lousy-ana," in the opinion of many. They had arrived in the dry season, so there was not much rain. The dust on the roads was dry and powdery, and stuck to everything. The men were issued dust masks to wear in their tanks, and many wore them everywhere. Their first surprise after getting their tents up was a swarm of young Filipinos competing to be hired as houseboys. For a few pesos a month, they shined shoes, made up the cots, and kept everything tidy. Women were hired very cheaply to do the laundry, which after a few days began to smell like carabao. It turned out that clothes were washed in carabao wallows. Everything picked up the odor, and after a week or so it went unnoticed.

The men did have some free time, in which they ran up against both the Regular army's prejudice against Guardsmen and the onerous uniform regulations of this tropical peacetime post. Tankers had to remove their overalls and change into the uniform of the day for urgent errands off the base; officers had to change into dress whites for dinner and drinks at the officers' club. Colonel Weaver and Major Miller's protests were for the most part unavailing.

The tankers did face less off-duty harassment on base than did the antiaircraft gunners from New Mexico. On November 4 the Japanese consul in Manila reported to Tokyo that "2–3000 brown soldiers" had arrived at Fort Stotsenburg, and that they were "not too friendly" with American soldiers. Other than his number estimate, which was high, the consul's comment was spot on. He was remarking on the Hispanics and Indians of the 200th Coast Artillery Regiment, who got into so many fights at the NCO club in response to racist comments that their CO declared it off limits, promising to build them their own, which of course never happened.

Most officers boycotted the officers' club in favor of the Manila night-life. The enlisted Guardsmen from all states frequented the local barrios, all of which had at least one bar and nightclub. A favorite nightspot was in Sopinbato, or "Sloppy Bottom." Almost as soon as they had erected their tents, Captain Write, CO of A Company, 192nd Tank Battalion, called a company meeting and had the senior base chaplain "put the fear of God and gonorrhea into the men." But STDs, primarily clap, quickly became a problem.

For entertainment on the post, the men listened to Don Bell's newscasts on KMZH from Manila. The jingoistic Bell was bombastic and brash and kept daring the four-eyed Japanese to attack. The men laughed, most agreeing with Bell's disdain for all Orientals—but Bell even kept up his taunts after the Japanese had attacked and destroyed the servicemen's belief in their own inherent superiority.

On November 21 the Provisional Tank Group (PTG) was formally activated under Col. James R. N. Weaver. It comprised:

- PTG Headquarters: 2 half-tracks, 2 jeeps, 1 sedan, and no trucks; the commander, 3 staff captains, and 10 enlisted men.
- 192nd Tank Battalion (Light): 54 M3 light tanks, 22 M2 and M3 half-tracks, TO&E allotment of trucks, trailers, jeeps, and motorcycles; 543 officers and men (on this date it gave up its D Company to the 194th Battalion for operations and administration, although the transfer was apparently never made official).
- 194th Tank Battalion (Light): 54 M3 light tanks, 22 M2 and M3 half-tracks, TO&E allotment of trucks, trailers, jeeps, and motorcycles; 543 officers and men (includes D Company of the 192nd Battalion).
- 17th Ordnance Company (Armored): equipment list not located; 148 officers and men.

The PTG was organized at Fort Stotsenburg as an independent tactical command under the Commanding General, USAFFE (MacArthur). It was associated with the USAFFE General Reserve (primarily the Philippine Division) administratively, but only MacArthur or his chief of staff, B/Gen. Richard Sutherland, could issue it operational orders. This peculiar arrangement did not match actual conditions on the ground and led to problems throughout the coming campaign. It has never been explained as other than a product of MacArthur's ego and controlling nature, but Alvin Poweleit's diary inadvertently adds more to the story.

On the afternoon of November 21, Colonel Weaver decided to pay a courtesy call on MacArthur and invited Dr. Poweleit along. Oddly, Maj. Wickord was not included, but Poweleit got Wickord's permission to go. MacArthur met them at the Manila Army & Navy Club and greeted Weaver like an old friend. Weaver ordered scotch and soda; the general, iced tea; and Poweleit, lemonade. They discussed tanks and their capabilities for nearly two hours, with MacArthur dominating the conversation. When the meeting ended and everyone departed, Weaver asked Poweleit his opinion of MacArthur. Poweleit responded that at first he wondered who the general was trying to impress with his verbosity and rhetoric. But after listening, Poweleit realized that MacArthur's "was not a superficial intellectual brilliancy, but a brilliancy of a deeper and more profound nature—the brilliancy of a thinker." Weaver wholeheartedly agreed.

What is the significance of this conversation for the present reader? First, MacArthur and Weaver were friends who respected each other's opinions; MacArthur may in fact have requested Weaver by name to command the armored division that he also requested. I have found no documentary evidence of this, but it seems plausible. Second, MacArthur and Weaver shared a vision of tanks as offensive Blitzkrieg weapons, intended for slashing movements through and behind the enemy's lines. Third, all of MacArthur's ground commanders were holdovers from the Philippine Department; many had been in the islands for years and had no knowledge of modern armored warfare. General King was the only one among them who believed war was imminent and seemed open to new ideas, but he was slated to leave Fort Stotsenburg for Manila on December 3 to become the USAFFE artillery officer. If given tanks to command, the others would probably fritter them away in small detachments to infantry units. (We have already seen Wainwright try to do this with Miller's battalion, weeks before the war.) MacArthur thus thought it best to keep the PTG under his direct control; Weaver of course agreed.

For a month or more the transports bringing reinforcements to the Philippines returned to the United States carrying military dependents. Washington obviously felt that the Far East was closer to war than did most officers in the Philippines. To boost the morale of men suddenly without wives, Brigadier General King at Fort Stotsenburg and Lieutenant Colonel Maitland at Clark Field ordered their officers to stop shaving. Then, on the day that *President Coolidge* left with the last of the wives and children, King ordered a full-dress dinner in the officers' mess. Most of the officers from the combat units were there reluctantly, staring at their drinks until a drum roll interrupted the clinking glasses. The bearded King stood up and announced, "Gentlemen, I have word that the tug pilot has just left the *Coolidge* and all the wives are at sea!" The band began playing, followed by what Dr. Poweleit called "a special feature of native dancing and singing." A young New Mexican lieutenant remembered it differently. He called the natives strippers and said that he saw more that night than he had ever seen before.

Major Miller gave Colonel Weaver a copy of the Alert Plan to approve, but Weaver rejected it. The plan was defensive; Weaver's orientation was entirely offensive, but after he met Wainwright he changed his mind and approved the plan.

M/Gen. Jonathan Wainwright was the senior USAFFE field commander, and when MacArthur gained full control of the Philippine defenses by disbanding the Philippine Department and merging their assets with those of the Philippine Army, he divided the islands into five corps-equivalent commands and offered the most important to Wainwright, along with a promotion to lieutenant general. Wainwright was a tough, wiry cavalryman who had been on Luzon since September 1940, when he had arrived to take command of the Philippine Division. This posting had been a surprise to Wainwright, who had been leading a cavalry brigade at remote Fort Clark, Texas, which he fully expected to be his last command. He had previously commanded the prestigious 3rd Cavalry Regiment at Fort Myers, Virginia, adjacent to Washington, D.C. In 1938 he had gone into General Marshall's black book as an old (fifty-five), hard-drinking cavalryman. Marshall was purging generals with any of these three characteristics from the army, but three years later Wainwright was in command of the North Luzon Force. One has to assume that Marshall felt that Wainwright's well-known affection for alcohol would not hurt him in the Philippines, and that his popularity with enlisted men would help morale in a theater that was destined to be forgotten. Wainwright's area of responsibility encompassed Lingayen Gulf, which contained the best beaches on Luzon and was considered the only suitable site for a large-scale Japanese invasion. His forces had to defend the beaches, and if forced to withdraw despite MacArthur's orders to hold to the death, fall back in an orderly fashion to Bataan. Wainwright was never known as a tactician, and Weaver's attempts to get his 108 tanks added to Wainwright's battle plan ended with frustration. Captain Poweleit confided to his diary, "I overheard Col. Weaver and Gen. Wainwright discuss tank warfare, and I am afraid that the General hasn't the slightest idea of their use. This could be very bad if they were committed to action without complete knowledge of their capabilities."

Poweleit's own preparations for the invasion that he expected had not stopped once he got off the *Hugh L. Scott*. He continued his Japanese language training for several days with a Japanese man he found working on the base, despite that man's unease. He bought a book on native flora and fauna in a nearby town and enlisted a native boy to find edible plants—cogon grass, papaya seeds, alibangbang (a small tree with edible, bitter leaves)—and animals—mudfish and earthworms—that were described in the book. He increased his pay allotment for home and took out a $10,000 insurance policy. During his workday he scouted Luzon by jeep and completed a 900-page Luzon sanitary survey for Colonel Weaver in less than a week. He also cadged a flight with a friendly B-17 pilot and noted many Japanese fishing boats in Lingayen Gulf, some unusually large. The pilot said that these had all been reported to USAFFE headquarters, with no result. On December 2, with most of the military now on alert, Poweleit suggested digging bomb shelters for 192nd Battalion headquarters. He was greeted with hoots of derision but ordered his own men to dig them for themselves—he had two medics stationed permanently with each tank company—and for his own medical detachment headquarters.

Colonel Weaver did what he could to prepare for what he believed would be the coming war of movement. He made several reconnaissance trips by half-track and jeep, confirming what Major Miller had found. He made preparations to stock tank gasoline in various dumps around Luzon. He got the armory to release ammunition but was unable to schedule any time on the firing ranges. He then approved Miller's Alert Plan, with Major Wickord's battalion added. The 192nd would be positioned north and east of the Fort Stotsenburg main post; the 194th was in the heavy cogon growth surrounding a small hill near Clark Field and on the grassy island between the two main landing strips. Not a night now passed without high-altitude overflights by unknown aircraft. 200th Coast Artillery (AA) searchlights assiduously tracked these. Blackouts were ordered for Clark Field and adjacent Fort Stotsenburg. Clark Field scheduled practice alerts for the day of November 30 and the night of December 2, and the tank units were invited to participate; the antiaircraft regiment for some reason was not. The day alert was full of near-collisions with air and antiaircraft assets, and it was obvious to Weaver that movement to positions during a night alert would be a disaster, especially to the 194th, which shared its alert positions with small ammunition and gasoline dumps around the hill and between the runways. On December 1 he ordered his tanks and half-tracks to return to their alert positions and stay there. They could be fed and supplied by the rear echelon trucks. There they stayed until the outbreak of war.

Japan's stunning defeat of Russia in 1905 had established its position as a major Asian power and led its rulers to plan for a dominant role in the western Pacific and eastern Asia. Japan's plans to expand into China (to obtain land), Malaya (to obtain rubber), and the Netherlands East Indies (to obtain petroleum and other strategic materials) were brought up sharply in July 1941. Japan had obtained the agreement of Vichy France to occupy its Indo-China colony. This would serve the Japanese campaign in China, but also out-flanked the Philippines and the important British colony of Hong Kong. President Roosevelt responded on July 26 by freezing all Japanese assets in the United States. Great Britain and the Netherlands East Indies quickly followed suit. Japan instantly lost 75 percent of its foreign trade and 88 percent of its oil imports. It had petroleum reserves sufficient for three years if at peace, less than half that if at war. Prime Minister Fumimaro Konoye frantically proposed that a peace treaty with the United States be negotiated in face-to-face meetings between him and President Roosevelt, possibly in Alaska. General Marshall and Adm. Harold Stark, Chief of Naval Operations, were highly in favor of these meetings, which would postpone war for at least the several months it would take to complete their planned reinforcement of the Philippines, but President Roosevelt, Secretary of State Cordell Hull, and Secretary of War Henry Stimson were adamantly against it. Low-level talks continued in Washington, but Konoye resigned on October 16 and was succeeded by Gen. Hideki Tojo. War was now inevitable. Stimson famously confided to his diary on November 25, "The question was how we should maneuver them [the Japanese] into firing the first shot without allowing too much danger to ourselves." General Marshall was concerned enough to send a "war warning" message to MacArthur on November 27:

> *Negotiations with Japan appear to be terminated to all practical purposes with only barest possibilities that Japanese government might come back and offer to continue. Japanese future action unpredictable but hostile action possible at any moment. If hostilities cannot, REPEAT cannot, be avoided the United States desires that Japan commit the first overt act. This policy should not, REPEAT should not, be construed to restricting you to a course of action that might jeopardize the successful defense of the Philippines. Prior to hostile Japanese action you are directed to take such reconnaissance and other measures as you deem necessary. Report measures taken. Should hostilities occur you will carry out the tasks assigned in Revised Rainbow 5 which was delivered to you by General Brereton. Chief of Naval Operations concurs and request you notify Hart.*

MacArthur passed on the gist of this message to select members of his staff. It stirred some to take action. Lieutenant Colonel Maitland ordered revetments for the B-17s on his overcrowded Clark Field built out of sand-filled gasoline drums and long, L-shaped personnel trenches gouged by a ditch-digging machine. Colonel Weaver claimed later that he did not receive this warning, but already had his PTG on a war footing. The message had one unanticipated and highly undesirable outcome—its carefully worded desire that Japan commit the first overt act was used by MacArthur to excuse the debacle that befell Clark Field on December 8.

The Imperial General Headquarters had completed their war plan by the first of November after about six months work. Japan's war aim was to capture the Dutch and British possessions in southeastern Asia and incorporate them in its Greater East Asia Co-Prosperity Sphere. It would prevent effective U.S. intervention by:

1. Destroying or neutralizing the U.S. Pacific Fleet in Pearl Harbor.
2. Depriving the United States of its base in the Philippine Islands.

3. Cutting the American line of communications across the Pacific by seizing Wake and Guam.
4. Establishing a powerful island-based line of defense: Kuriles-Wake-Marshalls-East Indies-Malaya-Indochina.

They did not plan to defeat the United States but force it into a negotiated peace on favorable terms to Japan. Their navy, superior to the combined forces of the British, the Dutch, and the Americans in the Pacific, would attack from the first day, and after attaining naval supremacy would aid the army in its conquests and patrol the line of defense. Most of the army was tied down in China, but that part devoted to the southern campaign, the Southern Army, would win out with speed and offensive spirit.

The Southern Army was divided into four corps-size numbered armies. Gen. Masaharu Homma's 14th Army was assigned the Philippines. Homma had only two infantry divisions, some supporting units, including two tank regiments, and one air group, equivalent to a numbered American air force. He was allowed only fifty days to capture the archipelago, after which the air group and half his infantry would be withdrawn for operations farther south. He and his staff had a good estimate of the size of the Fil-American army, but no knowledge of War Plan Orange, which called on it to withdraw to Bataan. The Japanese planned to land on Luzon north and south of Manila and encircle the city, at which time the Fil-American defenses were expected to dissolve. The Japanese were confident of success despite being outnumbered two to one. They had little respect for the Americans, and even less for the Filipinos.

The lack of respect was mutual. In the spring of 1939 the Joint Army and Navy Board (predecessor of World War II's Joint Chiefs of Staff) began pondering the need for, and effect of, alliances in the Pacific. It was decided that the loss of the Indies to the Japanese would be a casus belli even if American possessions were not directly attacked, and projected a war against Japan involving the United States from the outset in binding alliances with Great Britain, France, and the Netherlands (but not China) on behalf of "the interests of the White race [sic]." Fleet visits to Malaysian harbors and the reinforcement of Luzon would probably be enough to scare off the Japanese. This rosy optimism dimmed during the early days of World War II, when European successes by Germany—to which Japan was now allied—prompted the United States to adopt a secret Europe-first policy that wrote off the Philippines. The American plans for the archipelago's defense had always been based on bluff rather than reality—there were never enough Americans present to defend all 7,100 islands, and the buildup of the Filipinos' own defenses was barely underway. But MacArthur's ascension to high command in the Philippines in mid-1941 had brought a sudden change of attitude in Washington. He was promised, and received, reinforcements, and by December the Fil-American defenses included the largest concentration of American warplanes outside the United States and the first tank unit to leave the American continent since World War I. A Japanese landing fleet approaching Luzon would be punished by B-17s and submarines; its army would be met on the beaches by MacArthur's 100,000-man Philippine Army; and any survivors would be swept back into the sea by the M3 light tanks of the Provisional Tank Group. Those were MacArthur's plans.

CHAPTER 4

December 8

IMPERIAL JAPANESE NAVY AIRCRAFT BEGAN ATTACKING PEARL HARBOR a little before 8 a.m. on December 7, Hawaiian time—2:30 a.m. on December 8 in the Philippines. Pvt. Bud Bardowski was probably the first Provisional Tank Group (PTG) soldier to learn of the raid. He was pulling extra duty in the B/192TB headquarters half-track as punishment for punching out the company's first sergeant and was listening to music on a favorite shortwave radio station, San Francisco's KGEI, when an announcer broke in with a bulletin stating that Hawaii was under air attack. When Bud reported this news to the duty officer, he was told to ignore it; everyone was sensitive to radio hoaxes since Orson Welles's 1938 "The War of the Worlds" broadcast.

Word of the attack was soon being spread through official sources and by the Manila radio. Most of the tankers got some version of the story at breakfast. Major Miller found it was the talk of the officers' mess at 6:30 a.m., and after eating went to his office to await orders. The enlisted men had no mess hall but filled their mess kits at the kitchen and returned to their tents or vehicles to eat. Sgt. Jim Bashleben was eating in his tent when Cpl. John "Mouse" Massamino burst in shouting, "They bombed Pearl Harbor! We're at war with Japan!" He had heard the news on his radio in his own tent. Colonel Weaver apparently was waiting for some official word, but at 7:30 a.m. ordered his two battalion commanders, Major Miller and Major Wickord, on full alert.

Major Miller in turn ordered his company commanders to implement his Alert Plan. His 194th Tank Battalion tanks and half-tracks were already emplaced in cogon grass and foliage around two sides of

66

the crowded Clark Field and in a strip between the runways and were now manned by their full crews; his rear echelon was to leave Fort Stotsenburg, which Major Miller felt was too exposed, and take cover in the nearby jungle. Major Wickord's 192nd Tank Battalion was still parked near Fort Stotsenburg's main post area. Its natural defensive positions on the eastern and southern sides of Clark Field were privately owned and had been forbidden to it until today. No preparations had been made, and the men were told to scatter their tanks in the brush as best they could. Many did not have their full allotment of ammunition. Sgt. Al Allen belted .30 caliber shells for C Company by hand—the belt loader couldn't be found. The cannons of A Company's tanks had still not been cleaned of the Cosmoline that they had been soaked in to prevent rusting on the trip over. Sgt. Forrest Knox was in charge of putting A Company's weapons in order. Some of his men belted machine gun ammunition, while Knox himself cleaned the 37mm cannon bores. The battalion's single rammer staff was missing, so Knox used a piece of bamboo and a chunk of burlap soaked in aviation gas, which wiped out the Cosmoline and any residual oil. Removing oil from the gun barrels was forbidden, as this allowed them to rust quickly, but Knox told the complaining tank commanders that this was his way of doing the job, and he had cleaned all seventeen of the company's cannons by mid-morning.

Once the men were in place, they spent the morning listening to the radio, sharing rumors, and carrying out the standard army order, "Always work to improve your position." This meant camouflaging their tanks and half-tracks with brush and loading the cans of ammunition they were brought by Bud Bardowski and others (as part of his punishment, Bardowski and his radioman T/4 Frank Goldstein were ordered to fill the B/192TB headquarters half-track with machine gun ammunition and deliver it to the company vehicles). Their commander, Capt. Don Hanes, had both a tank and a half-track at his disposal, and chose to stay with the tank now and for the rest of the campaign. Capt. Fred Moffitt of C/194TB visited his men and ordered Pvt. Roy Diaz to move the fifty-gallon drums of aviation gasoline that shared the cogon grass with his tanks. Diaz found a truck, loaded the drums—he did not state how—and headed for the jungle. Capt. Walter Write of A/192TB brought some hard-boiled eggs to his men and told them to expect an attack by noon, although he did not say where he got his information. The attack they were preparing for was by Japanese airborne troops. Japanese bombers were not considered a threat and were to be handled by the antiaircraft guns and interceptors—P-40s took off and landed in a steady stream for several hours, although all had landed by 11:45 a.m. Capt. Jack Altman of D/19T2B told Sgt. Arnold Lawson that the tanks' priority targets were not Japanese paratroopers but transports landing on the airstrips to disgorge troops. Altman's tanks were to charge the transports, ram their tails, back up, and set fire to the transports with their machine guns. To Lawson this process seemed overly complex and silly.

Shortly after noon Colonel Weaver ordered the PTG to return to half alert, "as the skies over Luzon are clear," and send the men to lunch. Major Miller assembled his officers and told them that inasmuch as Weaver's message "was not stated as an order," Miller was going to ignore it for his 194th Tank Battalion and keep it in its alert position—combat vehicles fully manned and the rear echelon dispersed in the jungle. This was the first of several times Miller chose to defy the wishes of his superior officer. PFC Bernard FitzPatrick of A/194TB was in a tank next to the battalion command post and saw Miller send off his S-2 (Intelligence) officer, Capt. Ferris Spoor. Spoor was going to PTG headquarters for clarification. FitzPatrick heard later that while in Weaver's headquarters Spoor overheard an order from USAFFE stating that all aircraft on Clark Field were to remain on the ground—probably the reason Weaver decided to stand his own men down.

But where were the Japanese at this time? Ten minutes from Clark Field. Why were the P-40s and the highly vulnerable B-17s on the ground? Treatises have been written on this subject. The tankers' role in the coming debacle was only peripheral. It will pay us to study the timetables of the Japanese attackers and of the Americans in USAFFE who bore the principal responsibility for the defense of Clark Field. The Japanese originally planned to attack Clark and Iba Fields at daybreak on December 8 with naval medium bombers from their Formosan bases. This was four hours after the Pearl Harbor attack, but the increased accuracy of daylight bombing was felt to outweigh the danger from loss of secrecy.

Heavy fog over their two bases forced the Japanese to delay takeoff from 2:30 to 4 a.m. and finally to 8:18 a.m., placing their estimated time on target at 12:30 p.m., a full ten hours after the attack on Pearl.

The Japanese fully expected their own Formosan bases to be bombed by the B-17s that they knew were at Clark Field. However, the B-17s never came. This was not from lack of trying by Maj. Gen. Lewis Brereton, the commander of the Far East Air Force (FEAF). The American war clock in the Philippines began ticking at 2:30 a.m., when Adm. Thomas Hart's Asiatic Fleet headquarters received the famous radio message, "Air raid Pearl Harbor. This is no drill." Hart immediately warned his ships, staff, and USAFFE headquarters that America was at war. All but USAFFE acknowledged receiving the message.

Maj. Gen. Richard Sutherland, MacArthur's chief of staff, got the word at 3:30 a.m. from a commercial radio broadcast, probably the same one Bud Bardowski was listening to. Sutherland telephoned Brereton, who warned his own staff to break out their plans to attack Formosa and arrived at MacArthur's Manila headquarters for orders at about 5 a.m. Sutherland prevented Brereton from seeing MacArthur, who was supposedly in conference, but finally took Brereton's request into MacArthur's office. He returned saying that Brereton had MacArthur's permission to continue planning, but that USAFFE and thus FEAF was not to make the first overt action over the Philippines—this despite MacArthur's receipt of a War Department message at 5:30 a.m. confirming the Pearl Harbor attack and directing MacArthur to implement the tasks specified in Rainbow 5, one of which was to use the FEAF to conduct raids on Japanese facilities. A disgusted Brereton returned to his own headquarters and told his staff and L/Col. Eugene Eubank, the B-17 unit commander, to keep planning.

All this time the Air Warning Service (AWS) at Nichols Field was receiving reports of Japanese aircraft. At 8 a.m. the acting 19th Bomb Group commander at Clark Field had his B-17s take off and circle the area to avoid being caught on the ground. By 9 a.m. Aparri and Baguio in northern Luzon had been bombed by Japanese Army aircraft, and Davao in southern Mindanao had been attacked from a Japanese aircraft carrier. The first overt war actions over the Philippines had definitely been taken by the Japanese, and Brereton called Sutherland at 10 a.m., only to be rejected once again. MacArthur called Brereton at 10:14 a.m. and told him to plan for offensive action that afternoon. At 11 a.m. he called again and authorized reconnaissance flights over Formosa, followed by an air raid in the afternoon. That matched Brereton's own thinking, and at 11:20 a.m. FEAF Field Order 1 was teletyped to Clark Field recalling all B-17s to prepare for reconnaissance or bombing missions that afternoon. The circling B-17s all came in to land, and the crews went to lunch while the aircrafts were being serviced. Were the bombers lined up in a neat row, as some sources claim? Probably not, but the field was too small to disperse these large aircraft properly or move them under trees; there was no camouflage netting in the Philippines; and only two revetments were under construction. Two of the B-17s were in hangars to receive their olive drab paint; the rest stuck out on the airfield in all their aluminum glory, reflecting the bright Philippine sun for miles.

Performance of Col. Harold George's V Interceptor Command on this day was abysmally poor. It controlled one Pursuit Group, the 24th, under Col. Orrin Grover at Clark Field. The 24th contained five pursuit squadrons based on four airfields in the Manila-Clark Field area. There were ninety fighters, only fifty-four of which were modern P-40Es. The Interceptor Command's main source of reliable information was the radar set at Iba Field, which could determine a formation's direction and speed (with a little algebra), but not its altitude or size. From all indications the radar performed well on December 8 until it was bombed to oblivion. Colonel George did not let Colonel Grover scramble his planes until he estimated that the Japanese were fifteen minutes from Clark, which was not nearly enough time. In common with all other Americans in the Philippines, the two men grossly underestimated the performance of the men and machines of the Japanese Naval Air Force. They were also over-confident of their own fighters. The P-40E was a very poor interceptor, requiring ten minutes to reach 15,000 feet and then climbing no faster than 1,000 feet per minute between 15,000 and 20,000 feet and no more than 500 feet per minute from 20,000 to 25,000 feet.

After a morning spent in futile medium-altitude patrols and transfers between airfields, almost all of the fighters were on the ground at 11:27

a.m. when radar picked up a large formation over the Lingayen Gulf and reported it to the Air Warning Service. When George allowed Grover to scramble his fighters, he ordered four squadrons to the Manila area, although one did not receive the message. The 20th Pursuit Squadron, with the only fighters on Clark Field, was apparently forgotten, was never scrambled at all, and was destroyed on the ground. Clark Field, the most important target in the Philippines, had no air defense. In probably his most egregious error, Grover failed to warn the 19th Bomb Group, which shared Clark Field with him. At 12:20 p.m. the 24th Pursuit Group radioed to all its airborne fighters, "Tally Ho Clark Field! All pursuit to Clark! Messerschmitts [sic] over Clark!" It was far too late. No American fighter reached the altitude of the Japanese bombers, which returned to Formosa unscathed after their mission.

At 12:35 p.m. the rumble of many aircraft was heard approaching Clark Field from the northwest. Two perfect V-of-V formations of twin-engine planes came into view in the clear sky. The tankers had time to count them—most came up with totals of fifty-three or fifty-four—but could not identify them. They were blue or blue-gray, so could not be B-18s, the only twin-engine U.S. Army bomber in the Philippines. Several men shouted, "Hey! Look at all the Navy planes!" Sprinkles of confetti could be seen sparkling in the air beneath the aircraft. Someone yelled, "Bombs! Take cover!" just before the first one exploded. Blasts from 132-pound bombs walked down the main runway and into the field's permanent buildings. The main gasoline dump went up in a huge fireball. Panicked men ran in all directions. The tankers at Clark took cover in the "Maitland's Folly" slit trenches or in or beneath their tanks. They had no weapons that could be used against high-altitude bombers; this was the responsibility of the 200th Coast Artillery (AA), which had eleven of its twelve 3-inch guns sited on the approved northern and western sides of the airfield. The unit had received a few shells that morning but had not fired its weapons since it arrived in the Philippines. Green corrosion had to be filed off the shells before they could be loaded. The fuses were corroded to the shell bases and had to be knocked loose with wrenches. The old powder-train fuses could not be set for the altitude of the bombers, which were above 20,000 feet, and the shells that did explode—an estimated one of six—went off 2,000 to 4,000 feet below the formation. No medium bomber was hit by antiaircraft fire.

The arriving Japanese were not able to believe their good fortune. Clark Field seemed totally inactive at first—no antiaircraft fire, no interceptors—but on close examination many aircraft, including the highly respected B-17s, could be seen around its boundaries. The first formation, comprising twenty-six G3M2 Type 96 Naval Attack Bombers (later called "Nells" by the Allies) dropped 324 132-pound bombs in a closely spaced string, and after crossing the field, wheeled in formation in a broad left turn and headed back across Luzon. FPO1C Saburo Sakai, leading a flight of nine of the thirty-six A6M2 Carrier Fighter escorts ("Zeroes") watched Clark Field disappear in a brown carpet of bomb bursts and burst into tears of joy.

In the brief pause between the two bomber formations, Sergeant Al Allen of C/192TB, who had dived under a tank with a half-dozen other men, sheepishly climbed out, frightened to death, and was face-to-face with Colonel Weaver, one of the men who had shouted, "Look at those planes!" Weaver now stared at Allen and yelled, "Sergeant, you're out of uniform! Button those flaps!" Allen's one-piece fatigues had flaps to attach over his boots, and these were undone. Flustered and angered, Allen replied, "Yes sir!" and fastened the flaps. Weaver continued, "Take your motorcycle, find your company CO and make sure the tanks are under cover!" "Yes, sir!" again. Although this was far removed from Allen's regular duties, it was good to get orders. "Good luck to you, soldier" was the sendoff from the colonel. Only much later did Allen realize that the chewing out had been Weaver's way of calming him down—Allen observed that while his fatigues were dry, those of most men were wet.

The second wave of bombers—twenty-seven G4M1 Naval Attack Bombers ("Betties") continued the damage begun by the Nells and followed them in their wheel to the left. Nearly every permanent installation on the airfield had been destroyed, but most of the B-17s had survived to this point. The Zeroes continued their escort for ten minutes and then turned back to attack the airfield, as ordered. They approached the field from the south at fifty to one hundred feet, strafed with their 20mm cannon and 7.7mm machine guns, circled around to the south, and came back repeatedly. Their prime target was the B-17s, but they fired at any-thing that moved or fired at them. The antiaircraft gunners, tankers, and half-track crewmen all took shots at them. The antiaircraft gunners had decades-old 37mm cannons and .50 caliber machine guns, but their range finders would not track, their ammunition was corroded, and they apparently had no success. The tanks had turret-mounted 37mm cannon, but these could not track aircraft. They had .30 caliber machine guns on their turrets in antiaircraft mountings, and these were used. Best equipped were the tank battalions' M2 half-tracks, which had .30 and .50 caliber machine guns mounted independently on a ring that traveled around the entire bed.

Forrest Knox's experience with the tank-mounted antiaircraft machine gun was typical. He had finished cleaning the tank barrels, took his tank to its dispersal, and was standing near it when he saw an explosion on the hangar line, followed by billowing clouds of black smoke. When the sound reached him, he knew what it was and jumped in his tank, followed by a crewman. Knox closed the turret hatch and hunched down. The crewman asked, "What will we do now?" Knox replied, "Well, I don't think we do anything." The man said, "We can't stay here." Knox came back, "Sure we can." When the bombing stopped, Knox decided to take a look and tipped the hatch back. Zeroes were zooming past. Knox grabbed the machine gun, jerked the pin from the mount, and yelled for a box of ammo. He hooked the box on the mount, flipped its lid, chambered a round, and was ready to fire. He had no idea what the oncoming fighters were but recognized the "flaming red assholes" on their fuselages as Japanese. They were swarming past him like hornets, and he called for the crewman to come out of the tank and help him spot. The man stood on the front deck and looked forward, while Knox looked to the rear. He fired so much that the deck became slippery with casings, but he was off balance, the gun had no antiaircraft sight, and he had had no training in antiaircraft shooting. He believed that he did not lead his targets enough and did not hit a thing.

Lt. Ben Morin, a B/192TB platoon leader, was with his tank some distance from Clark through the entire raid. He had Cpl. John Cahill, his assistant driver, set up and fire the machine gun, but reported no success.

The only Zero claimed by a man firing from a tank was credited to Pvt. Earl Smith of C/194TB, but he received little publicity for it, did not survive prison camp, and details are unknown.

After the Clark raid the tankers claimed that their antiaircraft guns were too hazardous to use. Their mounting was so poorly positioned at the rear of the turret that a gunner firing it was completely exposed. Since the Japanese Navy strafers did not return after December 8th, the antiaircraft machine guns were not needed in the short term. Japanese Army planes were overhead daily but bombed from medium altitude, out of machine gun range. The tanks' antiaircraft machine guns were fine for infantry use—they had tripods that were stowed inside the tanks—and quickly disappeared, traded to the Philippine Army for goods wanted by the tankers.

After delivering their ammunition, Bardowski and Goldstein parked their half-track near their B Company comrades and were enjoying a lunch of cold cocoa when the Japanese bombers arrived. Bud and Goldy took cover until the Nells and Betties passed. When the Zeros began strafing, Bud pulled the half-track into the open to give them better shots at the fighters. The planes were flying in a straight line from south to north; most stopped firing once they had overflown their briefed targets on Clark Field. Bud took the half-track's .50 caliber machine gun and Goldy took the .30. They had plenty of ammunition, having saved some back from their delivery chore. The Zeros were flying at nearly 300 miles per hour but presented a nearly zero-deflection target if they failed to bank as they pulled away. Goldy recalled that Lt. George Van Arsdall from Headquarters Company shouted at them from his own tank, "Hey, stop shooting at them. Do you want to antagonize them?" He was ignored. (This same comment has been attributed to other officers from other units, but Goldstein attached a name to his, and I'm accepting it.)

Jim Bashleben drove his own half-track within shouting distance of Bud's and opened fire with his own .50 caliber, which jammed. Jim could not clear it but contributed to the battle by yelling encouragement at Bud. Bud was a good shot, had kept his weapon in perfect shape, and stitched the belly of one fighter with .50 caliber shells as it passed. The fighter burst into flames and crashed about a quarter mile away. Ben Morin stayed with his tank during the strafing and saw Bud's target roar past, its pilot showing a worried expression, and crash with a whoosh. The crash was witnessed by many other men from B Company and Headquarters Company.

As soon as the strafing was over, Bud and many others raced to the scene of the crash. The pilot's body lay near the plane. It was a scene that remained seared in the minds of many. Head and extremities were blown off; one hand was draped over a bush. Bud was looking for souvenirs, especially weapons. He rolled the torso over with his foot and retrieved the pilot's pistol just as the Japanese pilot's sphincter let go. Bud got fecal matter all over his foot and shouted, "You gotta watch these Japs. They'll shit on you even after they're dead." One tanker recalled that an unnamed chaplain tried to get the gawkers to bury the body but was ignored; one of them urinated on it instead. Bud returned to the B Company dispersal and was approached by an unknown field-grade officer, who asked, "Did you knock that plane down?" Bud acknowledged that he had, and the officer said he was putting him in for a Silver Star. Bud's company commander, Capt. Don Hanes, approved Bardowski's immediate promotion to sergeant, but was able to get the award downgraded to a Bronze Star. Hanes's relationships with his men, especially the brash and undisciplined Bardowski, were always bad, and it is probable that he resented Bud's gaining more publicity than the rest of his company.

The attack was over by about 2:20 p.m. The Provisional Tank Group's losses were relatively light. Personnel casualties were three injuries and one fatality, Pvt. Robert Brooks of D/192TB. Brooks was a draftee from Sadieville, Kentucky, who had been assigned to Company D at Fort Knox in line with the policy of placing men in companies originating in their home states. Brooks trained as a driver and had been assigned to Sgt. Arnold Lawson's tank a few days before the 8th. Brooks reached the tank late that morning, hung over, and asked to stay at the tank when Lawson and the rest of the crew went to lunch. When Lawson raced back to his tank after the bombers left, he found Brooks lying beside it, dead. A dud bomb had split apart when it landed twenty feet from the tank. A fragment had blown off half of Brooks's head and caved in his chest. Lawson didn't know why Brooks hadn't taken cover. He covered the body with a tarp and continued with the war.

Unknown to the men of Company D, Brooks was an African American, the only one in the group. He was light-skinned enough to pass for white, and apparently lied about his race when he was drafted. The U.S. Armed Forces were strictly segregated, and Brooks would never have been assigned to a white unit. He had kinky hair and was nicknamed "Nig," but the survivors did not learn his race until after the war, after learning the honor afforded Brooks. Private Brooks was the first Armored Force war fatality. Its chief, M/Gen. Jacob L. Devers, decided to dedicate the main parade field at Fort Knox in his memory. While making arrangements for the ceremony, it was discovered that Brooks's parents were poor black sharecroppers. When General Devers was informed of this fact, he said that no details of the arrangements would be changed, and in his speech he would touch upon the matter. The ceremony on December 23, 1941, was one of the most impressive in that first bleak month of the war: Troops and a division band passed a reviewing stand of nine generals, and after taps and the speeches, the flag was raised from half-staff. In his speech, General Devers said:

> *For the preservation of America, the soldiers and sailors guarding our outposts are giving their lives. In death there is no grade or rank. And in this, the greatest Democracy the world has known, neither riches nor poverty, neither creed nor race draw a line of demarcation, in this hour of national crisis.*

The news release announcing the ceremony noted that it was "[i]n answer to charges of racial discrimination leveled against the United States Army." Perhaps, but only fortuitously and temporarily. Robert Brooks was a unique case. Black tankers next saw combat in November 1944, in Patton's 3rd Army's segregated 761st Tank Battalion.

Clark Field was pocked with small bomb craters and littered with the detritus of a lost battle—the shells of burned-out aircraft, fragments of equipment, and body parts. Dr. Poweleit and his medics helped with the wounded at the Fort Stotsenburg hospital. The injured arrived by a variety of means—in ambulances, buses, trucks, and bomb carts. Poweleit recalled that "some of the bodies were terribly mangled; backs blown out, intestines hanging from the abdomen, heads sheared off." The tankers who could see the field witnessed a sad procession of bomb carts bearing men whose arms and legs hung over the sides, trailing blood.

The mission of the armor was still to repel Japanese airborne troops. Several tanks were moved to better positions on the incomplete south runway. Major Miller had hot meals brought to the tank and half-track crews of his 194th with orders that the officers were to have no priority over the enlisted men, a gesture that was remembered by the survivors. The men had little to do for the rest of the day but wait and try to recover their senses.

The Provisional Tank Group was the only combat unit to come through the Clark Field debacle in full shape for operations. The condition of its men ranged from fighting mad to shell-shocked; a few of them were never put back on combat status. But its tanks were untouched. Bernard FitzPatrick and others heard Radio Tokyo announce that night that the 194th Tank Battalion had been destroyed in the raid. This was good for a laugh, which was badly needed. FitzPatrick felt that the bomb carts had been targeted deliberately, possibly confused for tanks, but in reality the Japanese had no interest in the tanks. Their target was the FEAF, and in this one raid they eradicated the American plan for Philippine defense and gained total air supremacy for the coming land campaign. All of their bombers returned to Formosa; four Zero fighters were missing. Twelve of the nineteen 19th Bomb Group B-17s on Clark were destroyed, and five more never flew a combat mission. The 24th Pursuit Group lost thirty-four P-40Es, its only first-class pursuit, as well as nineteen P-40Bs and three P-35As. Nearly all of the permanent installations at Clark were destroyed, as was the only functioning radar unit in the Philippines, at Iba. No definitive personnel loss report was ever issued, but MacArthur's initial report said that 55 men were killed and 110 wounded on Clark; 22 killed and 38 wounded on Iba. Over a hundred civilians were also killed.

Over sixty years ago Louis Morton summed up December 8 in the official history: "The Japanese had removed in one stroke the greatest single obstacle to their advance southward." Yet with the exception of

Colonel Grover, none of the commanders bearing responsibility had their careers scarred. All were evacuated to Australia before the surrender. MacArthur was "near catatonia" that morning, in the words of biographer William Manchester; other historians have said that he was "numbed," "stunned," and "suffered a mild nervous breakdown." Yet MacArthur was awarded a Medal of Honor, was promoted to five-star general, and became proconsul of postwar Japan. His staff, claimed by historians to be "near fatal paralysis" that morning, stayed with him the entire war and was promoted every time that he was. Lewis Brereton was given ever-larger air forces to command. Three of America's greatest aerial defeats were suffered by forces Brereton commanded: Clark Field by the FEAF, Ploesti by the 9th Air Force, and Operation Market Garden by the First Allied Airborne Army. Harold George was killed in a ground accident on an Australian airfield. Eugene Eubank returned to the United States, where he was given successively greater commands and retired as a major general. Only Orrin Grover's career suffered. He received only staff postings and retired as a brigadier general.

The Roosevelt administration's machinations had made war with Japan inevitable, and after Japan and Germany had signed the Tripartite Pact, the desired war with Germany as well. Politically, events could not have been better planned, although American casualties were greater than desired. General MacArthur served the American people as a war hero; Admiral Kimmel and General Short as scapegoats (for Pearl Harbor), and the men of the Provisional Tank Group and the other Americans left in the Philippines as martyrs to the treacherous Japanese. Secretary of War Henry Stimson confessed after Pearl Harbor (and Clark Field), "My first feeling was of relief . . . that a crisis had come in a way which would unite all our people."

CHAPTER 5

The Lingayen Gulf Landings and the Fil-American Response

ON THE EVENING OF DECEMBER 8, WHEN THE LAST CLARK FIELD FIRE had been put out and the bomb carts had wheeled the last corpses to the cemetery, the Provisional Tank Group (PTG) found itself in better condition to go to war than most other units at Clark Field and Fort Stotsenburg. It had suffered but one fatality and three injuries and had sustained little material damage. The damage to the men's psyches, however, was a different matter. Most American military men in the Philippines, from MacArthur on down, considered the Japanese an inferior race, and felt that Japanese aircraft in particular were but poor imitations of obsolete western designs. The successful Japanese attack was a severe shock to all. Nearly all of the men in the field quickly regained their self-confidence, and their initial numbed fear was replaced by a burning desire for revenge. Men who had fled into the jungle around Fort Stotsenburg on December 8 returned sheepishly over the next few days and resumed their old jobs without attracting much notice. Several shell-shocked officers did lose their ability to function in leadership roles, however, and had to be given lesser duties. MacArthur came out of his funk and resumed his role as generalissimo with all his old panache, promoting several of his officers, including Colonel Weaver, to boost morale, but had great difficulty giving the Japanese full credit for their victory. His initial report to General Arnold in Washington stated that the Japanese aircraft were "at least partially manned by white pilots." His staff kept the canard alive as long as possible. MacArthur's S-2 (Intelligence) officer reported in an August

1942 interview, "The job was so well done that there is reason to suspect that the pilots of the planes were Germans."

The U.S. Army Chief of Staff, General Marshall, faced some difficult decisions as soon as he learned of the Pearl Harbor disaster. A large convoy was en route to Manila, escorted by the cruiser USS *Pensacola* and comprising seven cargo ships with the 27th Bomb Group aircraft, the 2nd Battalion of the 131st Field Artillery, which was ex-Texas National Guard, and a large amount of ammunition and other supplies. It was ordered to put in at Suva in the Fiji Islands and then to return to Hawaii. This decision was reversed on December 12, and the convoy was ordered to Brisbane, Australia. Marshall summoned B/Gen. Dwight "Ike" Eisenhower from his position as chief of staff of the Third Army at Fort Sam Houston and asked his advice on future plans. Eisenhower's opinions agreed with Marshall's, and Ike was immediately named to head the Pacific section of the War Plans Division, and later to head the entire division. Admiral Stark, the Chief of Naval Operations, confirmed Admiral Hart's opinion that the *Pensacola* convoy could not be safely escorted to the Philippines, and Ike recommended that it be unloaded in Brisbane and its cargo used to establish Australia as a new base of operations for America and the rest of the ABDA (American-British-Dutch-Australian) nations. This advice was accepted, although the 131st Field Artillery battalion was reloaded on the convoy's two fastest ships, headed for Manila, and made it as far as Java, where it was captured. The United States continued to reassure Great Britain that it was committed to a Europe First strategy, which meant that the Philippines were written off before the end of 1941. There would be no attempts to bring in convoys, though efforts would be made to send the theater small amounts of supplies by submarines, aircraft, and blockade runners.

The newly promoted Brigadier General Weaver accepted that the PTG's major mission was still defense against Japanese air landings and over the next few days shifted his men to guard a larger area. The 192nd moved into dry riverbeds on the southern side of the field; B/192TB was detached to the barrio of Dau to guard the rail line. The 194th moved northeast toward Mabalacat. The tank companies were mobile and self-contained; their maintenance crews and kitchens always operated from trucks. The men left their footlockers at Fort Stotsenburg and never saw them again; their contents were left to the Japanese and were featured in propaganda broadcasts several months later. The tankers spent a week chasing rumors of Japanese paratroopers. 2nd Lt. Albert Bartz of C/192TB accompanied a 26th Cavalry Regiment task force to Mount Arayat east of the fort and returned with three Japanese aviators and a badly wounded American fighter pilot who had been held by the natives since the 8th.

The Japanese Naval Air Force, supplemented by that of the army, concentrated on targets in the Manila area—Nielsen and Nelson air fields and the Cavite naval base—for the next week, but did return to Clark Field and Fort Stotsenburg several times to complete the destruction. On December 11 Lieutenant Bartz was caught without cover during a sudden attack on the C/192TB bivouac and had his clavicle broken by shrapnel. He was treated in a field hospital, shipped to Manila in a freight car with other wounded men, and was extremely fortunate to escape from the Philippines on the SS *Mactan*. The *Mactan* was a ramshackle 2,000-ton interisland cruise boat that the International Red Cross obtained to evacuate war wounded to Australia. The Japanese gave their permission, and in twenty-four hours the ship was given a coat of whitewash, and red crosses were painted on its sides and funnel. It left Manila on December 31, the last steamship to escape the embattled island of Luzon.

Two more PTG officers and four enlisted men joined Bartz on the *Mactan*. 2nd Lt. William Slicer was a Maywood tanker who had transferred from B/192TB to 192nd Headquarters as a liaison officer. On about December 12 he borrowed Al Allen's motorcycle and took it on an unauthorized jaunt to Manila to see a fight. He wrecked the motorcycle on the return trip and tore up his leg badly. Although the accident report was cleaned up, several 192nd survivors (e.g., Poweleit, Allen) said that he was drunk. He was evacuated to Australia and joined MacArthur's staff as an expert on Japanese antitank tactics. He fathered a child in Australia before returning after the war to the wife and children he had left in Maywood. He rejoined the Illinois National Guard and rose to become commanding officer of the 33rd Division Heavy Tank Company, which replaced B/192TB at the Maywood armory. He was called a "yellow

SOB" by the B/192TB veterans who had survived POW camp and was not allowed into their reunions for many years. In Slicer's official capacity he shared many speaking stages with Colonel Wickord. The easygoing and laconic Ted Wickord found these meetings distasteful, as recalled by Wickord's family.

2nd Lt. Emmett Gibson suffered his war-ending injury a little later in December. Gibson was a Maywood native who had been transferred to Wainwright's headquarters for liaison duties—according to Poweleit, he had "lost all confidence in himself." He was driving his liaison jeep on a rainy night. His passengers were his regular driver and a young Filipina whom, according to Gibson, he was taking home after a visit to her husband in the Fort Stotsenburg hospital. Crossing a bridge in the dark, Gibson rammed the rear of a bus carrying PA soldiers and flipped the jeep over, badly crushing a leg. He was taken to Manila, reached Australia on the *Mactan*, and was evacuated to the United States for further surgery, which left one leg two inches shorter than the other. He was wined and dined as a Bataan hero, wrote a popular series of Bataan articles for the *Chicago Herald-American*, and finished the war as a rifle instructor at Fort Benning. He returned to Maywood and joined the police department, rising to lieutenant before he contracted brain cancer and died at age forty-two.

The four PTG enlisted men on the *Mactan* were Pvt. Avid Danielson, who was injured in the Clark Field raid; Sgt. Edward Trebs and Pvt. Wesley Kerrigan, who were injured later by bomb shrapnel, and Pvt. Kenneth Booher, who was injured on December 26 in a battle on the Agno River.

In mid-December General Weaver received a surprise addition to his inventory of tracked vehicles. The SS *Don José* was a Philippine-flag freighter en route from Canada to Hong Kong when war erupted. It took temporary refuge in Manila Bay and downloaded its deck cargo on a deserted Manila lot in preparation for a run to Hong Kong. The cargo included the vehicles for a Canadian battalion garrisoning the British colony—fifty-seven Bren gun carriers and seventy-five GMC trucks. Bren gun carriers were light, fully tracked weapons carriers. They had crews of three, weighed only 3.75 tons loaded, and their ninety-horsepower Ford V-8 engines gave them a listed top speed of thirty miles per hour. Their thin armor (10mm or 0.4 inch front, 7mm or 0.3 inch side) would stop only small-arms fire, and the vehicles were more suitable for light cargo than combat. They were similar in function to American half-tracks but were smaller and more fragile and were rejected by all of the Allies except Great Britain and its Commonwealth, where they were ubiquitous. Their cross-country performance was good, and they would prove useful on trackless Bataan. They were close enough to "armor" that General Weaver's claim took priority, and he got forty of the carriers to distribute among his tank companies; the other seventeen went to the cavalry. The carriers did not have their Bren guns, but .30 caliber Browning machine guns were installed on them in the workshops. Every service arm wanted the GMC trucks, and according to one infantryman these were valuable additions to his unit. It is not known if Weaver was able to get any of them. The *Don José*'s attempt to escape the Philippines was unsuccessful. She was captured by the Japanese and destroyed by American aircraft in 1945.

Dr. Poweleit's dispensary routine returned to that of peacetime: treating diseases. Among the enlisted men at this time, the most serious were gonorrhea and syphilis. These men were sent to the Fort Stotsenburg hospital, only to be returned. Poweleit and his medics gave the men the standard medication: sulfapyridine and salvarsan. Bombing continued daily. There were few physical wounds, but the mental injuries were persistent. Dr. Poweleit noted that several of the battalion's officers suffered from post-traumatic stress disorder (PTSD), then known as shell shock. One officer, who was constantly drunk, asked Dr. Poweleit if the army would release him if he shot himself in the leg. The doctor told him it would be better if he shot himself in the brain.

On December 18 Dr. Poweleit and Major Wickord went to nearby Angeles to set up a prophylactic station with the prostitutes and stationed a medic there. Coming back, they stopped at a restaurant for lunch with Captain Write of the Janesville Company. Write commented, "This place is hot, the beer is terrible, and the peanuts are stale." The Filipino proprietor replied, "Captain, those are not peanuts. They are fried grasshoppers." Write spat out his beer and grasshoppers and walked out, leaving the check for Poweleit and Wickord. Grasshoppers would become delicacies for the men in the coming months.

Newly promoted Sgt. Bud Bardowski and T/4 Goldy Goldstein decided to increase the firepower of their B/192TB Headquarters half-track. They acquired two .50 caliber machine guns from a wrecked P-40 and engaged two Filipino welders to fabricate a joint mount for the two guns that would allow them to fire vertically. The aircraft Brownings had a much higher rate of fire than the ground model. The result was the islands' best single weapon against strafers. The air force asked to borrow the half-track and its crew for airfield defense. Captain Hanes was all too willing to let Bardowski and the half-track go, but kept Goldstein to run the company's radio net. Unfortunately for Bardowski and his lust for combat, the strafers never returned; Japanese Army bombers were overhead every day, but they bombed from medium altitude, well out of range of Bud's .50 calibers. Even worse for Bud, he missed the entire two-week Central Luzon campaign and its exhilarating war of movement.

Goldstein's duties remained the same for the entire campaign. He was responsible for Company B's tank radios. He radioed every tank in the company every morning to check reception. If there was no reply, he had to find the tank and fix the problem. After he lost Bardowski and the half-track, he switched to the headquarters jeep. He fabricated a radio direction finder from scraps and used it to locate his tanks. He signaled every tank from two locations and could pinpoint every tank that replied by triangulation. He was the only man in the group who knew the exact location of every B Company tank. Captain Hanes was notorious for over-controlling his men, issuing them detailed orders from his position on what he claimed was the front line. Only Goldstein knew that Hanes was nowhere near the front, but was transmitting from far to the rear—information that Goldstein claimed he kept strictly to himself.

Lingayen Gulf, on the northwestern coast of Luzon, had long been considered the prime landing site for any invading force targeting Manila—it had seen such service before and would again. Its wide beaches debouched onto the Central Luzon Plain, a deforested, highly cultivated alluvial flatland 40 miles wide and stretching 120 miles across the island to Manila. MacArthur's strongest beach defenses, or at least the greatest number of defenders, were located at Lingayen Gulf.

On December 10 the Japanese landed regiment-size forces on Luzon at Aparri and Vigan, far north of Lingayen Gulf. Lieutenant General Wainwright considered these to be only feints to prompt him to disperse his forces and did not respond. These landings in fact had two purposes: One was to seize airfield sites for the short-range Japanese Army aircraft; the other was to furnish a force to send down the northwestern Luzon coast to roll up the flank of the defenders expected to be waiting at the main landing site farther south.

On December 12 the Japanese made a small landing at Legaspi, in far southern Luzon. General Parker's South Luzon Force (SLF), with two Philippine Army divisions, was smaller than Wainwright's North Luzon Force (NLF), which had four plus the cavalry regiment and part of the Philippine Division, which was a unit of the regular U.S. Army even though two-thirds of its men were Filipinos. USAFFE felt that the tank reinforcements it planned for Parker should get underway early. Brigadier General Weaver was summoned to USAFFE headquarters in the morning and told to send one of his two tank battalions to the SLF. He chose the 194th, as it was the more experienced, with seven weeks more service in the islands, and it would have two difficult night marches ahead of it. Major Miller was notified, and although he was unhappy that none of his men had any knowledge of the area, got them underway that evening. They were to bivouac at the Calumpit Bridge on the northern end of Manila Bay when they arrived and remain there under cover the next day. In Major Miller's words:

> The strain on the drivers and vehicles, particularly tanks, is severe enough in daytime driving. To drive at night, without lights, in continuous rain, and against other traffic is enough to give anyone a case of the severe jitters. It should be remembered that the tanks and half-tracks had no windshields. To drive (just one) . . . vehicle in this manner is not so bad, but we were moving as a mechanized unit, by platoons. We had to maintain intervals of space and time between vehicles and units as much as humanly possible.
>
> Then began the nightmare. A number of tanks and other vehicles went off the road—into ditches and over fills—some to regain the

roadway under their own power—others needing help. One tank crew went over the shoulder and turned bottom side up. The crew miraculously escaped serious injury. . . . As we went through San Fernando, at one of the turns, several tanks missed the turn and went down the road to Bataan. I was riding in a jeep that night and luckily checked the column. A guide had been posted by the reconnaissance detachments, but . . . some tanks missed him . . . we started in pursuit and . . . guided the vehicles back. We finally reached the bivouac area around 6 AM. . . . We had to bivouac in three separate areas in order to obtain adequate cover. The Calumpit Bridge is located in extremely open country with numerous rice paddies.

Cpl. Bernard FitzPatrick of the 194th's Company A, the Brainerd Company, took part in this movement and remembered the stress of driving on the "wrong" side of the road—the Filipinos drove on the left—in a blackout in drizzling rain.

The trip of the 194th the next night down the better roads near Manila apparently went more smoothly than that of the 12th–13th, and by the morning of the 14th the tanks, half-tracks, and other vehicles had passed Manila and the heavily bombed navy yard at Cavite, which looked and smelled like death, and moved into a bivouac area south of Manila that was near the SLF headquarters and well camouflaged with mango trees. From there they patrolled against saboteurs and awaited further developments.

The 192nd now prepared to take the field from its Fort Stotsenburg base. The USAFFE supply officers began releasing the ammunition, gasoline, and spare parts for which Major Miller of the 194th had been fighting since his arrival in the theater in September, but the field exercises for which he had wanted them would never be carried out. The 192nd, which was so new in the theater that it was still unpacking and had not even test-fired its cannons, was assigned to Major General Wainwright's North Luzon Force (NLF). Brigadier General Weaver recalled that he tried to get permission to send the battalion all the way to the Lingayen area, but was turned down by General Sutherland on the grounds that the NLF "had too much up there already." Weaver did succeed in caching

30,000 gallons of gasoline at Gerona and had Wickord move the rest of the 192nd to join B Company in new field bivouacs near Dau. Weaver and his small staff then left for Manila, where they set up shop near the USAFFE staff. The 192nd armor remained near its new bivouacs. Its recon units checked out the roads and bridges to the north; Sergeant Allen of C/192TB went as far as Lingayen Gulf on his motorcycle.

It was a week before there was any significant enemy activity in the NLF's area. A Japanese trawler was spotted steaming slowly across Lingayen Gulf on the morning of December 21, and NLF headquarters was alerted. The ship was taking soundings in preparation for the landing of Gen. Masaharu Homma's 14th Army, which would begin coming ashore that night. Eighty-five transports would land 43,110 men on three beaches. The beaches where the Japanese landed were farther north than they had planned owing to bad weather or poor navigation, and the landings missed the prepared beach defenses. General Homma had heard that the Americans had armor on Luzon, and made sure that one of his two tank regiments, the 4th, came ashore in early morning with its thirty-eight Type 95 Ha-Go light tanks. This reliable 7.5-ton 1934 design had a 37mm main gun with a good armor-piercing round and was equal to the Americans' much newer M3s. His other regiment, the 7th, had fourteen Type 95 Ha-Go light tanks and thirty-four Type 89B medium tanks. The latter had low-velocity 57mm guns and were considered more suitable for infantry support.

General Wainwright had difficulty learning the true course of events. He knew only that his troops defending the beaches, two divisions of green Philippine Army (PA) infantry, were fleeing. The two divisions did not in any sense meet the invaders on the beaches, as had been MacArthur's intent. Although the enemy was landing to the north of the prepared defenses, the Filipinos began streaming to the rear at the first rumors of Japanese. The only beach defenders to hold their ground were two batteries of 75mm self-propelled mounts (SPMs), which were under direct USAFFE command and not Wainwright's. Three SPMs were destroyed there, and the other five had to retreat north to Baguio, where they were disabled. At 7 a.m. Wainwright climbed aboard his battered 1936 Packard to visit the headquarters of his two divisions, only to find

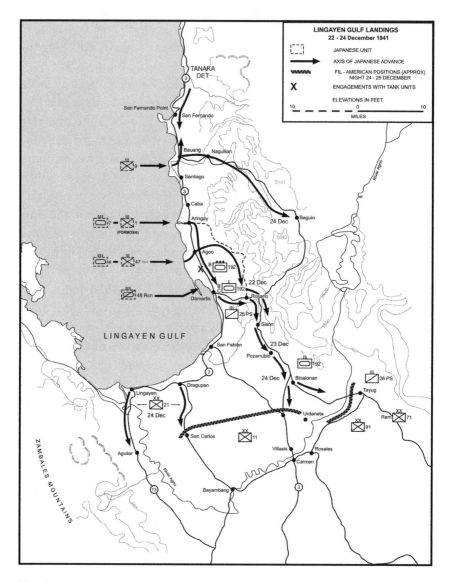

Map 2

them crumbling. He sent his immediate reserve, the 26th Cavalry Regiment (PS), toward the front. He badly needed the 192nd Tank Battalion but would have to ask MacArthur. Incredibly, his only means of doing so was over a public telephone. Borrowing a nickel, Wainwright frantically tried to get through to his chief. The closest he could get was the general's chief of staff, M/Gen. Richard Sutherland. In no mood for Sutherland's usual pompous and condescending tone, Wainwright came straight to the point. "Brougher's division [11th Infantry Division (PA)] is being cut to pieces, and I need a tank battalion now," he screamed into the phone. "Give it to me, or the Japs are going to be serving tea in Manila before you can spit. All I've got is Pierce and his 26th Cavalry to hold them long enough to get my people off the beaches. I can't give Weaver the order—he's still under your direct command. I need armor now!"

"I am unable to authorize that," Sutherland answered smoothly. "At present, we are committed to defend every inch of our sacred soil in the Philippines, and we cannot carelessly expend our reserves."

Now near apoplexy, Wainwright shot back, "I'm the goddamned corps commander, and if you don't let me fight the way I see it from here in the field, those little bastards will be in your lap in hours. Until then, for God's sake, give me permission to use these forces up here as I see fit."

Sutherland replied coolly, "I will ask the general," and abruptly hung up. Shortly thereafter, a call came in for Wainwright on the 71st Infantry Division's main communications line. "This is Sutherland," came the flat voice. "The general has already instructed General Weaver to dispatch a company of tanks from the 192nd to the Rosario-Damortis vicinity to support your defenses."

"A company!" exploded Wainwright. "I'm facing maybe two entire Jap divisions, maybe more, with one depleted regiment of horse cavalry!"

"I'm sorry, General Wainwright, but that is all we can commit to you at present."

The previous evening General Weaver had alerted Major Wickord to begin moving the 192nd northward, while Weaver came from Manila to Wainwright's headquarters to control them. Wickord had an immediate problem with his C Company, the Port Clinton Company. Its commander, Capt. Robert Sorensen, had fainted and lost self-control and had to be replaced by 1st Lt. Harold Collins, its senior platoon leader. Wickord then sent his combat elements—three light tank companies and the headquarters platoon—toward the forward NLF headquarters, but they did not get far. Sgt. Forrest Knox, a tank commander in Company A, the Janesville Company, did not know that his driver had night blindness—they had never driven at night—and learned of it only when his tank veered off the road and bottomed out in a ditch. The rest of the column stumbled along, only to find that some of the necessary gasoline dumps were empty, while at others, USAFFE supply officers were still unwilling to release their precious fuel. Wainwright would thus not have gotten the entire battalion on the 22nd even if MacArthur had permitted it. Wickord picked B Company to press on to Rosario and Wainwright. Malicious rumor had it that the Maywood Company was chosen because it was Wickord's old unit. Capt. Donald Hanes, the company commander, pooled his gasoline, refueled the five tanks of Lt. Ben Morin, his junior platoon leader, and sent them forward to meet the battalion's obligations. Wainwright had been promised a company of fifteen to seventeen light tanks by USAFFE as reinforcement; what he got was one platoon of five tanks and their general.

Morin's tanks were met at Manaog by the company's gasoline truck and topped off from drums. It was now pitch dark, and Ben ordered his men to sleep the rest of the night beside their tanks. They climbed in the tanks when it started raining. At six in the morning he radioed his company commander and said, "Still in original position, awaiting our orders." Captain Hanes replied excitedly, "Get out of there! Get out of there!" Morin's platoon resumed its journey and reached Rosario at nine o'clock, under observation by Japanese reconnaissance planes most of the way. Ben did not know to whom to report in Rosario, but General Weaver quickly found him. He was to carry out a simple "reconnaissance in force," since Weaver knew no more of what lay ahead than any other American commander. Morin was to locate the enemy, identify and engage them if possible, and then return to Rosario—again, if possible.

Ben Morin led his platoon of five M3 light tanks west out of Rosario at eleven in the morning at twenty-five miles per hour, in the same order in which they had arrived. Morin placed S/Sgt. Al Edwards, his second-in-command and most reliable man, in the number 2 position, one hundred yards behind Morin. The other three tanks, commanded by Sgt. Larry Jordan, Sgt. Willard Von Bergan, and Sgt. Ray Vandenbroucke, were equally spaced behind Edwards. Four of the tank commanders, and all of Edwards's crew, had graduated from Maywood's Proviso High School within a few years of each other, and thus were members of a true brotherhood in arms. Morin was to turn north when he reached the Lingayen Gulf coast at Damortis, continuing on Highway 3, and engage the Japanese when they were found. This would probably be before he reached Agoo, eight miles north of Damortis. The Japanese had been coming ashore since daybreak, but Morin was told that they had probably not landed any tanks or artillery. In all honesty he did not know what to expect, but felt that this was probably a suicide mission. Morin was leading his tanks in single file down a narrow road. He had never seen combat but knew that he was likely to be ambushed. As platoon leader he had painted a white "1" on his tank, making him a conspicuous target, and he told himself that this was what he was paid for.

Morin recalled later that shortly after leaving Rosario his force was attacked by Japanese aircraft. These dropped only fragmentation bombs, which dinged the tanks but did no damage. The tanks reached Damortis and turned right toward Agoo, eight miles to the north. Although they were now on what was called the coastal highway, this apparently ran somewhat inland. Morin did not remember seeing the ocean or any Japanese shipping or landing operations. At times the road was closely hemmed in by jungle underbrush; elsewhere it dropped off sharply to rice fields on both sides.

Shortly after leaving Damortis Morin saw a scout car of the 26th Cavalry parked under a tree by the side of the road. The lieutenant in command was examining the road with his field glasses. Morin stopped his column and asked, "Where are the Japs?" The lieutenant replied, "About half a mile up the road." The tanks buttoned up and rumbled forward at fifteen miles per hour. Morin fired a trial shot down the road from his 37mm cannon—the first time it had been fired in the Philippines—and the gun locked in recoil, jammed and out of service. The recuperating cylinder had apparently never been filled with oil, a problem with all of the battalion's tanks. Morin's M3 would enter the forthcoming battle with an effective armament of four .30 caliber machine guns: two in the sponsons, one in the bow gun mount, and one mounted coaxially with the main gun in its turret.

The small column next encountered Japanese infantry on the road. The tanks' fire sent the enemy jumping for the ditches. The M3s charged at them, firing all of their operable guns. To make effective use of the fixed sponson guns, Morin alternately kicked the left and right shoulders of his driver, Pvt. Louie Zelis, signaling him to pull the levers stopping the left and right tracks in turn. The toe of Morin's boot traced a circle in the small of Zelis's back, cueing him to fire the guns; the other tank commanders probably did the same. M3s had no intercoms, and their radial engines, suspensions, and tracks were so noisy that communication within the tank was only possible by visual or physical means.

The five tanks serpentined down the road, firing continually. In Ben's tank, only the sponson guns gave no problems. These were always tricky to load, but radioman Pvt. Steve Gados kept the belts straight, and Zelis was able to fire 1,000 rounds. The bow gun kept jamming, but Cpl. John Cahill still managed to go through several belts of one hundred rounds each. And Morin's machine gun jammed also, badly enough that he had to cock it manually before each shot. Shortly thereafter—the survivors' memories are vague—Morin's "white 1" was struck by a cannon shell on the left side of the hull. The hit knocked the driver's access door loose. A few seconds later a second hit tore the door away and left it dangling over the front hull plate. Zelis was now completely exposed, and Morin signaled him to pull to the right side of the road and stop so that the men could attempt to put the door back in place.

Soon a Japanese tank came charging out of the brush, collided with the left front of Morin's stopped tank, and apparently left the scene. The Americans were now back in their tank, and Zelis reversed into the road and tried to go forward. The left track had been knocked off its drive sprocket by the collision and no longer had any power. The right track, now at full speed, whirled the tank around and off the road to the left, fifty to seventy-five yards into a dry rice field. Shells began to hit the right side of the tank. One pierced the armor into the engine compartment and apparently hit the battery; the engine and all electrical equipment quit immediately. The engine caught fire. The white smoke entering the crew compartment was something new to Ben and prompted him to yell, "Gas!" which was an order for the men to don their gas masks. Zelis suspected a more conventional gasoline fire. The M3 had no automatic fire extinguishers, but Zelis was able to reach and press the buttons for the manual extinguishers, which eventually smothered the fire with foamite.

Through the smoke Morin could see Edwards lead his tank and the other three past him. Ben hoped for a successful continuation of their attack, but a few minutes later the American tanks came back and continued to the rear. Edwards did not try to rescue Ben's crew, who had made no effort to escape their heavily smoking tank; Edwards assumed all were dead. He was probably also affected by the sudden death of his bow gunner, Pvt. Henry Deckert, a company cook who had begged his way onto a tank crew. A Japanese shell that had penetrated the unarmored bow gun mount had decapitated Deckert. His head rolled around on the floor while his torso sprayed the crew compartment red with blood. All of the four returning tanks were damaged severely enough to be abandoned at Damortis, and all the tank commanders were injured slightly. They reported that a 47mm antitank gun had hit Morin's tank, and that they themselves had caused severe damage to one Japanese medium tank, but that most of their 37mm shells bounced off the tanks' sloping hull armor. They also reported that the Japanese tanks had no turrets. General Weaver repeated all of this to Washington, in the first American wartime intelligence report on Japanese armor. The Japanese tanks were in fact all standard Type 95 Ha-Go light tanks with turreted 37mm main guns. The Imperial Japanese Army had a 47mm antitank gun under development, but the first two of these did not make it to the Philippines until the next April.

Ben Morin and his crew were left alone in their stifling hot tank, under continuous fire. The men all suffered minor burns from their own ejected shells and from hot shrapnel that left their coveralls smoldering. Ben remembered saying, "Keep your chins up, men. We'll get out of this!" After what seemed to Ben to have been fifteen minutes the firing stopped, and through their vision slits the men could see four Japanese light tanks approaching. Ben opened his hatch and quickly raised his hands. Upon gestures from the Japanese he climbed down from the tank and surrendered his crew. They knelt in front of their tank while the Japanese tankers relieved them of their sidearms to the clicking and whirring of newsreel photographers. The four Americans were then bound hand and foot, and each was tied to the rear deck of a Japanese tank—Ben was impressed at the resourcefulness the Japanese showed by having rope available.

The Japanese tanks headed north to Agoo, Ben's original objective. Each of the Americans had a guard on the rear deck with him. Ben's was an officer who kept his pistol pointed at Ben for the whole trip. Steve Gados was on the tank behind Ben; his guard was an enlisted man with a short sword that he held against the back of Steve's neck. One sharp turn by the tank would have resulted in Steve's decapitation, so Ben felt fortunate that his own guard was an officer with a pistol. The men could now see Lingayen Gulf, which was filled with ships and landing craft in the far distance. They also met Japanese infantry marching south down Highway 3 toward Damortis.

In Agoo the Americans were taken down off the tanks, given water from a canteen and small rice balls to eat, and directed to lie down in a small band shell, still bound hand and foot. They were then taken one by one to be interrogated. The Japanese intelligence officer's technique was not harsh, but the interpreter's words, the first English Ben had heard from the Japanese, chilled him: "You are not prisoners. You are captives."

The first American tank battle of the war had ended—in an American defeat. The tankers had suffered their first land combat fatality and had lost their first four captives. Morin's crew was spared the starvation diet the rest of Company B had to endure during the Bataan siege and the hideous conditions of the Death March, and all survived the war, albeit with feelings of guilt at having surrendered in their first combat.

C Company had inexplicably beaten the rest of B Company to Rosario. General Weaver took its new company commander, Captain Collins, west to Damortis in his half-track to reconnoiter sites from which the tanks could cover the 26th Cavalry Regiment's retreat. Weaver then withdrew to Rosario, turned command over to Major Wickord, who had arrived with the gasoline trucks and the rest of his battalion, and returned to Manila. C Company's tanks took up their positions but were ordered to withdraw in the late afternoon, leaving the cavalry to face the oncoming Japanese tanks alone. William Gentry watched in horror as the Japanese tore the cavalry formations apart with cannon and machine gun fire. He heard bullets thud into horseflesh and the resulting screams. Terrified, riderless animals raced about madly before collapsing, many in the narrow road where they were run over by the last of the American tanks as they raced past. One hundred and fifty cavalrymen and an equal number of horses were slaughtered before the rest escaped across a wooden bridge. The bridge was then blocked by the unit veterinary truck, which was set afire by three cavalry officers, who were later awarded the Distinguished Service Cross for their valor. The four surviving tanks of Morin's platoon were abandoned in Damortis, reducing B Company's tank strength on this first day of combat by one-third.

Captain Hanes's delay in reaching Rosario with the rest of B Company saved them from having to take part in this sorry episode. This is how *The West Point Atlas of American Wars* summed up the PTG's first ground battle: "The American tankers, operating much too independently, had not been of much assistance." Relations between Weaver and his tankers and Wainwright and his cavalrymen were irreparably broken on the 22nd. Who ordered the tanks to retreat? Collins said it was the commander of a Philippine Army infantry division who wanted the tanks out of his way. Wainwright and his men were convinced that it was Weaver. Weaver denied this in his postwar report, but nonetheless supported the retreat order because the timely withdrawal of his tanks preserved them for future use, only coincidentally at the expense of the cavalry, a wasting (and obsolete) resource. Weaver's report noted frequently how he was able to thwart the infantry commanders when they tried to misuse his precious tanks. The infantry commanders in the field knew only that they had difficulty getting tanks when they needed them. December 22 was the first time that this problem arose, but was by no means the last. Weaver was a hard man with firm ideas on the proper use of armor, frequently and bluntly expressed. The men of the PTG paid the resulting price for the squabbles among the generals.

CHAPTER 6

Retreat across the Central Luzon Plain

GENERAL MACARTHUR'S PLAN TO REPEL THE ENEMY ON THE BEACHES did not survive the first day of the Japanese landings at Lingayen Gulf. He radioed General Marshall on December 22 that the Japanese were landing 80,000 to 100,000 men, that he had only 40,000 men to oppose them, and that he might have to revert to WPO-3, the plan he had rejected six months previously, and withdraw to Bataan. (The true sizes of the opposing forces were almost the reverse of these—43,000 Japanese versus 75,000 to 80,000 Filipinos and Americans.)

The American commanders in the field did not learn of MacArthur's shift in thinking immediately; as far as they knew, the emphasis was still on forward defense. However, Wainwright told USAFFE on the 23rd that further defense of the beaches was impracticable and requested permission to establish a defensive line on the Agno River. He asked for the Philippine Division to be released from USAFFE reserve for use in a counterattack, but was refused. The defense of the Agno River was authorized; this line had been reconnoitered in the 1930s as part of the original War Plan Orange scenario. Later on the 23rd Wainwright was told by USAFFE, "WPO-3 is in effect." USAFFE headquarters would move from Manila to Corregidor. Wainwright's NLF was to delay the Japanese at five successive lines before withdrawing into Bataan on January 8. Parker's SLF was to withdraw west and north around Manila to Calumpit Bridge across the Pampanga River, to San Fernando and then Bataan. This "double retrograde movement" was very tricky, especially since the Philippine Army was unable to hold its ground, and all movements had to be made at night because the Japanese had complete mastery of the air.

(This was Wainwright's principal claim to fame as a tactical leader and was successful enough to be studied postwar in the War College.)

Although MacArthur's early decision to revert to WPO-3 was correct, its execution on the strategic level was badly flawed. The role of the USAFFE supply officer (S-4) in WPO-3 was to stock Bataan for a long siege. Supplies had been moved forward in Luzon to comply with the "defend the beaches" plan. Orders to empty these forward depots did not begin reaching them until after December 23, and execution was slowed by a shortage of trucks and clogged roads. The S-4, Brig. Gen. Charles Drake in Manila, was given 1,300 men and seven days to move supplies for 80,000 fighting men and an unknown number of civilians. He sent 300 barge loads from warehouses to Bataan and Corregidor; MacArthur ordered him to fill Corregidor's quotas first.

On the 24th MacArthur ordered Fort Stotsenburg evacuated and its supplies destroyed, too early in the opinion of many, and although its quartermaster saved 50,000 gallons of gasoline, much material was lost. The next day the depot at Tarlac issued its supplies to all comers and prepared for evacuation, without orders. Combat units were on their own to prepare for the future, and some showed more initiative than others. The 17th Ordnance Company sent a detail to Clark Field and secured a number of drums of aviation gasoline for the PTG's tanks. Maj. Charles Canby, the 194th Tank Battalion executive officer, found 12,000 gallons of gasoline and six truckloads of food to bring to Bataan, and the 194th was better fed during the coming siege than most of the other units.

There were two main causes for the panicky retreat: the loss of the Far East Air Force on December 8 and the utter failure of the ill-trained, ill-equipped Philippine Army to hold the Japanese. MacArthur never publicly acknowledged the poor performance of the army he had done so much to organize and train, but every American who served with the Philippine Army units noted it. Another reason for the quick withdrawal was MacArthur's desire to spare Manila from destruction. His fondness for the Filipinos was probably why USAFFE delayed preparing Bataan for a siege. It would mean abandoning Manila, the main population center—and MacArthur knew that this would demoralize the civilians.

Wainwright's withdrawal plan for the NLF called for one-day delays on five lines one night's march apart. The lines were anchored on natural features and had been reconnoitered before the war. Each bisected the main north-south highway, Route 3, which ran from Manila past Fort Stotsenburg to Rosario, where it turned and ran parallel to the coast. D-1, the first line, began near Aguilar in the Zambales foothills and ran east to Urdaneta on Route 3. D-2 ran along the Agno River, with its center point at Carmen. The Agno was not as imposing a barrier as it appeared on the map. There were roads and cleared fields along only part of the south bank; elsewhere the jungle reached down to the water. Japanese infantrymen could ford the river in many places and disappear into the jungle. D-3 was anchored in the west at Ste. Ignacia in the Zambales and ended in the east at San Jose on Highway 5. D-4 ran beside several major towns and was sometimes called the "Tarlac Line." It began at San Miguel, passed Tarlac, La Paz, Zaragoza, and Carmen, and ended at Cabanatuan on the Pampanga River. D-5 was the only line intended to be fortified and ran from Fort Stotsenburg north of Mount Arayat and the Candaba Swamp to Sibul Springs, east of Route 5. The retreating forces of the NLF and the SLF were to merge at San Fernando and take Route 7 into Bataan.

Major Wickord's 192nd Tank Battalion reached the Pozorrubio-Rosario area on December 22–23, just in time to fall in behind the Philippine Army retreat. The battalion passed through Urdaneta with only a brief stop on the notional D-1 line and was ordered to fan out when it reached the Agno River at Carmen. The headquarters and the medical detachment crossed and set up shop south of the river. The 26th Cavalry Regiment formed the rear guard alone and was totally worn down on the 24th while holding off the Japanese at Binalonan. According to Wainwright: "Here was true cavalry delaying action, fit to make a man's heart sing." Its commander, Clinton Pierce, was promoted to brigadier general, but the regiment had lost one-third of its men and horses since Damortis, failed to hold in its next combat on December 26, and was withdrawn to Bataan.

A/192TB was the last tank company through Urdaneta, and its CO, Capt. Walter H. Write, stopped his jeep to help some 11th Division

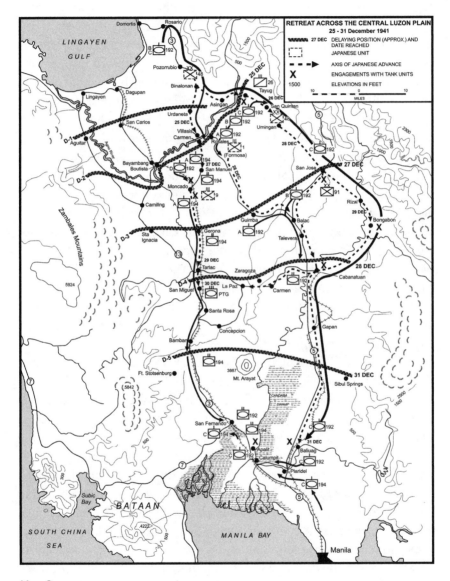

RETREAT ACROSS THE CENTRAL LUZON PLAIN
25 - 31 December 1941

27 DEC   DELAYING POSITION (APPROX.) AND
          DATE REACHED

          JAPANESE UNIT

X   AXIS OF JAPANESE ADVANCE

          ENGAGEMENTS WITH TANK UNITS

1500   ELEVATIONS IN FEET

Map 3

men lay land mines that had been fabricated by the USAFFE Ordnance Department. These were primitive, extremely dangerous affairs consisting of a wooden box with six sticks of dynamite, a lantern battery, and a detonator. The lid was propped open by two metal cleats. The weight of a vehicle would pop the cleats out, and closing the lid would complete the circuit and explode the mine. Write accidentally let the lid of one mine close and it exploded between his legs, blowing off both arms and one leg and blinding him. After applying tourniquets, Sergeant Knox carried Write to the nearest first-aid station, where he died a few hours later, still attempting to issue orders. He was buried by the side of Route 3. One of his last wishes was for red roses on his grave. Pvt. Carl Nickols, a supply truck driver, was unable to find roses, but decorated the grave with red wildflowers just before the company pulled out with the sound of Japanese vehicles in the background. Write had been an inspiring commander who led by example. According to Knox, he was "too brave for his own good. He wouldn't give a job to someone else that was considered above and beyond the call of duty." Walter Write was the first U.S. Army tank officer killed in action in World War II. The morale of the Janesville Company dropped with his loss and, according to some survivors, never recovered. Lt. Kenneth Bloomfield was named permanent CO after acting in that capacity for two weeks.

Lieutenant Colonel Miller, who had been promoted on December 19, was ordered to leave his C Company with the South Luzon Force and lead the rest of his 194th Tank Battalion to the Agno River (D-2) line. Their trip from Manila in the daytime was undisturbed by air attacks and took less than a day. Miller met General Weaver at Carmen on the 24th and received his orders. His two companies would man the twenty-five miles to the west of Carmen; Wickord's three companies the sixteen miles to the east. The units maintained the same relative positions during the withdrawal, with the 194th using Route 3 and the 192nd, Route 5. Wickord was promoted on this date to lieutenant colonel. He was thus junior to Miller by five days, and Miller would make use of his seniority several times in the days to come. In addition to the PTG, the D-2 Line was manned by the 21st Division, 11th Division, and the 92nd Regimental Combat Team of the Philippine Army, and (for a few days) the 26th

Cavalry Regiment of the Philippine Scouts. The line was not continuous but made use of suitable terrain on either side of the Agno.

Suitable placement of the tanks was the subject of frequent disputes between Wainwright and Weaver, who from the 25th had the assistance of his new executive officer, Lt. Col. Thaddeus Smyth. Smyth's last service with a combat unit was in the 7th Infantry Division at Fort Lewis in Washington State, but he had much experience with armor, having instructed the engine and chassis classes at the Tank School. Weaver had located Smyth on the quartermaster's staff at the port of Manila. Smyth became the second (and last) West Point officer in the PTG. He was given the job of coordinating the movement of tanks to Bataan with a minimum of losses.

Lieutenant Colonel Miller was very unhappy with his orders from General Weaver. A/194TB, the Brainerd Company, was well positioned on the south bank of the Agno for ten miles west of Carmen, but D/192TB, the Harrodsburg Company, at the far west end of the line, was separated from the others by jungle. The company was split up, with one platoon north of the river. Its only contact with other Fil-American units was by radio. Miller quizzed Weaver as to when they would pull back and was told the orders would come in the morning. Miller remained with A/194TB, while Weaver withdrew to PTG headquarters in San Miguel.

Most of the men on the line received hot dinners Christmas morning, the best meals they would receive for years. The food had spoiled by the time it got to D/192TB, indicative of the company's isolation, and the Harrodsburg tankers made do with iron rations. The line west of Carmen came under mortar and artillery fire in late morning. The tanks returned fire, but their armor-piercing 37mm shells were useless in indirect fire, although they were effective against observed targets. The 75mm cannon of the SPMs were much better, and there was a battery of these half-tracks with the 194th. They would pull up between the tanks, fire a few rounds, and move on; they pulled out for good in the afternoon. The tanks frequently had to reposition themselves before the Japanese could get the range of the SPMs with their 105mm howitzers.

As the day went on, the Japanese began digging trenches on the north riverbank and exposed themselves on sandbars looking for shallow spots in the river. The tanks and unattached men moved closer to the south bank to take them under fire. Miller estimated that 500 Japanese were killed at this time, but a mortar shell burst in a tree above Sgt. Herb Strobel's tank before Strobel could button up, and shrapnel mangled Strobel fatally while a piece of shell embedded itself in the driver's foot. Lieutenant Colonel Miller was knocked down by the blast but got up, lifted Strobel out of his tank, and put him and the driver into a truck that was headed for an aid station. Miller knew that Strobel was fatally wounded. He was the first fatality whom Miller had known personally back in Brainerd. Strobel had driven a milk truck, and Miller kept telling himself, over and over, "Herb won't deliver milk anymore."

Two of the men on the riverbank were also casualties of the Agno River stand; they failed to return to their vehicles when these pulled out that night and remained MIA. In mid-afternoon Miller drove to Weaver's San Miguel command post (CP) in his bloody uniform, failed to get any new orders from Weaver, and retired to his own CP in Gerona.

Just before nightfall Capt. Edward Burke, the Brainerd Company CO, unable to reach any higher commands by radio, took the company's only jeep east toward Carmen. Nearing the town, he got out and was struck by Japanese machine gun fire while standing beside his jeep. Lt. Harold Costigan, commanding the nearest tank platoon, opened fire with his machine guns and was answered by a torrent of Japanese fire. It was obvious that the town had been abandoned by the Philippine Army and that Route 3, the battalion's escape route, was probably blocked. Costigan ordered his platoon to follow him into town, turn right onto Route 3, and try to break through any Japanese obstacles. He could not see Burke or his sergeant and assumed they were dead; Burke, however, had rolled into a roadside ditch and was taken prisoner the following morning. Costigan's four or five tanks charged up the road, all guns blazing. They overran an incomplete Japanese roadblock and went on into Carmen, where all but the last tank successfully turned right onto Route 3, under fire by a full arsenal of Japanese guns.

Sgt. James McComas, his driver blinded by smoke and haze, missed the turn and proceeded east out of town alone. He found a road running south at Rosales, turned, proceeded cross-country to Route 3, and roared down it at full speed, engine knocking (one cylinder had been blown out). He was stopped outside the 194TB command post at Gerona by Miller and his G-3, Maj. Eddie Johnson, who got the story and ordered a road-block established; McComas was sent to the rear in his crippled tank.

Costigan lost one tank to a thermite bomb, which a Japanese soldier had tossed onto one of the tank's many flat surfaces; the bomb burned through the plate to ignite the ammunition supply within. Sergeant Oliver and his crew bailed out and were picked up by the following tank. The platoon reached Weaver's command post at San Miguel shortly after McComas. Costigan had a difficult time persuading General Weaver that his retreat had been legitimate—according to Miller, Weaver threatened him with a firing squad—and was soon sent north to join Miller.

Lieutenant Colonel Miller carefully established his roadblock on Route 3 north of San Manuel with his own M3, that of Major Johnson, the best of Costigan's tanks, and a command post half-track—everyone else was sent to the rear. Several of Capt. Gordon Peck's SPM half-tracks approached them across a cane field and were incorporated in the block, their 75mm cannons becoming its major components. The Americans laid their guns in fixed positions, covering the entire highway and ditches from several angles. A number of Filipino stragglers approached the block and were sent to the rear. At about 2:50 a.m. a large motorized column was heard. Its leading vehicle was seen coming down the road with dimmed lights. Miller and Johnson opened fire at about 150 feet. The SPM then raked the road. The one-sided action continued for fifteen minutes; Miller believed that the Japanese fired only one shell. After the fire subsided, Miller decided that it was time to withdraw—the Japanese would surely bring up infantrymen to resume the attack, and Miller had none to defend his almost-blind tanks—and bumped Johnson's tank in a prearranged signal. The block was reestablished at Moncada and maintained until two trains carrying Filipino infantry crossed the highway. There were two bridges at Moncada spanning a steeply banked river. After telling the local infantry commander that more tanks were expected and receiving assurances that the bridges would not be blown, Miller and his tankers withdrew to Gerona on the next defensive line, D-3. The Japanese withdrew to Carmen and fortified it in anticipation of a counterattack. They temporarily abandoned Route 3 as an axis of advance and next moved southward on Route 5, to the east.

The 194th Battalion tankers left behind on the Agno River line spent the rest of the night in uneasy silence. The next morning Captain Altman of D Company went east to find out if Captain Burke had received any orders—his own radio was jammed. When he learned that Burke was missing, he sent Lieutenant Hummel toward Carmen in a half-track to investigate. Firing was heard, and the half-track came roaring back and stopped in the middle of the road. The crew bailed out, grabbed the half-track's guns, and ran toward Altman and the men around him. Lieutenant Hummel had been shot in the neck and was holding his fingers over the entry and exit wounds until he could get medical help. A sergeant was also wounded in the neck, and the half-track was immobilized with a punctured radiator, an overheating engine, and a locked crankshaft.

As senior officer on the scene, Captain Altman took command of A Company's eight tanks—2nd Lt. Albert Hook's and 2nd Lt. James Hart's platoons—and his own thirteen and proposed an escape plan. The tanks would proceed directly south across some sugarcane fields until they reached a carabao trail that Altman believed paralleled a railroad track he knew of that eventually crossed Route 3. Lieutenant Hart trailed the column and, after trying unsuccessfully to persuade other members of his platoon to join him, destroyed his tank and headed west with his crew on foot. They succeeded in joining a nascent guerilla band in the Zambales Mountains. Hart was promoted to guerilla captain and survived until killed in a 1943 Japanese raid. Two of his crewmembers were likewise killed as guerillas; Pvt. Rudolph Bolstad survived and in 1944 was evacuated on the submarine USS *Narwhal.*

The rest of Altman's convoy proceeded in fits and starts as trails branched off from the one they were trying to follow. Altman overturned his tank trying to reverse it at one dead end and had to destroy it. The other nineteen succeeded in reaching the railroad line and followed it until it crossed Route 3 north of Moncada. They raced south on Route 3, only to find to their utter chagrin that both bridges had been blown. Altman ordered the guns and ignition systems disabled, but did not destroy the tanks, intending to return and salvage them. Darkness had fallen before the men addressed the task of crossing the river. They swam, scrambled across the bridge girders, or in the case of Sgt. Bernard Fitz-Patrick, who couldn't swim, floated across in a life preserver constructed of empty canteens. The men then improvised litters for the wounded and marched south on Route 3, eventually reaching American outposts at Tarlac, north of the D-4 line. Ninety men were returned to duty; Altman had lost only Hart's crew. Altman drew six Bren gun carriers from the PTG to remain operational as a company. Surplus tank crews were split up and sent to the other companies. After the surrender, the PTG commanders held an investigation in prison camp to study the loss of Company D's tanks. Altman was held blameless. He had reached Moncada fifteen hours after battalion headquarters and fourteen hours after the last infantry had crossed the bridges. No Company A or headquarters tank had been left behind to protect the bridges and guide Company D. In his bitter postwar memoir, Miller attempted to lay the blame on Weaver, for placing his tanks in a "rat trap." Weaver's mild rebuttal, which was not published but disappeared into the army's files, pointed out that Miller had moved back from the San Manuel roadblock while under no enemy pressure and following no orders, and that Miller himself should bear the blame for abandoning his Company D.

2nd Lt. Weeden Petree's platoon had also been abandoned, but Petree was much luckier. He was stationed north of the Agno River in the section where the south bank was covered in thick jungle. Altman apparently made no attempt to contact him before pulling out. Petree judged the situation correctly and evacuated to the west. He apparently reached Route 13 at Bayembang and followed it all the way to Tarlac without losing a man or machine.

Lieutenant Colonel Wickord's 192nd Battalion had an easy time on its withdrawal from the D-2 line. The infantry commander in his sector told Wickord that the infantry would be pulling back in the evening of the 26th and advised (or ordered) Wickord to conform to his movements. Rather than checking with Weaver or with Miller's 194th Battalion to his west, Wickord assumed that the move was general knowledge and pulled back at 9 p.m., the headquarters and Companies A and B on Route 5, and Company C on Route 8 farther east. The medical detachment and (presumably) the headquarters moved all the way south to Cabanatuan on the D-4 line; the fighting elements stopped on the D-3 line, where Company C fought a noisy skirmish at San Jose. Lieutenant Colonel Wickord may or may not have been chastised for his failure to contact the rest of the PTG on the 26th, but he took the lesson to heart, and his headquarters was noted for the rest of the campaign for clear communications.

The D-3 line was manned for only one day before the NLF fell back. General Weaver and Lieutenant Colonel Smyth had quickly established a tactical doctrine for the tanks, which worked well until the force entered Bataan. The M3 light tanks were to cover infantry movements, sweep enemy avenues of approach, and halt enemy tank movements (always important to Weaver). When stationary they were to deploy on alternate sides of the roads at curves and bends to achieve maximum sweep of their weapons with a minimum of exposure. They were always to leave a route of escape, and withdrawals were to be made one tank at a time, each covering the next. The SPM half-tracks were to be used whenever available. These were in Philippine Army (PA) artillery units and did not report to General Weaver, but relationships in the field between the artillerymen and the tankers were always outstanding. The tank-infantry command relationship was never resolved. Weaver's insistence that all orders to the tank battalions go through him was undercut quietly by Wickord and Miller, who assigned liaison officers from their own staffs to the infantry units they were working with. This eased day-to-day relationships, and the prickly Weaver was called in only when the infantry commanders asked the tanks to perform tasks that were too risky or beyond their competence.

The next line, D-4, was reached in good order on the morning of December 29. It ran through several major towns and was occupied from left to right by the 21st Division (PA) at Tarlac, the 11th Division (PA) from Tarlac to Cabanatuan, and the 91st Division (PA) at Cabanatuan. Miller's weak 194th Tank Battalion supported the west end of the line; Wickord's 192nd, the east. General Wainwright planned to hold D-4 for several days to allow the SLF to complete its retreat from Manila, but it had to be abandoned quickly. The Japanese shifted the main axis of their advance east to Cabanatuan on Route 5—which not only outflanked

Wainwright's defenses but also provided the shortest route to Manila, which was still the main Japanese objective. The 91st Division collapsed and fled south on Route 5. Wickord's three companies were on both sides of the Pampanga River at Cabanatuan and performed their practiced role as rear guard. A Company moved west to prevent the Japanese from rolling up the rear of the D-4 line, B Company moved south on Route 5, while C Company was on the next road to the east, Route 8. MacArthur's headquarters pulled Miller's two companies, now down to twenty tanks, out of the D-4 line and sent them south past the unmanned D-5 line to Apalit, where they were to form a backstop for the critical Calumpit bridges, which had to be held long enough for the SLF to reach Bataan. A composite company comprising Company B and Company D joined Miller at Apalit; General Jones, the area commander, ordered the 91st Division, bolstered by the artillery and C/192TB, to hold off the eastern Japanese wing as far north as possible, preferably at Baliuag.

THE BATTLE OF BALIUAG

C Company first had to reach Baliuag. The company was moving down Route 8 and needed to turn south onto Route 5 at Cabanatuan. Sgt. John Rowland, the senior half-track commander in the 192nd Battalion reconnaissance platoon, scouted Cabanatuan on the evening of December 28 and discovered the presence of Japanese, who had reached the barrio by Route 5 and were setting up artillery to cut off C Company. Rowland's radioed warning allowed the leading elements of the company to bypass the ambush and follow Route 5 to Gapan. 1st Lt. Bill Gentry's trailing platoon circled behind the roadblock and attacked it from the rear, overrunning the Japanese field pieces before they could be manhandled around to face the onrushing tanks. Gentry's platoon sustained no losses; Japanese losses are unknown but were rated as "considerable" in American histories and communiqués.

Gentry and his men put enough distance between themselves and the enemy to stop for fuel and provisions ten miles south at Gapan. They were covered in grime and bone-tired, having been without sleep since C/192TB had become the rear guard for the eastern wing of the Fil-American Army. This was in headlong retreat from Col. Seinosuke

Sonoda's eastern Japanese column, which comprised a battalion of General Tsuchibashi's 48th Division supported by the 7th Tank Regiment and a company of engineers. It was coming down Route 5, the shortest route to Manila, and by chance was heading for Route 5's intersection with Route 3 at Plaridel and beyond it the Calumpit bridges, the capture of which would block General Parker's South Luzon Force from entering Bataan and also head off General Wainwright's North Luzon Force, which was coming south by a more westerly route. General Jones scrambled to set up a defensive line at Baliuag. Jones commanded two Philippine Army divisions, but the 71st was down to 200 effectives; most of the missing men had headed for their homes. He now had the 91st Division, the 71st Field Artillery Battalion, a handful of Philippine Army 75mm SPM half-tracks—and Company C's M3 light tanks.

Lieutenant Gentry reached Baliuag from Gapan on the evening of December 29 and planned a full night's sleep, but before morning was told by Capt. Harold Collins, his company commander, that for the third time in a week his platoon was to be given a critical mission—and this time it was the most critical mission for the United States Army Forces in the Far East (USAFFE). The defense of the barrio was to be Gentry's responsibility. He had the long-range support of the field artillery and the SPMs and was given tactical control of Lt. Marshall Kennady's tank platoon of five M3s and Captain Collins's company headquarters element of one M3 tank and one M2 half-track.

Bill Gentry, a twenty-three-year-old Kentuckian, had had a good war. He and two friends had joined the National Guard tank company in his native Harrodsburg in 1936, mainly because its machinery and the money fascinated them. Gentry managed to finish one year of college but was fated to remain on his family's farm as a hand, so was glad when the tank company was federalized in November 1940 as Company D of the 192nd Tank Battalion. He applied for and received a commission as a second lieutenant, was named head of the Fort Knox radio school, and reached the Philippines as the 192nd Tank Battalion communications officer. He made favorable impressions on Colonel Weaver and Brigadier General King, but the onset of war fated him to remain within the 192nd.

Capt. Robert Sorensen, who had brought the tank battalion's Company C overseas, fell apart completely on December 22, the day of the Japanese invasion, and had to be relieved. Maj. Ted Wickord, the battalion commander, chose 1st Lt. Harold Collins, the company's senior platoon leader, to be the new commander. To fill Collins's old role, Wickord picked 1st Lieutenant Gentry from his own staff. The senior platoon leader served as the company's executive and maintenance officer, and Gentry's experience made him a good fit. He reached the company at Rosario on the Lingayen Gulf just in time to begin the rapid retreat that ended in Bataan. Collins proved to be a weak leader, and Gentry wound up in effective command of the company, although he never claimed that role for himself. According to Gentry, Collins was personally brave and could follow orders, but could not make decisions. Collins was afflicted with what Gentry called the "10,000 mile stare," which was far worse than combat artist Tom Lea's "two thousand yard stare" later in the war— it reached all the way to Collins's home in Ohio.

Company C received fuel, ammunition, and rations in Gapan and then proceeded to Baliuag, where they bivouacked south of town and planned the first full night's sleep in days. But Captain Collins was awakened in the middle of the night by the radio operator, who said, "I've got a message here. I've had them repeat it and repeat it, and I get the same answer every time." Collins asked, "What's that?" The reply, "Hold at all costs." Collins got everyone together, and when asked what the message meant, replied, "Well, if I get killed, Bill's in command, and if he gets killed, Marshall's in command, and we go right on down to the last man. We're gonna stay here until we get orders to pull out. It says, 'Hold at all costs,' and we're gonna stay here until we're told to pull back."

On the morning of the 30th, the approaches to Baliuag were scouted by the recon troops; by Capt. John Morley, the battalion intelligence officer (S-2), who had taken over the platoon half-track with the best radio; and, according to his account, by Gentry himself. I assume, but can't confirm, that all of the Highway 5 bridges across the Angat River and its tributaries and canals were destroyed—ample time and explosives existed—but a narrow-gauge railroad bridge leading into the western outskirts of Baliuag was left intact. Planking would be required before tanks and other heavy equipment could cross, but the Japanese attack would then be funneled into the narrow streets of the barrio, where Gentry's tanks would be waiting. Was the bridge deliberately left unblown as bait to attract the Japanese? This would have been the most adept tactical move in the campaign; unfortunately I can't confirm it. No surviving American commander took credit for the decision.

Lieutenant Gentry spent rest of the 30th positioning his defenders. He placed his five tanks beneath nipa huts about 1,000 yards south of the bridge. The huts were eight to ten feet above the ground on bamboo stilts. Gentry's men had a clear view of the bridge across drained rice paddies. The tanks were camouflaged with foliage and bamboo mats and proved invisible to the Japanese infantry, which began crossing the bridge that evening and camping on the south side. 2nd Lieutenant Kennady's five tanks were similarly camouflaged on the other side of town; Captain Collins's company headquarters blocked the only road exiting the town to the south. 2nd Lt. Everett Preston's platoon of five tanks was sent south with a gas station road map to find unblown bridges or fords; according to Gentry, Preston's orders were to cross if possible and attack the Japanese from the rear. This is odd in two respects: Recon was a job for the recon platoon's half-tracks, not the invaluable tanks; and Preston's platoon was too small to be an effective attacking force. At any rate, Preston was unavailable for the defense of Baliuag. According to Gentry, Preston got lost and never made it back to Baliuag. When he was located the next day, he was still trying to find a way across the river.

On the morning of the 31st, Japanese infantry of the Sonoda Force continued crossing the railroad bridge, watched closely by Lieutenant Gentry. The Philippine Army's fifteen 75mm artillery pieces from the 71st Artillery Battalion and half-dozen SPMs began to shell the landing site. The Japanese infantrymen dug in and waited for their Type 89B medium tanks, which in turn waited for the engineers to lay planking on the bridge. By mid-morning the Philippine Army infantrymen could wait no longer and began heading south for Plaridel, without orders from General Jones. The Japanese began moving into the town and established an observation post in the largest church without seeing any Americans, who had set up their own observation site in the tower of a multistory building that may have been another church or the city hall. Captain Burholt, the battalion operations officer (S-3) was among the staff officers present.

Sgt. Al Allen, the C Company recon platoon sergeant, was also there. The twenty-one-year-old Allen had enlisted the previous January and was assigned to C Company. Allen was sharp and inquisitive, and was a good fit for the company's reconnaissance platoon, where he quickly rose to sergeant and the senior enlisted man. By the Baliuag battle he had already lost his first motorcycle to Lt. William Slicer, who took it on an unauthorized drunken spin to Manila and destroyed it by crashing into a tree. Allen made sure that his replacement Harley-Davidson was hidden securely in the observation post. The officers with him had binoculars, good observation perches, and a working radio. After the shooting began, they kept battalion headquarters well informed, leaving Gentry free to conduct the battle.

Map 4 was hand-sketched by Bill Gentry for the Kentucky Historical Society twenty years after the war and was redrawn for this book using a modern ©Google Map. The population of Baliuag has grown from 2,000 to 3,000 in 1941 to over 150,000 in 2015, and the railway and its bridge are gone, but Gentry's memory for landmarks and scale was perfect. The bridge spanned a canal, and not the Angat River itself.

The shooting did not start until about 5 p.m. According to Gentry's account, Captain Morley drove into town in a jeep accompanied by Collins and parked outside Gentry's hide. Gentry told them to go back the way they came as quietly as they could, but he could see that the Japanese in the church steeple were agitated and assumed Japanese investigators would soon arrive; Gentry thus began his attack as soon as he felt Morley had cleared the town. He sent the prearranged signal to Kennady and the artillery, radioed his own men, burst from cover, and opened fire. His main targets were the enemy artillery park and medium tanks, two of which immediately burst into flames.

The Japanese tanks turned out to be much less effective against armor than the Type 85 Ha-Go light tanks that had bested Lt. Ben Morin's B Company platoon on the 22nd. The mediums' 57mm guns fired only high-explosive ammunition, which could not penetrate armor, even that

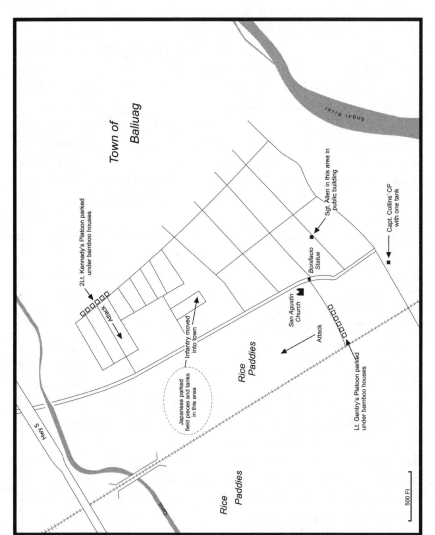

Map 4

as thin as on the M3. The Japanese infantrymen had no antitank weapons, and their small-caliber rifle and machine gun fire plinked harmlessly off the American tanks' hides. As the Japanese tanks raced into town, Gentry's tanks immobilized the parked artillery pieces without wasting armor-piercing 37mm ammunition on them—wheels were broken off, barrels were knocked askew, and trails were overrun. The M3s then wheeled into town.

For once in the war American tankers were in complete control of the battlefield, and they took advantage of it. The Japanese tanks and an estimated 400 to 500 infantry fled into the town, away from Lieutenant Gentry, only to come under fire from Lieutenant Kennady's platoon. Sergeant Allen reported that the tanks chased each other up and down the streets, but the American M3s did most of the chasing, being much faster and more agile than the Japanese Type 89Bs. Gentry reported that the turrets of the Japanese tanks could traverse only a few degrees, although in theory they were fully traversable. We can speculate that the Japanese gunners, untrained in tank-to-tank combat and stunned by the surprise attack, simply could not hand-crank their turrets quickly enough to follow the speeding American tanks, which sustained no damage from the 57mm Japanese tank guns. The careening tanks did considerable damage to the barrio, smashing through the bamboo huts and setting them on fire with tracers, and knocking great chunks of masonry off the permanent buildings. The equestrian statue of Andres Bonifacio that dominated the town square lost its head to a shell fired by Sgt. David Duff, who told Sergeant Allen later that the head was an aiming point for bore-sighting his cannon.

After neutralizing the enemy tanks, the Americans turned their attention to the infantry; the four .30 caliber machine guns on their M3s, more in number than on any later U.S. tank, were ideal for slaughtering exposed men, and were reported to have killed most of them, driving the survivors back toward the bridge.

The battalion headquarters was tuned in to Gentry's radio frequency and burst in with words of encouragement, like cheering on a football team. Sergeant Allen, the only C Company member among the battalion brass in their observation post, left early to report to battalion headquarters, either under orders or because, as he said, he wanted to protect his precious new motorcycle. He proceeded alone south down Route 5 until he chanced on the rear echelon of the 194th Tank Battalion in Plaridel. These men were directing C/194TB and various supply and Philippine Army units that were heading north on Route 5 from Manila, turning west onto Highway 3 at Plaridel, and reorganizing behind the Calumpit bridges over the Pampanga River. Sergeant Allen convinced the 194th supply officer (S-4) that the rumbling that could be heard was artillery in Baliuag, and that the Fil-American rear guard would soon be coming down the highway, followed by the Japanese. Allen was ordered to find the 194th commander, Lt. Col. Ernest Miller, and give him the news. Miller was loathe to believe Allen until the S-4 arrived and confirmed his story. The rumbling had grown louder, and the distinctive roaring of the M3s' radial aircraft engines could be heard in the distance. Miller got his men to Calumpit, and all of them made it across the bridges safely. Miller's bitter postwar memoir, *Bataan Uncensored*, does not mention that this escape was only made possible by the 192nd Battalion's victory at Baliuag, an omission that angered Al Allen for the rest of his life.

C Company stopped firing at about 6:30 p.m. when it ran out of ammunition, and pulled south of town to its earlier bivouac. Gentry took a minute to inspect a Type 89B that had been immobilized on the town square and shot at by every passing M3. The corpses of the four Japanese tankers were inside the tank, which was perforated by forty to fifty 37mm holes—many of the armor-piercing shells had come in one side of the tank and out the other. His report stated that the American M3s were superior to the Japanese mediums in all respects. The Philippine Army artillery resumed firing on the Japanese, by now back north of the river; this was the rumbling heard in Plaridel. They ceased fire soon before nightfall, limbered their guns, and headed south, followed at about 10 p.m. by C Company, which had finally been released, either by General Jones or General Weaver.

The Japanese reentered Baliuag cautiously and followed the Fil-American forces at a distance. The Philippine Army rear guard at Plaridel held the Japanese off briefly and then headed for Calumpit. Gen. "Skinny" Wainwright waited impatiently on the western side of one bridge, accompanied by Colonel Skerry, his engineering officer; General Stevens, commanding the 91st Division (PA); and General Weaver. Wainwright delayed his final order to blow the bridges to allow groups of stragglers to cross. At 6:15 a.m. on New Year's morning, only one Philippine Army engineering unit was unaccounted for, and Colonel Skerry closed the switch. Seven tons of dynamite exploded, dropping the twin spans into the broad Pampanga River. The Fil-American Army was only a few days away from entering the Bataan Peninsula, where all believed the U.S. Navy would relieve them—but as the Japanese more realistically put it, they were just "entering the sack."

The Japanese confirmed the loss of only one Type 89B, but Colonel Sonoda alerted Japan that its 57mm gun was inadequate against the M3 light tank. He knew that the Type 1 47mm was in development and requested that it be put in a tank. These were installed in a few Type 97 Chi-Ha medium tanks, and two arrived in the Philippines in time for the Corregidor invasion.

Bill Gentry and his men were treated as heroes when they finally reached battalion headquarters. C Company's only casualty was one man who sprained his ankle jumping from his tank to tell his story. The Americans were credited with destroying eight Japanese tanks and killing several hundred men in Baliuag. The validity of this claim is, of course, unknown, as the area was evacuated after the battle, but the performance of the American armor definitely impressed the Japanese, who did not again use their own armor aggressively until the final days of the campaign. This was the first victory in the war by American land forces, an event eagerly looked for in the United States. Frank Hewlett of the United Press interviewed Lieutenant Gentry in the hospital two weeks after the battle (he was down with a fever), and Hewlett's account of the "ten little tanks spitting death" was picked up by news media across America. Baliuag was a clear-cut victory and very important in bucking up home-front morale in January 1942, when war news around the world was almost all bad. For his performance on December 31, Bill Gentry was awarded a Silver Star, one of the few in the campaign.

The minuscule battle was overwhelmed by later events and soon forgotten by everyone in the Philippines who had not taken direct part.

General Wainwright's version in his memoir is so confused and poorly written that it is totally useless as history. Morton's official history devotes one page to the engagement, which it calls "The Battle for Plaridel." The tiny group of American tankers had won a victory at Baliuag when victories were very rare. This deserves to be remembered, and under its own name.

The celebrations had to wait a few days, as C Company had to perform its well-practiced role as rear guard one more time. When it reached Apalit, the first Route 3 barrio past the bridges, it was ordered to relieve the portion of the 194th Battalion that had been serving as a backstop at Apalit. Miller's force was pulled farther back to San Fernando, the next critical road junction. C Company found ammunition trucks at Apalit, provisioned, and established a blocking position across Route 3. Bill Gentry recalled:

The area is all open rice paddies. The rice had been harvested and was in large stacks in different places. Since we felt the attack would probably come at night, when we moved into position we zeroed our guns on these rice stacks so that the first round of ammunition from the 37mm gun would be tracer ammunition that would go thru a rice stack. This would give us a light to see the Japanese.

We spaced our tanks about a hundred yards apart or more and, since we were the only troops in the area, we kept up a constant chatter of shouting between tanks in order to make the Japanese know that there were troops up in front and to hold up their advance. They moved equipment and troops across the bridge from dusk until about midnight. At this particular point, they had advanced up within just a few yards of us. In fact, some houses directly in front of us, the Japanese had collected in back of these houses until we felt that there just wasn't room for any more. We could see them setting up their mortar positions out a little ways and they dropped the first volley of mortar fire right over in amongst our tanks and we had four men that picked up a few pieces of shrapnel in this first volley from the mortar. At this particular point we opened fire by setting the rice stacks on fire and gave them machine gunning. Then later on, as we leveled off the troops

in front of us, we started using the 37s on equipment we could see fur-
ther out. In fact, we were down to the point where we were shooting
single Japanese with single rounds of 37mm. At about two o'clock in
the morning we were completely out of ammunition, even though we
had started with more than our normal load of ammo. And we pulled
back, under orders, to San Fernando, where we refueled and filled up
with ammunition.

C/194TB (THE SALINAS COMPANY) IN SOUTHERN LUZON

Capt. Fred Moffitt's C/194TB tanks and a handful of SPMs were the
only armored backing in the South Luzon Force, which came under Gen.
Albert Jones's command when Gen. George Parker left on December 24
to establish the Bataan defenses. That same morning, the Japanese landed
7,000 troops of the 16th Division on the shores of Lamon Bay, southeast
of Manila. They were to form the southern wing of a pincer attack on
Manila, but they faced worse obstacles from water, mountains, and jungle
than the men coming from Lingayen Gulf; Homma considered them
second-rate troops and did not expect much from them. Furthermore,
they were actually outnumbered by the SLF, so should have been bottled
up easily on the coast. However, Jones had inherited a poorly positioned
force and was bedeviled by the Philippine Army units' inability to hold.
He placed Moffitt's tanks behind what passed for defensive lines, with
contact between positions maintained by half-track patrols.

On the 26th the Filipinos at Lucban began falling back without
orders, and their advisor, an American major, ordered Lt. Robert Needham's platoon of five M3s to go up a narrow trail toward Pils, traveling
like hell and firing their guns. Needham requested a preliminary reconnaissance, but the major assured him that he had definite information
that the Japanese had nothing larger than .50 caliber machine guns, and
that the purpose of the tankers' demonstration was to impress his men
and raise their morale. Needham led his tanks down the jungle road in
offensive patrol formation, spaced to maintain visual contact. Needham's
tank disappeared around a sharp bend and gunfire broke out; Sgt. Emil
Morello in the second tank accelerated just in time for an antitank shell
to pass behind him. He rounded the turn, did not see Needham's tank

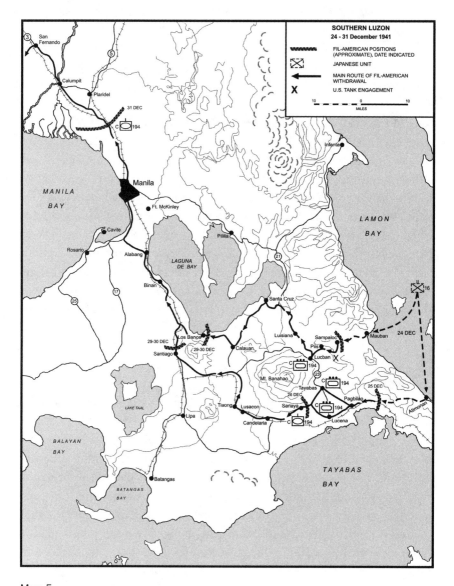

Map 5

thru his vision slit, and ordered the other tanks to follow him at full speed, cannons and machine guns blazing. They now faced a roadblock of felled trees, partially hidden by a smokescreen from a fire of green wood. Morello's driver barreled the tank over the roadblock, only to encounter a 77mm gun set up in the middle of the trail. Morello did not hesitate, but crashed into the gun, scattering the crew. The four tanks proceeded down the trail, taking fire from both sides, until the trail widened enough to allow the tanks to turn around. They then turned, still in trail, and reversed course. They continued to exchange fire until they reached the area where Needham's tank had last been seen. Morello's tank then took a direct hit that knocked off the idler sprocket and sheared off rivets that ricocheted around inside the tank. One went through the neck of Pvt. Eddie DeBenedetti, wounding him severely. The tank rolled over a bank and came to rest upright in a rice paddy. Morello ordered his crew to shut off the engine, lock the hatches, and feign death.

Sgt. Glenn Brokaw's tank, next in line, took hits that fatally injured Brokaw and killed the rest of his crew. The other two tanks were also destroyed, but the crews survived. Needham's tank, the first hit, had plunged off the road into a rice paddy. Needham's legs had been severed by the first antitank shell, and he quickly bled to death. His three crew-members were gunned down when they tried to escape the tank.

Morello's survival strategy worked, however. Japanese tried to open the hatches, but possibly seeing DeBenedetti's blood, concluded the crew was dead and left the area. Several parties examined the tank later in the day and came to the same conclusion. That evening the Japanese constructed a camp with a field kitchen only twenty feet from the tank. Morello's men had no water, the tropical sun beat down on the tank all day, and the men resorted to licking the red-hot metal for moisture. At about 3 a.m. a Philippine Army artillery barrage hit the area, doing considerable damage. The Japanese pulled out at about 5 a.m., and two hours later Morello and his men carefully climbed from their tank, carrying their sidearms and ammunition into the jungle. They escaped random encounters with the Japanese, picked up two wounded crewmen from Needham's other tanks, pooled their resources, and hired a Filipino guide for 100 pesos, got through the Japanese lines, and reached Manila on New Year's Day. There were no Fil-American combat units around, but Eddie DeBenedetti and the other two wounded were left at the Philippine General Hospital, and the three others caught the last *banca* out of Manila for Corregidor. There they were put in the hospital for three days, then taken to Mariveles at the southern tip of Bataan by boat and dumped off. They stayed there for a few days before hiking north to find the 194th Battalion bivouac. After a heartfelt reunion with their amazed comrades, they rejoined C Company. Emil Morello was awarded a Silver Star for his outstanding performance in this episode, as was Lieutenant Needham.

Lieutenant Needham's combat, which cost five tanks and twenty MIA and KIA, was apparently the only major engagement for Captain Moffitt's company in southern Luzon. The rest trailed General Jones's infantry as it headed north. Some of the Americans were as jumpy as the average Philippine Army recruit. Cpl. Frank Muther recalled:

I was the last tank to leave the area and given orders to hold until all the Filipino troops passed our area, then hit the enemy and leapfrog to our next position. All day long Filipino troops were streaming by after being driven off the beach by the massive Jap attack. These Filipinos were so poorly trained that they were given a rifle and sent to the front. One soldier came to me; his gun was covered in blood, and he wanted to know how to fire it. Opening the bolt, I could see that the Cosmoline wasn't even cleaned out of the barrel, although he claimed to have killed some of the Japs before he was overrun. When the troops stopped coming I knew it would be our turn to stop the advance along the road. The waiting got too much for our sergeant and he constantly wanted to pull out, but our orders were to hit and run. I was cutting some bamboo to better camouflage the tank, for we had a good field of fire about 200 yards down the road. My plan was to wait for the column of troops to come within range and then open up on them. We had two sponson guns, a 37mm cannon, and one bow gun. I could just see 2400 rounds per minute and the 37mm ripping into the attacking forces. While I was cutting the bamboo, the sergeant kept saying we had to get out or we would be killed, and the driver became jittery. With that I slammed the bolo knife on the tank and said, "I'll cut your damn head off if you don't shut up." With that he started crying, crawled back into the tank, and was useless for the next five days before he got to the rear echelon. The radio signal in the tank sounded, and I jumped in and took the message. "Pull out and proceed with Plan Orange"; that was the code to move out.

MacArthur declared Manila an open city on December 26, to spare it from destruction. The Japanese bombed it on December 27 and 28, resulting in one war crimes charge against General Homma that MacArthur was able to make stick. They did not bomb the retreating SLF as it passed around Manila on the 30th; Japanese pilots then and later lacked the authority to deviate from their briefed targets. C/194TB was the trailing unit and succeeded in making a one-hundred-mile road march in six hours at night. Although they were ordered not to enter the city, which was now displaying lights to demonstrate its status as demilitarized, Captain Moffitt decided to pass through it; he did not know the bypass route, had only a gasoline station map to go by, and besides, who would know? All went well until Corporal Muther, a radioman who was being forced to drive his tank owing to the mental failure of two crewmen, dozed off and lost the tank he was following. He jerked the tank to full speed, awakening the rest of the crew. He vaguely recognized the landmarks and thought he was on Rozas Boulevard. He confirmed this by a glimpse of the Rozas statue, surrounded by a crowd of spectators, which he was headed straight for. He shouted and pulled back on both levers, prompting the regular driver to shout, "Let go of the left lever, Frank!" He did, and the tank went into a violent spin, missing the crowd but bottoming out on a pillar at the base of the statue. Locking pins sheared, and the tank shed a track. The crewmen jacked up the tank and worked feverishly to replace the track. The job was finished by noon, but the tank shed the track again the first time it moved forward. The driver then noted that the rear idler was buckled—a workshop repair now out of the question. The crew immobilized the tank: The gunner dropped the breech into a nearby river, the driver smashed the controls with a hammer, and Muther dismantled the radio and scattered the parts. They then hitched a ride with the Headquarters Company of the 26th Cavalry Regiment (PS), who had returned to Manila to pick up their quota of Bren gun carriers, which had been trapped at the outbreak of war as described earlier. The tankers reached their company in bivouac on the east side of the Pampanga and joined it in crossing the Calumpit bridges on the night of December 31.

INTO BATAAN

In the last few days of 1941, C/192TB was at Baliuag, C/194TB was trailing the SLF on its retreat north of Manila, and the rest of the PTG helped bolster the defenses on the main approaches to Bataan. On the retreat from D-4, Sgt. Ray Mason's Company B M3 was disabled by Japanese fire. Mason and his crew exited the tank and attempted to surrender. The Japanese ordered the men to run toward their own lines and then opened fire with a machine gun. Mason was killed immediately; the other three men were injured and hid in a sugarcane field. Pvt. Quincey Humphries was probably found and killed by the Japanese, and was carried as MIA; Pvt. LD Marrs was taken prisoner and survived the war; S/Sgt. Walter Mahr was found by the Filipinos the next day and returned to duty after his wounds were treated but died in POW camp.

The Kanno Detachment, primarily a battalion of the 2nd Formosa Infantry Regiment and a battalion of mountain artillery, moved west on the arterial road behind the D-4 line, which here was still manned by the 11th Division (PA). A platoon from Captain Bloomfield's A/192TB was drawn up on both sides of this road east of Zaragoza. At 3:15 a.m. on December 30, a tanker observed a column of bicyclists coming down the road. This was the leading element of the Kanno Detachment, which were taking no precautions at all. The tankers sprang their ambush—one source says they were outside their tanks, firing their tommy guns—and mowed down eighty-two Japanese before they could retreat. The tank commander, fearing infantry infiltration, ordered the Delagrot River bridge blown. The order was carried out, despite the tanker officer's junior status. Apparently, the engineer blew the bridge and left with his men, trapping the 3rd Battalion of the 11th Infantry Regiment on the east side.

According to B/Gen. W. E. Brougher, the division commander, 394 of his 500 men were killed, most mowed down while wading across the river or attempting to climb its steep banks; the survivors and other members of the division formed a defensive line on the west bank of the river and held even when the Japanese brought artillery, including one antitank gun, forward. After this gun knocked out one tank, the platoon leader ordered his remaining tanks to the rear. This order could not be countermanded, as the tanks did not report to the 11th Infantry Regiment. General Weaver in his postwar report stated that the tanks' withdrawal was standard operating procedure once their position was revealed; tanks were not pillboxes and had to retain their mobility. The Filipinos were reinforced by more division infantry and held off the Japanese until Wainwright ordered them to fall back. The Janesville tank platoon leader is identified as "Lt. Nat Grand" in Brougher's memoir, a name not found in the PTG records, but is probably Brougher's clever way of disguising "National Guard." Incidentally, William Brougher and James Weaver became great friends and roommates at POW camp.

2nd Lt. William Read's M3 was the platoon's rear guard on its withdrawal. The tank was hit and damaged by a mortar round. Read exited the tank and was helping the rest of the crew get out when a second round cut off Read's legs. Read's wounds were obviously fatal, but the crew sheltered him under a bridge, and two of them went for medical help. Neither returned, and Pvt. Ray Underwood stayed with Read's body, cradling it in his arms as the Japanese took over the area. Japanese officers were said to have been impressed by Underwood's solicitude toward his officer, which would have been very unusual behavior in the Japanese army, and treated Underwood well, although Japanese enlisted men treated him as brutally as they did every American prisoner.

Most of A/192TB and the 11th Division turned south at La Paz, reached Route 3, and took it south to the D-5 line, which was fully occupied by the dawn of December 31. One platoon of five tanks and two SPMs tore through the badly damaged town of Tarlac, losing one tank and crew to Japanese fire. The survivors tried to reach the 21st Division (PA). A blown bridge stood in the way, and the tankers and artillerymen had to abandon their vehicles and swim the stream; their tanks and SPMs were destroyed later by Philippine Army artillery. It has proved impossible to identify this platoon; it was either that of "Nat Grand" or one from

Miller's battalion that he had been ordered to leave behind to reinforce the long front occupied by the 11th Division and A/192TB.

Dr. Poweleit's 192nd Battalion medical detachment was stationed south of Cabanatuan at San Isidro, off Route 5 and the Pampanga River. After the morning air raids, he noted vehicles moving southward down the highway, and also moving across the fields in the distance. Finally Capt. John Morley from the 192nd Battalion headquarters staff came up cross-country in a Bren gun carrier and told him that San Isidro had been evacuated. They were to take their equipment down to the river, ditch it, and swim across. Poweleit didn't like that idea and decided to get on the road and find a bridge south of Gapan. Unfortunately, Gapan had already fallen to the Japanese, but Poweleit's few trucks raced through the barrio without taking fire. He caught up to the Fil-American convoy five to six kilometers south of Gapan and trailed it for a while, ditching his trucks from time to time to avoid strafers. The first Pampanga bridge Poweleit came to was surrounded by sightseers. A truck had been towing a Bren gun carrier, which had clipped a bridge support and flipped over onto the bank; its nose was under the water. Dr. Poweleit dove into the water and fished out an air force private, who could not be revived. A second passenger, Sgt. Jacques Merrifield of the 192nd Battalion communications section, was being given artificial respiration; Dr. Poweleit took over and had him taken to a hospital, where he recovered (but with lifelong back problems). He had lost his dog tags, which turned up later on the body of a dead American soldier. Merrifield was listed as KIA, and his father, a Maywood preacher, announced his death from the pulpit; his survival was not reported to the United States for a year. A third passenger, PFC Charles Jensen, a B/192TB medic, had been thrown overboard with Merrifield, and the two had thrashed downstream until coming ashore at a river bend. It was Jensen who was giving Merrifield artificial respiration until Dr. Poweleit came to relieve him; Jensen then blended into the crowd. Dr. Poweleit was later awarded a Silver Star for this incident, a very rare award for a noncombatant; Jensen received nothing.

The western end of the D-5 line occupied a strong natural position behind the Bamban River. The 11th and 21st Divisions (PA) and A/192TB reached it in time to build fire trenches, set out barbed wire

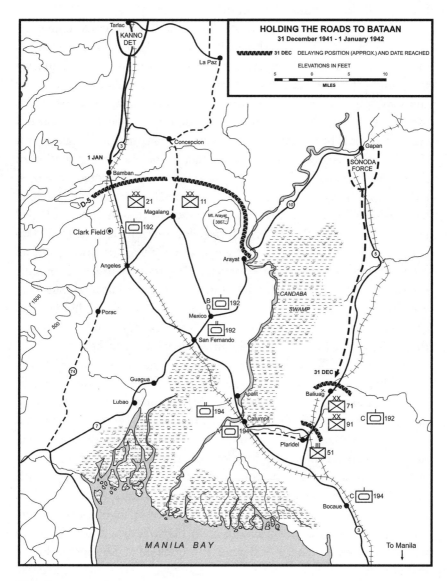

HOLDING THE ROADS TO BATAAN
31 December 1941 - 1 January 1942

〰〰〰 31 DEC DELAYING POSITION (APPROX.) AND DATE REACHED

ELEVATIONS IN FEET

MILES

Map 6

and stakes, and clear fields of fire. It was ordered to hold while the rest of the NLF passed through on Route 3 to San Fernando, a crossroads town from which Route 7 branched south to Bataan.

Traffic began backing up in San Fernando as early as December 27. Eventually the jam extended three miles north of the town and seven miles to the south, from which direction the SLF was arriving from Manila via the Calumpit bridges. The town's streets were clogged with army trucks and cars, ambulances, carabao-drawn carts, and brightly painted buses carrying both civilians and PA soldiers. Before the war the Luzon bus companies had been organized into provisional motor battalions for the Philippine Army divisions, which had no organic transportation of their own. This had been a good decision, but the buses could have been put to much better use carrying provisions to Bataan; the soldiers could have walked. The civilians were a huge problem that the USAFFE had not foreseen. MacArthur did not turn them back, and eventually 20,000 entered Bataan, requiring food, shelter, and medical attention from an army that could not even care for itself. The traffic jam was eventually resolved by the military police. Most movements were at night, but there was no way to disguise the thousands of vehicles during the day, and although Japanese Army aircraft crossed over Routes 3 and 7 every day, they did not attack; if they had, the massacre would have been terrible.

Lieutenant Colonel Miller reached San Fernando on January 1 with part of his 194th Battalion, sent out patrols, and was in action immediately. A platoon reached the barrio of Mexico northeast of town, heard noises, and took cover. Japanese tanks, apparently Type 89B mediums, approached without advance reconnaissance and stopped in an open field to check their location. The M3s opened fire and, in a hot, one-sided engagement, destroyed five tanks without loss. The next day USAFFE ordered the PTG to cover the Fil-American army's withdrawal into Bataan from San Fernando to Layac, a distance of slightly over twenty miles, and then enter bivouac. The main highway was Route 7, which was the only paved road into Bataan. It originated at San Fernando and had already been in heavy use for several days. General Weaver chose Lieutenant Colonel Miller for this task. Although the 194th was down to thirty operational M3s, Weaver considered Miller, a civilian engineer, well suited to handle the many bridges and other obstacles on this swampy route. Miller directed the last Philippine Army units to reach San Fernando and C/192TB coming from Apalit south onto Route 7, followed them, destroyed the first bridge south of town, and set up his next defensive position at Guagua.

The Guagua line was extended west with the 11th and 21st Divisions (PA) and ended at Porac, which was defended by part of Lieutenant Colonel Wickord's 192nd. Miller's small force was pressured by Japanese forces coming down Route 7 and by others approaching from the swamps to the east. By January 4 Japanese artillery was in position and pounded the 194th all day. Japanese aircraft were also active but remained ineffective. USAFFE sent the 11th Infantry Regiment and Lieutenant Bloomfield's A/192TB east from Porac to reinforce Miller. They could not reach Guagua directly and lost three tanks in the effort; traveling cross-country, Bloomfield's depleted unit finally reached Route 7 south of Guagua in time to cover Miller's withdrawal and was attached to the 194th.

On January 5 USAFFE ordered a rare daylight withdrawal from the Porac-Guagua line. Wickord's tanks left Porac on a secondary road, Route 73. Miller's tanks pulled out onto Route 7 one by one as rear guard for the eastern units. Flank support was provided by two of Captain Moffitt's C/194TB M3 tanks and four of Captain Peck's SPMs. Moffitt observed a force of 750 to 800 Japanese coming down a road to Lubao, accompanied by machine guns, mortars, and towed artillery. The Japanese were led by three Filipinos carrying white flags, but these did not prevent the Americans from opening fire, killing several hundred Japanese and forcing the survivors to crawl away. The rest of the 194th and the attached A/192TB set up a roadblock south of Lubao; the position was surrounded by turnip fields rather than the more common rice paddies, bamboo groves, or jungle, and promised clear fields of fire. At nightfall those men not on duty hollowed shallow ditches in the soft soil to rest their weary bodies and tried to sleep beneath a full moon. Lieutenant Colonel Miller was kept awake by the tossing and turning of his intelligence officer, Lt. Ferris Spoor. Shortly before 2 a.m. the two officers heard soldiers challenge what sounded like a Filipino. Moments later, shots were fired, and a Japanese soldier shouted, "We are the peepul who are not afraid to die

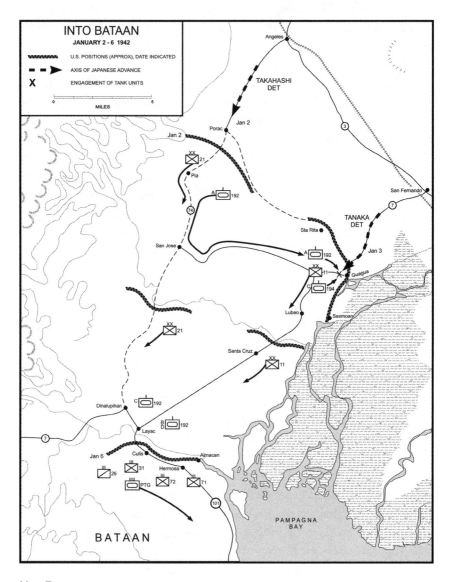

Map 7

by boolets." Following this exclamation he proceeded to grunt and moan in Japanese, causing both officers to smile from the perverse humor. A second shot silenced the soldier.

American soldiers scrambled to their tanks, half-tracks, and carriers. Japanese soldiers could be seen advancing across the open field in bright moonlight. A cloud of gas proved to be an attempted smokescreen, which blew back into the Japanese lines. The battalion opened fire and the usual slaughter occurred. Tracers flew through the air and small fires flared up. One was near U.S. positions and directly threatening the highly flammable M3 tanks. Lieutenant Petree and his platoon were near the fire. On his own initiative, Petree dismounted his tank and put out the fire. As he ran back to his tank, he was shot down. Noticing the manner in which the officer dropped, Miller drew a line to the rear of his battalion's position and saw a white patch in a tree. Miller and one of his men swung the turret-mounted .30 caliber MG around and blasted the tree. A badly mangled, white-shirted body dropped to the ground. Petree survived his wounds for a week but eventually died. He and Sgt. Henry M. Luther, who retrieved the tank, were awarded Silver Stars. By 3 a.m. the Japanese gave up the attack and withdrew, leaving hundreds of dead and wounded in the turnip field. Japanese forces ceased all local operations for the rest of the night.

Enemy pressure resumed the next morning along both Routes 7 and 73, which met at Layac Junction, just north of a bridge across the Culo River, which marked the northern boundary of Bataan province. On the night of January 6–7, the 192nd Tank Battalion followed the 194th across the bridge, and it was blown. The battle of Bataan was about to begin.

CHAPTER 7

The Siege of Bataan

THE PENINSULA OF BATAAN EXTENDS LUZON'S ZAMBALES MOUNTAINS south into the Pacific and separates the South China Sea from Manila Bay. It blocks the port of Manila from the ocean and is thus of strategic importance. The U.S. military recognized this, and from the earliest days of War Plan Orange, Bataan was to be the site of the last-ditch defense of the Philippines. Bataan's geography lent itself to a defensive stand. Twenty miles wide by twenty-five miles long, Bataan is split down the middle by a chain of sharp-sided extinct volcanoes, the largest being Mount Natib in the north (4,222 feet or 1,287 meters) and Mount Bataan in the Mariveles Mountains in the south (4,722 feet or 1,439 meters). The mountains descend almost to the sea on the western side but flatten out into a broad plain on the eastern side, where nearly all of the population lives. Many streams originate in the mountains and flow through gullies and ravines to the sea. At this time a single paved highway, Route 110, the East Road, snaked down the eastern coast, passing through the province's towns before curling back north at Mariveles on the southern tip, becoming the West Road, which was little more than a trail paved in gravel; it lost even that improvement halfway up the western side. The only east–west road of importance ran from Pilar to Bagac, through the valley separating Mount Natib from the range containing Mount Bataan.

The weather was typically tropical, with temperatures exceeding 100 degrees F (38 degrees C) in the day and in the mid-70s (24 degrees C) at night; the rainy season ran from May to October and the dry season from November to April. The relative humidity exceeded 75 percent all year.

All of Bataan but the eastern strip was a typical tropical jungle—huge hardwood trees sixty to eighty feet tall laced together with thick liana vines, with secondary growth of giant ferns and bamboo thick enough to block passage by humans not equipped with bolo knives. Wild animals abounded—pigs, monkeys, pythons, and poisonous snake species beyond counting. The fetid jungle rot was home to numerous insect species—large black blowflies swarmed during the day, replaced at night by ravenous mosquitoes that carried dengue fever, typhus, filariasis, scabies, and malaria. Bataan was the worst province in the Philippines for malaria; this could be kept in check with quinine, which unfortunately turned out to be in short supply. The eastern plain was arable and grew rice, bananas, and coconuts. Fishing was good on the eastern side; fish farms were also common. The U.S. Navy employed a few men and women, but most of the population outside the towns were subsistence farmers. There was no industry. An attempt had been made at logging, resulting in a number of dead-end trails starting on the highway and ending in the jungle, but malaria had run off the lumber companies.

Military supplies on Bataan were short at the beginning of the siege, and conditions rapidly became worse. A January 3 inventory showed that there was only a thirty-day supply of unbalanced field rations for 100,000 men on hand, and on January 5 MacArthur approved the recommendation of his quartermaster and ordered all troops and civilians on Bataan and Corregidor placed on half rations. The new ration totaled 2,000 calories per day for Americans, far too little for combat soldiers to function at the required efficiency. Historians have concluded that the worst error made by MacArthur and the USAFFE staff during the Philippine campaign, far worse than losing half of the Far East Air Force on the first day of the war, was their failure to make the withdrawal of food stocks to Bataan their highest priority after the reversion to WPO-3 was ordered on December 23. Food that had been stored on Bataan before the war as called for in WPO-3 had been dispersed throughout Luzon as part of MacArthur's "defend the beaches" strategy. Bataan was only thirty miles from Manila across Manila Bay, and most of the Manila warehouses were emptied successfully, but much of their food was shipped to Corregidor rather than Bataan, on orders from USAFFE. A shortage of vehicles and drivers, premature panic, and what can only be described as sloth by USAFFE staff officers slowed the return of supplies from central Luzon to Bataan. Supplies at the two major inland bases, Clark Field and Fort Stotsenburg, were destroyed to prevent capture, much sooner than necessary.

Two especially egregious examples of the prewar mindset still prevailing in the Philippines are frequently quoted: 10 million pounds of rice in the Government Rice Central warehouses at Cabanatuan were lost because of a law prohibiting the transfer of rice from one province to another, and at Tarlac the seizure of 2,000 cases of canned food belonging to Japanese nationals was forbidden. The movement of other supplies such as ammunition was more successful, and the PTG was extremely fortunate that six carloads of tank replacement parts were released from the ordnance depot in Manila in time to reach Bataan. The gasoline inventory proved adequate once strict rationing was imposed; little vehicular movement was necessary while besieged. Other standard items of issue such as clothing, mosquito nets, and especially medicine were always in short supply. But it was the shortage of food and the resulting enervation and disease that brought the men of Bataan down.

The Bataan defense force underwent a major reorganization on January 7. General Wainwright took command of the West Sector, which became I Philippine Corps. General Parker relinquished command of the entire Bataan defense force to MacArthur on Corregidor and assumed command of the East Sector, now II Philippine Corps. The boundary between the two corps ran down the middle of the peninsula from Mount Natib in the north to the Mariveles Mountains in the south. The southern tip became the Service Command Area under B/Gen. Allen C. McBride. The main line of resistance (MLR) ran from Mabatang north of Abucay on the east coast to Mauban on the west coast, but the central portion over Mount Natib was unmanned; USAFFE believed the thick, mountainous jungle was totally impassible to any military force, and there was no contact between I Corps in the west and II Corps in the east, even by patrols.

Before General Homma's 14th Army reached Bataan, he reported to Tokyo that the campaign was winding down. The Imperial General

Headquarters took away his best division, the 48th, and ordered it to the Netherlands East Indies along with the 4th Tank Regiment and the 5th Air Group. Homma was left with the 16th Division (which he never liked), the 7th Tank Regiment, fewer than seventy aircraft, and the newly arriving 65th Brigade. This 6,500-man unit was originally meant for garrison duties, and its own commander considered it "absolutely unfit" for combat, but when it got to the Bataan area in good order after a forced march from Lingayen Gulf, Homma assigned the brigade the task of seizing Bataan. One column was to proceed down the west coast, while another, larger force under the brigade commander, L/Gen. Akira Nara, was to make the main effort south down the East Road from Hermosa.

After entering Bataan, Lieutenant Colonel Miller's 194th Tank Battalion stopped behind the Culo River, while Lieutenant Colonel Wickord's 192nd Tank Battalion continued down Route 110 to the MLR. The 194th was now on the Culis-Hermosa line, but was never given orders or a specific role. This line was drawn up in WPO-3 and was intended to delay any attackers from the north for several days to allow the defenses in the rear to be strengthened. Command was given on January 3 to B/Gen. Clyde Selleck, who had his own 71st Division (PA), the 31st Infantry Regiment (US), and the 26th Cavalry Regiment (PS). Selleck apparently did not request the support of either the II Corps heavy artillery (which would have been provided) or the tanks (which would probably have been withheld).

The Japanese attacked on January 7, and the line collapsed in less than a day. The tired and dispirited Filipino infantry, who made up most of the defenders, had done little to improve their positions in the few days they had; the 31st Infantry Regiment, the only all-American infantry unit in the Philippines, fled ignominiously in this action, the first they had seen since the war began; and the cavalry, on the far western end of the line, had to pull out early or be trapped. Miller also pulled his tanks out early, on his own authority, but suffered no repercussions from Weaver, his superior officer. Weaver never favored tying down his tanks in fixed positions, and considered line defense a "gratuitous mission," in his own stilted language.

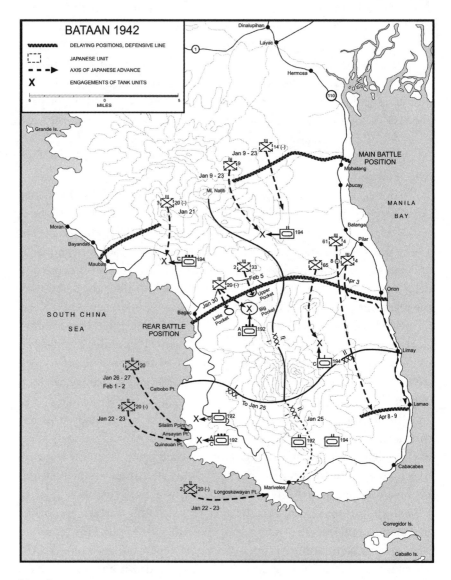

Map 8

Miller's men joined Wickord's in several days of relaxation behind the MLR. The free time was welcome, and the men liked being fed from their own kitchen trucks, but the meals themselves were appalling. Two meals a day were served, at 8 a.m. and 4 to 5 p.m. The 194th was in better shape for food than the 192nd. The former unit had spent some time on their own, especially in the Manila area, and the men appropriated food that Miller sent back to the rear echelon, which was used to supplement the official ration. Wickord's battalion had not been so lucky. Their early dispatch to the field, lack of civilian vehicles, and detachment by companies to infantry divisions that were indifferent to their needs prevented them from saving up any food for future use. The new 2,000-calorie-per-day rice-based half-ration was inadequate to keep active men, especially young ones, at full strength, and deficiency diseases, especially those of the eyes, began to appear quickly.

The PTG tanks were sent south to the 17th Ordnance Company in the Service Command Area for long-overdue heavy maintenance. Tracks were worn down to bare metal. Engines were well past the 400-hour run time specified for a full rebuild—most had been idling or running constantly for the previous month. The company was well equipped for this kind of work, with 10-ton wreckers, shop trucks, welding and machine shops, and a good supply of spare parts, up to and including complete engines, and in a few days could have a filthy piece of wreckage running as good as new. The PTG's losses of armored vehicles—primarily from abandonment—forced Weaver to reallocate them during this period. The 194th Battalion tank companies were reduced from seventeen tanks to ten, and platoons from five tanks to three; the 192nd Battalion units were similarly reduced in size, although it had lost only ten tanks to date in contrast to the 194th's twenty-six.

Early in the siege MacArthur ordered Maj. Claude A. Thorpe to pass through the lines and form a guerilla force on Mount Pinatubo near Fort Stotsenburg. The initial force included Pvt. George M. McCarthy, who had come to the Philippines with the Janesville Company but had been a military policeman since before the war. McCarthy was the only former PTG member in the twenty-four-man unit and was one of three to survive until repatriated in January 1945.

THE ABUCAY LINE

General Nara wasted no time attacking Bataan with his 65th Brigade and its three small regimental combat teams (RCTs). One RCT under Col. Yunosuke Watanabe traveled west across the peninsula on Route 7. It was to seize the small U.S. naval base at Olangapo on the west coast, turn south, and capture Moron and then Bagac; little or no resistance was expected. The 65th Brigade headquarters and two of its RCTs were to attack the Abucay Line of General Parker's II Corps on the east coast. Nara began his attack at 3 p.m. on January 9 with a massive artillery barrage, and was surprised when it was answered in kind by the Filipino artillery. The Philippine Army infantry divisions had gained enough experience to hold prepared positions, and fighting seesawed back and forth along the line for two weeks. Weaver refused to allow his tanks to be used on the line itself— "it would be using an elephant to kill flies"— but the tanks and their crews were used to assist the Philippine Scouts' very effective 155mm cannons. There were only six of these heavyweights, which were difficult to emplace and camouflage, but the Japanese reconnaissance planes were unable to find them. They proved to be better than the artillery of the Japanese, and during the Death March following the campaign, Japanese infantrymen pointed out their shrapnel scars to the American prisoners, attributing them to the "ichi go go" (one-five-five).

Possibly coincidentally, General MacArthur visited Bataan from Corregidor for the only time on January 10, the day after the Japanese attack began. The general and his chief of staff, General Sutherland, stopped by I Corps and II Corps headquarters, spoke to Wainwright and Parker, and sought out a few subordinate commanders whom MacArthur knew, including B/Gen. Weaver. He saw Dr. Poweleit, whom he remembered from their meeting in November, and expressed sympathy for the condition of the men. Sutherland, for his part, complained to both Wainwright and Parker about the discontinuous defensive line—Mount Natib was not even patrolled—but did not receive a favorable response. The commanding general and his coterie left Bataan that evening; MacArthur did not set foot on the Luzon mainland again until late 1944. Sutherland returned in two weeks to order a full-scale retreat to the Rear Defensive Position.

MacArthur decided that his bedraggled, underfed men on Bataan needed bucking up, and on January 15 USAFFE issued the following mimeographed communiqué:

HQ USAFFE, Fort Mills, P.I.
January 15, 1942
Subject: Message From General MacArthur
To: All Unit Commanders

The following message from General MacArthur will be read and explained to all troops. Every Company Commander is charged with the personal responsibility for the delivery of this message. Each head-quarters will follow up to insure reception by every company or similar unit:

"Help is on the way from the United States. Thousands of troops and hundreds of planes are being dispatched. The exact date of arrival of reinforcements is unknown as they will have to fight their way through Japanese attempts against them. It is imperative that our troops hold until these reinforcements arrive.

"Our supplies are ample; a determined defense will defeat the enemy's attack."

(signed) MacArthur

Carl H. Seals, Col. A.G.D.
Adjutant General

This message, dripping with MacArthurian hyperbole, was egregiously false. MacArthur in his *Reminiscences* blamed its errors on "poor reception" of a Roosevelt broadcast. But although Roosevelt promised that reinforcements were being dispatched to the Pacific as rapidly as possible, he was careful not to name their destination. MacArthur twisted the president's words for his own purposes. It is impossible to tell from his records, but his near-pathological optimism may have led him to believe for the next full month that the navy would be coming to his relief. Then one of Roosevelt's fireside chats let everyone in the Philippines know that no help was coming.

Colonel Watanabe's RCT on the west coast kept to its ambitious schedule. Without opposition it captured the Olangapo naval base and Fort Wint, which guarded the entrance to Subic Bay, and captured a quantity of American naval stores and cannon—the amount is disputed in the American records. Watanabe met his first opposition on January 15 at Moron, where he defeated the last American cavalry charge (by the 26th Cavalry Regiment [PS]), and on the 18th came up against the prepared Mauban Line. Homma was pleased at the progress being made in the west and decided to reinforce it. A regiment-size battle group was established from elements of the 16th Division in Manila and dispatched to Moron as the Kimura Detachment under M/Gen. Naoki Kimura, who took command of all forces in the west, about 5,000 men, and reported directly to Homma.

On January 21 one of Kimura's battalions found a weak point on the eastern flank of the Mauban Line, infiltrated the line, and established a strong roadblock on the only major road suitable for transporting supplies and heavy equipment. The I Corps infantry were trapped in their defensive positions. Their efforts to destroy the roadblock were unsuccessful, and Wainwright requested USAFFE to send tanks. Captain Moffitt's C/194TB was chosen. On January 22 one of his platoons was ordered to break through the block from the south and establish contact with the Filipino infantry on the line. The single-file tank attack was given no infantry close support or advanced reconnaissance and was doomed to failure. An infantry skirmish line did precede the tanks, but the Japanese closed in behind them and laid pie plate mines on the trail. The first two tanks struck mines, badly damaging their idlers and tracks. The tankers evacuated without casualties, and everyone pulled back. The disabled tanks were towed out the next day and used for spare parts. The PTG executive officer, Major Smyth, wrote a blistering report to USAFFE condemning Wainwright's "gross mishandling" of tanks as "mobile pillboxes." This could not have helped the frosty relationship between Weaver and Wainwright, especially when Wainwright took command of all Fil-American forces in the Philippines after MacArthur's departure for Australia. Further attacks by dismounted cavalry and infantry could not break the roadblock, and on January 25 Wainwright's infantry had to exfiltrate from the Mauban Line on foot along the beach, leaving behind their artillery (including an entire battery of SPMs), transport, and all heavy equipment.

RETREAT TO THE ORION-BAGAC FINAL LINE

II Corps in the east did a creditable job of holding the Abucay Line, but Japanese patrols soon found that the Fil-American defenses played out at Mount Natib, and General Nara began sending troops to the forbidding mountain. Less than a battalion of enemy troops in their rear encouraged the Filipino infantry to begin leaving their positions. On the 22nd General Sutherland returned to Bataan and ordered I Corps and II Corps to retreat to the Pilar-Bagac Line on January 23–25. This line would guard the only road across the peninsula, which ran in a valley between the Mount Natib and Mount Bataan ranges, but its defenses had not yet been prepared. The I Corps retreat was anticipated and went smoothly, albeit with the loss of most of its equipment. The situation in II Corps was much less sanguine—it was described as utter chaos, made worse by the USAFFE decision to withdraw the Philippine Division from II Corps at this time and place it in army reserve. The PTG resumed its practiced role in stabilizing the retreat. B/Gen. Weaver's orders read:

> *Tanks will execute maximum delay, staying in position and firing at visible enemy until further delay will jeopardize withdrawal. If a tank is immobilized, it will be fought until the close approach of the enemy, then destroyed; the crew previously taking positions outside and continuing to fight with the salvaged and personal weapons. Considerations of personal safety or expediency will not interfere with accomplishing the greatest possible delay.*

The 192nd Tank Battalion backed up the eastern portion of the II Corps line, centered on the East Road, which was still holding. The 194th Tank Battalion supported the western portion of the line, which was rapidly collapsing. Lieutenant Colonel Miller was named Clearance Officer, to whom each infantry commander was to report after his unit cleared the line. Miller said that bringing out the Philippine Army units was like herding a flock of sheep. The men pushed and shoved and maintained no semblance of military order, but remained eager to please and good-naturedly obeyed orders that were forcibly expressed. They continued to the rear and eventually took up their positions in the new line. The tanks and supporting SPMs set up ambush positions and were able to cause some damage to the advancing Japanese. On the night of January 25–26, Miller placed some available SPMs on a small knoll on the south side of an east–west road; his tanks and half-tracks lined the road itself. When the Japanese were detected approaching through the cane fields on the north side of the road, the SPMs laid down an indirect barrage with their 75mm cannon. Miller wrote later, "The result was astonishing. The Nips poured out like fleas off a dog. As they appeared, they were picked off by the tankers and half-track gunners." According to Miller, as many as 1,000 Japanese corpses littered the cane field the next morning. The battalion did not lose a single vehicle, and Miller considered this to be the most important and successful operation in which his unit had participated.

That same night, a platoon of three D/192TB tanks was sent forward to locate a missing infantry battalion and direct it to the rear. This mission accomplished, the tiny unit dug in and held off the Japanese for an entire day before returning to Captain Altman's company. PTG headquarters ordered the rest of Miller's battalion to take up positions that turned out to be in front of the new Fil-American outpost line; the unit retreated successfully the following day. One tank missed a turn, ditched, and had to be destroyed. Weaver ordered the PTG's 10-ton wrecker to recover a second, but it did not arrive until Miller had ordered the battalion to take to the road.

The new line was to have run from Pilar clear across the peninsula to Bagac, but Pilar, the eastern terminus of the east–west road, had to be abandoned temporarily. The eastern end of the line was stabilized at Orlon. The 90,000 men of the Fil-American Army were now crowded into 200 square miles of inhospitable terrain. Everyone understood that this was to be the final line of resistance, and it was laid out with great care. Fields of fire were cleared, earthworks were constructed, and home-made mines were strewn with abandon. All the barbed wire that was still available was strung. The new line was pushed forward when the Japanese fell back in mid-February, and then held until the final Japanese push in April.

The PTG was ordered to guard the east coast and gained several weeks for rest and maintenance. The broad eastern beaches were obvious landing sites and were defended by the armored group's tanks and half-tracks and the Philippine Army's SPMs and part of its field artillery. Japanese air supremacy did not allow the erection of permanent fortifications on the beaches. The mobile armor patrolled at night and pulled back into bamboo groves before daybreak. This was light duty, broken by one bizarre and heartbreaking incident. Japanese reconnaissance planes—all were "Photo Joe" to the Americans—flew the beaches daily, trying to locate the well-camouflaged Americans. One plane was especially persistent on February 3, circling the B/192TB hiding place and interrupting the men's sleep. Sgt. Wally Cigoi, a tank commander, finally lost control, drove Sgt. Frank Goldstein's half-track onto the beach, and opened fire with Goldstein's twin .50s, which he and Bud Bardowski had installed after the Clark Field air raid. Cigoi missed and Joe flew off, returning twenty minutes later with four dive-bombers that approached out of the sun and plastered the area. At the end of the attack three men were dead, and six more lay injured. Goldstein cut off one man's leg with a pocketknife but could not save him. I do not know if Cigoi was forced to pay any price for his rash, stupid act, although his tank was taken away from him shortly thereafter. Goldstein relived the attack in his nightmares for the rest of his life.

THE BATTLES OF THE POINTS AND POCKETS
General Homma was indeed interested in amphibious landings behind the Fil-American lines, a tactic being used with great success by General Yamashita in Malaya, but preferred Bataan's wild western coast rather than the defended eastern beaches. As early as January 15 he had suggested landings to M/Gen. Naoki Kimura, his western commander. By January 21 Kimura felt the time was right; he believed Bagac would be captured shortly, and from there he could take the east–west road into the rear of II Corps. A landing south of Bagac would protect the southern flank of his main force as it turned east. The job was assigned to the 2nd Battalion of the 20th Infantry Regiment, but its commander was given

only a day to prepare for the mission, and it was totally botched. The battalion left Moron in barges the night of January 22 for Caibobo Point, guided through the blackness by a single small-scale map. It encountered Lieutenant John Bulkeley's PT boat on a routine patrol; Bulkeley sank one barge and scattered the rest into two groups.

One group of 300 men landed at Longosawayan Point, the southernmost tip of the peninsula and adjacent to Mariveles harbor and town, causing somewhat of a panic in the Service Command Area. This finger of land is heavily forested, its tall hardwood trees tied together with thick vines and undergrowth. The local defenders were a mixed force of sailors, marines, airmen, and Constabulary troops (ex-policemen) under the command of Brigadier General Selleck. Only the marines had any infantry training, and Selleck's congeries of troops could make no headway against the Japanese, who dug in quickly, even though thoroughly lost. Selleck asked for reinforcements, including tanks, but these were fully occupied with the retreat from the Abucay Line. He did receive a battalion of Philippine Scouts and their artillery, and this force, aided by a bombardment by Corregidor's eight 12-inch mortars, wiped out the Japanese to the last man. It was not in time to save Selleck's career. He was demoted to colonel and relieved by Col. Clinton Pierce, the commander of the 26th Cavalry (PS) and a Wainwright favorite. Brigadier General McBride's Service Command Area was abolished at this time, and the line dividing the I Corps and II Corps areas of responsibility was extended to the southern coast.

The rest of the Japanese landing force, comprising some 600 men, came ashore at Quinauan Point, about halfway between Mariveles and Bagac. Its geography is just as forbidding as Longosawayan Point, but it contained a track that ended at West Road, so was perfectly suited for cutting off the retreat or reinforcement of I Corps, although the men who landed had no idea where they were. The newly promoted Brigadier General Pierce obtained a battalion of Philippine Scouts to supplement his airmen, sailors, and marines, but Pierce made little progress until much of the 192nd Tank Battalion was transferred to I Corps with twenty-three tanks after the Abucay campaign was complete. Weaver and MacArthur planned a combined armor-infantry operation over the telephone, and

Weaver sent Pierce a platoon of three C/192TB tanks, which made five unsuccessful attacks on February 2. Weaver took part in these attacks, for which he was awarded the Distinguished Service Cross, and observed that the Scouts trailed too far behind the tanks. The next day ended with a fifty-yard advance; half of the Scouts were casualties. A new local commander enlisted the aid of two more tanks and a radio control car commanded by A/192TB's Capt. Kenneth Bloomfield to coordinate their movements, and the combined attack on the 4th began forcing the Japanese back to the coast. Bloomfield was written up for a Silver Star for his skill in controlling the attack.

The underbrush had by now been shot away, clearing fields of fire. Lt. John Hay of C/192TB was credited with devising the most successful tactic. Six airmen with musette bags full of hand grenades rode the tanks of his platoon. The tanks forced the Japanese into their foxholes, and the airmen dropped grenades in after them. An infantryman with a walkie-talkie accompanied each tank to direct it. Hay led up to five attacks per day until this and the later Pockets campaign ended, and was awarded two Silver Stars. The Japanese perimeter continued to shrink, and the last Japanese were killed on the 8th. In the words of General Homma, the entire 2nd Battalion of the 20th Infantry Regiment had been "lost without a trace."

Homma still felt that the west coast promised a quicker end to the campaign than attacks against the fixed defenses in the east. On January 25 he sent L/Gen. Susuma Morioka to Mauban with the rest of his 16th Division and ordered him to take command of all Japanese forces in the area. Morioka immediately ordered one company from the 20th Infantry Regiment's 1st Battalion to reinforce the battalion fighting at Quinauan Point—the Japanese knew nothing of the landing at Longosawayan Point. The company left Olangapo at midnight on January 27 on several landing barges. But like their predecessors, they could not identify their landing site in the dark against the solid mass of woods, and they landed between Anyasan and Silaiim Points, 2,000 yards short of their objective. Wainwright did not know the Japanese strength but did know that they could access the West Road and became quite concerned, sending the usual mixture of airmen, Constabulary troops, and Scouts to the area.

The dozen M3 light tanks of C/192TB were assigned to this particular incursion after their arrival in I Corps, but their single-file attacks were not decisive at this time.

The Japanese company survived long enough for General Homma to order the rest of the hapless battalion to reinforce it, this time under its commander, Major Kimura. Kimura received his orders on January 31 and sailed the next evening. In one of the biggest intelligence coups of the campaign, a copy of Kimura's orders was captured in an officer's dispatch case on the east coast in time for it to be translated and a combined air-land-sea mission mounted to destroy Kimura's small convoy coming down the west coast. P-40s and PT boats killed at least half of the 500-man battalion. The rest ran into a thoroughly prepared Fil-American infantry force as they stumbled ashore in the Anyasan-Silaiim area. The Japanese formed a defensive perimeter and fought back ferociously, but the evolving tank-infantry attacks pushed in the Japanese lines, and on February 9 Kimura's superior authorized him to break out, either reaching the sea to be rescued by small boats or slipping through the I Corps lines to the north. The message was air-dropped in sealed bamboo tubes that also contained emergency drugs and rations. Delighted Filipinos captured many of these tubes. Most of the Japanese were slaughtered, either at the coast or attempting to pass through the lines, and by February 14 the battle was over. A promising concept had been marred by terrible execution. The net accomplishment after three weeks of heavy fighting was the total destruction of the 1st and 2nd Battalions of the 12th Infantry—of the 900 men dispatched, 34 survived. The threat to I Corps from the sea had been eliminated.

The 14th Army mounted conventional attacks against the Pilar-Bagac Line during the three weeks of the points battles. The 65th Brigade's attack on the western end of the II Corps line met with some success but eventually stalled, and on February 8 General Nara was ordered to withdraw to his original positions. In the west, Wainwright's I Corps MLR passed through such heavy jungle that it could scarcely be called a line. Adjacent units were not in contact, lines of fire had not been cut, and General Morioka's 16th Division located an undefended stretch and sent a battalion-size force under Col. Yorimasa Yoshioka through it.

The Japanese could move freely behind the Fil-American lines, but were soon hopelessly lost in the bewildering jungle, which was crossed by deep ravines dug by swift-moving streams. Yoshioka's force split in two and on January 28–29 formed defensive perimeters that the Americans called the "Little Pocket" and the "Big Pocket." The Big Pocket was a mile behind the MLR, near the intersection of two major trails that the Fil-Americans needed for communications and supply. It was also called the Tuol Pocket for the area's major ravine, which was two miles long by three-quarters of a mile wide and some 200 feet deep. The Japanese quickly dug fox-holes and tunnels, placed their machine guns behind fallen trees, and destroyed several patrols that tried to cross the area. When Wainwright formed an estimate of the size of the Japanese force, he asked for help from USAFFE. Artillery and mortars proved to be of little use; the heavy foliage hid the Japanese from both indirect and direct fire, and tree bursts and duds caused friendly casualties. This became an infantry battle, with crucial help from the 192nd Battalion's tanks, all of which had recently been assigned to I Corps.

The battles on the points farther south had prior call on most of the battalion's tanks, and the attack on the Big Pocket was made from the south by single platoons along the one trail into the area. The first platoon to arrive was Lt. Arthur Holland's from A/192TB. The infantry commander first asked the tanks to charge off the trail alone, but common sense prevailed. When buttoned up for combat, the tank crews were virtually blind; their M3s had no periscopes, and they had to look through tiny armored glass slits. When combat got underway on February 2, Philippine Army infantry accompanied the tanks, but far behind them. The tanks could only rush a few yards into the undergrowth, and if they did not crash into a tree, bottom out on a log, or lose a tread to an anti-tank mine, return to the starting line, their crews totally unaware of the details of what they had just experienced. The next day the Philippine Scouts unit that was now assigned to the tanks stayed closer, but these men were vulnerable to fire from both the Japanese and the tanks' own machine guns. Sgt. Leroy Anderson's tank was taken under heavy fire from a machine gun dug into the roots of a huge banyan tree. Anderson ordered his driver to ram his tank as far up the tangled mass of roots as he could, but the roots kept the defenders from being crushed by the tank, and none of his guns could depress enough to reach the enemy. Lt. Willibald C. Bianchi, a Scouts battalion staff officer who had come along with the infantry platoon, was hit twice in the hand while firing his M1 rifle from behind the tank. Clutching his pistol, he climbed onto the tank and managed to unlatch its antiaircraft machine gun and lay it onto the target. He continued firing after being hit in the chest by machine gun fire. A Japanese antitank gun found the range and hit the tank, blowing Bianchi off. Anderson and his crew exited the now-blazing tank with their personal weapons and destroyed the machine gun nest. Lieutenant Bianchi was carried off on a stretcher but returned to duty in six weeks; he was killed in 1945 on a Japanese prison ship. He was recommended for the Distinguished Service Cross (DSC), which was upgraded to a Medal of Honor, one of only five awarded in the 1941–42 Philippines campaign; these went to three members of the Philippine Scouts, General MacArthur, and General Wainwright. Sergeant Anderson received a DSC, the first draftee in the war to be granted this high award. Anderson was a Wisconsin native who had been assigned to A/192TB, the Janesville Company, after basic training. He too did not survive to return home; he died in the sinking of a prison ship in October 1944.

Sgt. William McAuliffe's tank was the next to be lost. A mine blew in its floor and badly injured McAuliffe. Lieutenant Holland's platoon was now out of serviceable tanks, and B/192TB's Lt. Edward Winger and his four tanks replaced it. Winger led the first attack the following morning. His tank was hit by a flamethrower, the first time the Japanese had used this weapon in the Philippines. The tank did not catch fire, but the crew were temporarily blinded and bailed out. The Filipinos identified Winger as German for his shock of blond hair and shot him. His driver, Cpl. John Massimino, tended to Winger, while Sgt. Bud Bardowski in the following tank exploded the flamethrower's fuel tank and attempted to salvage Winger's tank, whose flames had gone out. Bardowski dragged the towing cable from the front of his own tank to the rear of Winger's, but found that the cable had been shot apart, leaving only the hook, and had to carry Winger's tank's cable back to his own tank and attach it. After pulling Winger's tank to safety, Bardowski continued the day's attack, destroying an antitank gun and running over a machine gun nest; its crew's entrails stank up the tank's treads for days.

Bardowski's exploits on February 6 brought him a Bronze Star. It took three days for Corporal Massimino to get his commander to a hospital, which could not save him; gas gangrene had already infected his abdominal wounds. Both Massimino and Winger were awarded Silver Stars. General Weaver wrote up Ted Wickord for a Silver Star for a similar tank-towing incident on the same date.

Meanwhile the Japanese had attacked the MLR from the north in an attempt to reach their encircled comrades; they broke through the line but could not reach the Big Pocket. Although the Fil-Americans could not re-form their line behind the Japanese, the Americans called this new penetration the Upper Pocket, although it was only a salient. The battle to eliminate the Big Pocket was now going well, but on the 7th a new American infantry commander decided to eliminate the three pockets one at a time, beginning with the Little Pocket. This took only a few days with the help of a few tanks. The surviving Japanese slipped out of encirclement on the night of the 8th–9th, but stumbled into a Philippine Army unit and were destroyed to the last man. The Filipinos then took on the Upper Pocket and reduced its size by three-quarters.

On February 15 attention returned to the Big Pocket. Armor was still represented by the B/192TB platoon, but Philippine Army units had replaced the Scouts. One company in particular distinguished itself today. It comprised Igorot tribesmen from northern Luzon. Many companies were segregated by tribe, primarily to ease language and discipline problems. According to Bill Gentry the Igorots were still headhunters at heart, collecting jawbones from the "dom Jops" and scoring their prowess by the size of their collections. That morning four M3 light tanks inched their way forward through the trackless jungle, impeded as before by fallen trees, bamboo thickets, creepers, vines, and a tangled mass of aboveground banyan roots. Their mission was to wipe out the surrounded Japanese detachment, which was entrenched in the dense undergrowth. The tanks were ill-suited for this role, and several had been lost after throwing their tracks or bottoming out on invisible tree stumps. The buttoned-up tankers could see very little through their vision slits and were totally dependent on the infantry to help blaze a trail and find the enemy. The Philippine Army and Philippine Scouts infantry originally given this task had failed. Today it was the turn of an Igorot company from the Philippine Army. Their officer asked and got permission for the tribesmen to climb aboard the tanks, which they did with enthusiasm even though this would expose them to enemy fire. Today's advance came with war whoops and waving bolos. The infantrymen directed their tanks by beating on the turrets with sticks. They helped cut the trail with their bolos, and when they spotted Japanese in their holes among the banyan roots, dispatched them with pistol fire from the tanks or by dismounting and attacking with their knives. Bud Bardowski was highly impressed by the Igorots' indifference to incoming fire. Bardowski had always placed a high value on audacity; he had joined the National Guard under the assumed middle name Roland, to honor the medieval French knight. By nightfall the pocket's size had been reduced by half. The next morning's attack met no resistance; the surviving Japanese had slipped back to their own lines during the night, leaving behind several hundred rotting corpses.

Japanese Withdrawal

More Japanese made it back to their lines than the Americans estimated, some 377 of the 1,000 who had originally broken through the MLR. The 20th Japanese Infantry Regiment had entered the Bataan campaign with 2,690 men; 650 survived, most of them sick or injured. Homma's 14th Army had suffered 7,000 casualties since the Bataan campaign began on January 7. The survivors were wracked with malaria and dysentery, the army was short of medicine, and rations were cut in mid-February from sixty-two to twenty-three ounces per day. Homma decided to withdraw, capture the rest of the Philippines, tighten the blockade, swallow his pride, and request reinforcements to take Bataan. On February 15 the Japanese withdrew to higher and more defensible ground. This was a great boost to Fil-American morale; theirs was the first offensive victory over the Japanese Army on any front since the war had begun. As Homma suspected, his career was essentially over; he was allowed to complete the conquest of the Philippines but was recalled to Japan in August 1942 and never received another command.

USAFFE used the lull in the fighting to improve its positions and introduce formal training, especially in tank-infantry tactics. The men were growing noticeably weaker and prone to diseases, especially those resulting from vitamin deficiencies. Slight injuries such as skin scratches became infected and refused to heal. Dr. Poweleit observed that the younger men had more health problems than did the older veterans and attributed this to the lack of protein. Their morale was still good, however, until President Roosevelt's fireside chat of February 23 (the 24th in the Philippines), in which he said:

> *Immediately after this war started, the Japanese forces moved down on either side of the Philippines to numerous points south of them—thereby completely encircling the Philippines from north, and south, and east and west. It is that complete encirclement, with control of the air by Japanese land-based aircraft, which has prevented us from sending substantial reinforcements of men and material to the gallant defenders of the Philippines. For forty years it has always been our strategy—a strategy born of necessity—that in the event of a full-scale attack on the Islands by Japan, we should fight a delaying action, attempting to retire slowly into Bataan Peninsula and Corregidor. We knew that the war as a whole would have to be fought and won by a process of attrition against Japan itself. We knew all along that, with our greater resources, we could ultimately out-build Japan and ultimately overwhelm her on sea, and on land and in the air. We knew that, to obtain our objective, many varieties of operations would be necessary in areas other than the Philippines.*
>
> *Now nothing that has occurred in the past two months has caused us to revise this basic strategy of necessity—except that the defense put up by General MacArthur has magnificently exceeded the previous estimates of endurance, and he and his men are gaining eternal glory therefrom.*

Even the youngest and most naïve soldier on Bataan could understand what the president meant by "gaining eternal glory." General MacArthur's promises of convoys with "thousands of men and hundreds of planes" were lies. The convoys were going elsewhere. The men in the Philippines were going to be sacrificed for the greater good of the war effort.

On the same day that Roosevelt's address cost MacArthur all credibility with his men, the president ordered MacArthur to leave Corregidor for Mindanao, and then Australia, to take command of a new "Far East" region. Singapore had fallen; ABDACOM, the old American-British-Dutch-Australian joint command, was doomed; and the area was in chaos. According to MacArthur, he first drafted a rejection (of a presidential order!) but then accepted it on the conditions that he could take his staff with him and could delay his departure until "the time is right." The time came on March 12, and his departure was filled with MacArthurian touches that have been reported elsewhere in great detail. Roosevelt and Marshall had good reasons for wanting MacArthur out of the Philippines: Capturing a newly minted four-star general would be an unimaginable propaganda coup for the Japanese, and MacArthur's reputation and seniority suited him for joint theater command, although the latter was a concept just being worked out. Neither man wanted MacArthur back in the United States (each had his own reasons), and Australia was the perfect place to park him.

Rumors of his departure from the Philippines spread quickly on Bataan. Some of the men were bitter that he hadn't visited Bataan since January 10 and attributed this to physical cowardice. This may not have been true—he had demonstrated his personal bravery often during World War I—and it has been speculated that he was in fact exhibiting moral cowardice: that he did not want to face the men he had let down, and whom he was letting starve. Sgt. Bernard FitzPatrick and another radioman in the 194th Battalion communications shack expressed their feelings in a poem to be sung to the "Battle Hymn of the Republic." It spread across the peninsula in a single day and was traced back to the battalion headquarters area. Lieutenant Colonel Miller apparently suspected FitzPatrick, a musician and something of a nonconformist, and sent a runner to the shack to make inquiries. FitzPatrick told the man that the verses had been brought to him by a Greek soldier, Anonymous, and sent him on his way; the question of authorship never came up again. The song grew longer after it was learned that MacArthur and his large staff were leaving by PT boats. It is much less well known than "The Battling Bastards of Bataan," which is just as bitter but does not mention MacArthur and is thus "safe." The poem by Bernard FitzPatrick, a tanker, is worth repeating here. It is titled "USAFFE Cry of Freedom," and, ironically, Ernie Miller quoted it in full in his memoir:

> *Dugout Doug MacArthur lies ashaking on the Rock,*
> *Safe from all the bombers and from any sudden shock.*
> *Dugout Doug is eating of the best food on Bataan,*
> *And his troops go starving on.*

Chorus:
> *Dugout Doug, come out from hiding,*
> *Dugout Doug, come out from hiding,*
> *Send to Franklin the glad tidings*
> *That his troops go starving on!*

> *Dugout Doug's not timid, he's just cautious, not afraid.*
> *He's protecting carefully the stars that Franklin made.*
> *Four-star generals are rare as good food on Bataan,*
> *And his troops go starving on.*

> *Dugout Doug is ready in his Chris-Craft for to flee,*
> *O'er the bounding billows and the wildly raging sea,*
> *For the Japs are pounding on the gates of old Bataan,*
> *And his troops go starving on.*

> *We've fought the war the hard way since they said the fight was on,*
> *All the way from Lingayen to the hills of old Bataan,*
> *And we'll continue fighting after Dugout Doug is gone,*
> *And still go starving on.*

MacArthur reached Australia on March 17. Before leaving he split the Philippine theater into four commands, all to report to him in Australia via Col. Lewis Beebe, a new deputy chief of staff who was left on Corregidor. General Marshall in Washington was not informed of this setup. He assumed that command would pass to the next most senior general, Wainwright, and began addressing all Philippine communications to him. When Marshall learned of MacArthur's arrangement, he thought it was unworkable nonsense, and in a few days Wainwright was promoted to lieutenant general and given a new command, U.S. Forces in the Philippines (USFIP), with four subordinates reporting to him. There was now an overall commander on Bataan, General King, with General Jones commanding I Corps (replacing Wainwright), and General Parker retaining II Corps. Although Wainwright could communicate with Washington directly, he would report formally to MacArthur, who remained commander of USAFFE.

MacArthur did not object publicly to the command setup Marshall imposed on him. On March 23 MacArthur issued his famous "I shall return" communiqué, with its typical emphasis on the vertical personal pronoun. Japanese radio branded MacArthur a deserter and a coward; Marshall responded by convincing Roosevelt to award MacArthur a Medal of Honor, which might have been one of the things for which MacArthur had negotiated before he accepted his departure orders.

Wainwright moved into MacArthur's old office in a Corregidor tunnel, but had nothing in common with him. MacArthur had spent his days in his office writing self-serving communiqués and left the conduct of the battle to his chief of staff. Wainwright visited the front lines almost daily, checking positions and making small talk with all ranks. When asked why he constantly put himself in danger, Wainwright replied that he had nothing to offer his men but his presence. The surviving tankers remembered him fondly, despite General Weaver's low opinion of his tactical competence.

Most men on Bataan eventually came to believe that MacArthur could do more for them in Australia than from Corregidor and was needed for bigger things. Washington did not forget them completely, as MacArthur intimated in his communiqués once he reached Australia, but Japan closed the ring around the Philippines so quickly that efforts to send aid were almost entirely unavailing. The last civilian cargo ship reached Corregidor on February 27. The navy refused to send warships other than submarines, which did bring seven small loads of critical items such as food, antiaircraft fuses and shells, and ammunition. These mercy missions soon ended; the navy argued that their combat ships were needed for combat. Ten aircraft reached Mindanao with minuscule cargoes that included quinine and morphine. In February Roosevelt sent a personal friend to Australia with unlimited funds to hire blockade runners. These became impossible to find after the Japanese took the Indies, and only six ships eventually set out. Three of these got through, but only to Mindanao or Cebu. Ten thousand tons of cargo were off-loaded, but only 1,000 tons of food reached Corregidor and Bataan; this was enough to feed the 80,000 servicemen and 26,000 civilians for four days.

The food shortage and reduced rations had immediate consequences. The men were fed twice daily. A typical meal was boiled rice and salt with occasional gravy and pieces of meat. There was some canned food, which was doled out sparingly. When canned meat ran out, the next option was carabao, the local water buffalo. Abattoirs were set up to slaughter and butcher them, and eventually 2,800 made their way into the cooking pots. The meat of these animals, which had spent their lives wallowing in slime, did not become tender or palatable even after marinating overnight and much pounding by the cooks. The cavalry's 250 mounts and packhorses and 48 mules came next and were much preferred to carabao. These were followed by the peninsula's pigs and chickens, wild and domesticated; fish; and any wild animal that could be found, including snakes and their eggs, lizards, and monkeys.

Deficiency diseases such as beriberi and scurvy showed up early owing to the lack of vitamins. Wild fruit and any fruit or vegetables growing or stored on the abandoned farms disappeared early. Dr. Poweleit advised the men of the 192nd to forage for certain leaves and grasses that his research found were beneficial, and he and the men who listened to him, primarily the officers, remained disease-free. But in March he reported to Lieutenant Colonel Wickord that the men had lost about thirty to forty pounds. They were listless, and their eyesight was failing. Pvt. Charles

Jensen of the 192nd Battalion medical detachment recalled that the men knew they were doomed when MacArthur left, but kept fighting from the simple desire to live. Their emotions numbed by hunger and permanent stomachaches, the men shuffled around "like zombies."

On March 12 General Parker reported that the combat efficiency of his II Corps was 20 percent and dropping daily, and General Wainwright estimated that 75 percent of I Corps was unfit for action when he turned it over to General Jones that same day. Rations had been cut in February to 1,500 calories per day, and again in March to 1,000 calories per day. Wainwright tried to impress on Marshall the gravity of the situation, and that 90,000 soldiers and 20,000 sailors and civilians faced starvation. Marshall was shocked and failed at first to believe the numbers; MacArthur's florid obfuscations had implied that he had only half that many men. When MacArthur received copies of this correspondence, he tried to blame the food shortage on Wainwright's inability to enforce discipline; things did not seem that bad when he, MacArthur, had left the islands. Marshall's reply to this was probably unprintable and did not leave Washington. Shortly before the final Japanese offensive began, Wainwright told Marshall that the food on Bataan would not last past April 15, and that this was "at one-third ration, poorly balanced, and very deficient in vitamins." If supplies did not reach him by that date, his troops would be starved into submission.

Fighting over food is not mentioned in many contemporary accounts, but it did occur, and as always in the armed forces, rank had its privileges. Sgt. Forrest Knox of A/192TB recalled:

> One day our CO got on the radio and told our tank crews that the mess sergeant had a big pan of baked beans waiting for us when we came back. Everyone on the net heard him and the rear-area officers came flocking like flies on a turd. That talk of hot baked beans must have driven them hogs about half crazy. Our CO, of course, invited the colonel to help himself. Then it was seconds, thirds, and fourths. The tanks came in around 4 p.m. There were a few beans left in the pan where they had burned onto the side so hard the officers couldn't scrape them loose with their spoons. Funny thing, a man's reaction

Hercules towing a 40th Tank Company six-ton M1917 tank—Salinas, 1920s or 1930s. PHOTO COURTESY OF TOM LANG

A 40th Tank Company six-ton M1917 tank on the Camp San Luis Obispo firing range, 1920s or 1930s. PHOTO COURTESY OF TOM LANG

A 40th Tank Company six-ton M1917 tank being loaded on a tank transport at Camp San Luis Obispo, 1933. PHOTO COURTESY OF TOM LANG

A 40th Tank Company six-ton M1917 tank in a ditching exercise at Camp San Luis Obispo, 1920s or 1930s. PHOTO COURTESY OF TOM LANG

Capt. Ernest Miller inspecting a new M2A2 tank in Brainerd in early 1937. His 34th Tank Company received the first two produced. PHOTO COURTESY OF MINNESOTA MILITARY MUSEUM

A new 40th Tank Company M2A2 undergoes field maintenance at Camp San Luis Obispo, 1937. PHOTO COURTESY OF TOM LANG

The hood has been removed on this 40th Tank Company M2A2, showing its 250-horsepower Continental air-cooled radial engine. PHOTO COURTESY OF TOM LANG

M2A2 tanks borrowed by A/194TB at Fort Lewis in 1941. They carry a variety of unit markings. PHOTO COURTESY OF MINNESOTA MILITARY MUSEUM

Pvt. James Bashleben jumping a motorcycle at Fort Knox in 1941. This photograph was featured in a war bond poster. PHOTO COURTESY OF SHARON NAKAMURA

Zenon "Bud" Bardowski of Gary, Indiana. AUTHOR'S COLLECTION

D/192TB M2A2s crossing the Salt River at Fort Knox, 1941. PHOTO COURTESY OF MERCER COUNTY PUBLIC LIBRARY

A 4x6 ten-ton wrecker. These were the pride of the battalion maintenance platoons. This example was from the field artillery and was photographed at Fort Knox in 1941. PHOTO COURTESY OF IDA RUPP PUBLIC LIBRARY

Bud Bardowski in a typical pose with a B/192TB M2A2, probably photographed at Fort Knox in 1941. PHOTO COURTESY OF BATAAN PROJECT

M3 tanks transferred to the 192nd Tank Battalion from the 753rd sit on flatcars at Camp Polk, Louisiana. PHOTO COURTESY OF BATAAN PROJECT

B/Gen. James R. N. Weaver, commander of the Provisional Tank Group. PHOTO COURTESY OF BATAAN PROJECT

Col. Theodore Wickord, commander of the 192nd Tank Battalion. AUTHOR'S COLLECTION

Col. Ernest B. Miller, commander of the 194th Tank Battalion. PHOTO COURTESY OF MINNESOTA MILITARY MUSEUM

Sgt. Albert Allen Jr., C/192TB. PHOTO COURTESY OF IDA RUPP PUBLIC LIBRARY

Sgt. James Bashleben, B/192TB. PHOTO COURTESY OF IDA RUPP PUBLIC LIBRARY

Capt. William H. Gentry, D/192TB and C/192TB. PHOTO COURTESY OF BATAAN PROJECT

Lt. Ben Morin, B/192TB. PHOTO COURTESY OF BATAAN PROJECT

Sgt. John Rowland, HQ/192TB. PHOTO COURTESY OF BATAAN PROJECT

Pvt. Lester Tenney, B/192TB. PHOTO COURTESY OF BATAAN PROJECT

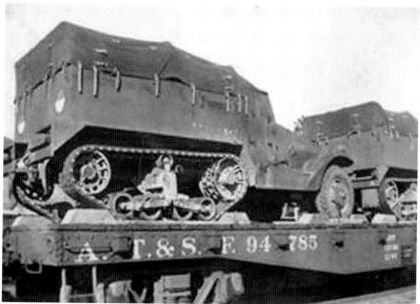

M2 half-tracks transferred to the 192nd Tank Battalion from the 753rd sit on a Santa Fe flatcar at Camp Polk, Louisiana. PHOTO COURTESY OF IDA RUPP PUBLIC LIBRARY

Men of C/194TB leaving Angel Island for the San Francisco docks on September 8, 1941. PHOTO COURTESY OF EDDIE JOHNSON

The SS *President Coolidge*, which carried the 194th Tank Battalion to the Philippines in September 1941. PHOTO COURTESY OF MINNESOTA MILITARY MUSEUM

A barracks at Fort Stotsenburg, where the 194th Tank Battalion was quartered from September to December 1941. PHOTO COURTESY OF STEVEN BULL

Capt. Eddie Johnson and Lt. Ted Spaulding of the 194th Tank Battalion Headquarters on a quick recon trip to Lingayen Gulf, November or December 1941. PHOTO COURTESY OF EDDIE JOHNSON

Capt. Eddie Johnson of the 194th Tank Battalion Headquarters enjoying the poinsettias on Luzon, autumn 1941. PHOTO COURTESY OF EDDIE JOHNSON

A member of the 194th Tank Battalion showing off a python killed near Clark Field in November or December 1941—this would have been a delicacy on Bataan two months later. PHOTO COURTESY OF EDDIE JOHNSON

Capt. Eddie Johnson and some of C/194TB's M3 light tanks at Fort Stotsenburg, November or December 1941. PHOTO COURTESY OF EDDIE JOHNSON

The M3 tank of A/194TB's Sgt. Glen Nelson, parked under a palm tree on Clark Field after the battalion was dispersed in early December. Nelson was selected for officer training and left the Philippines a few days later. PHOTO COURTESY OF MINNESOTA MILITARY MUSEUM

A Philippine Army 75mm self-propelled mount (SPM) on Luzon. These formed an effective partnership with the Provisional Tank Group. PHOTO COURTESY OF IDA RUPP PUBLIC LIBRARY

B/192TB M3 tank commander receiving orders from a motorcycle messenger somewhere near Clark Field. PHOTO COURTESY OF IDA RUPP PUBLIC LIBRARY

M3 tank of the Provisional Tank Group passing through a Filipino village somewhere on the island of Luzon. PHOTO COURTESY OF IDA RUPP PUBLIC LIBRARY

Members of the 192nd Tank Battalion take a break on their half-track somewhere on Bataan. From the left, the five men who are clearly visible are Cpl. Albert DeCurtins, Pvt. Clement "Joe" Martini, Sgt. Howard Hasselkus, S/Sgt. Walter Mahr, unknown, and Pvt. George Hardtke. All of the men identified died while Japanese POWs. PHOTO COURTESY OF IDA RUPP PUBLIC LIBRARY

Truck convoy carrying supplies somewhere on Luzon. PHOTO COURTESY OF IDA RUPP PUBLIC LIBRARY

A Type 95 Ha-Go Japanese light tank being tested in the United States. This is the type of tank Ben Morin's B/192TB platoon fought at Damortis. PHOTO COURTESY OF IDA RUPP PUBLIC LIBRARY

A Japanese propaganda photograph supposedly showing ex–Provisional Tank Group tanks captured on Luzon. Note that only the first three tanks are American M3s; the rest are Japanese. PHOTO COURTESY OF IDA RUPP PUBLIC LIBRARY

Bud Bardowski in his racecar at Indianapolis, 1946. AUTHOR'S COLLECTION

to an outright insult like that. The crews looked at the pan and just walked quietly away. I never heard one of them swear. That was the part that fascinated me. Hunger was a nagging thing that never went away. You could ignore it most of the time; when it hurt was when you realized that some hog had taken advantage of you and eaten your rations. Well, our CO paid as high a price as possible a month later on "The March."

Bataan was a perfect breeding ground for the anopheles mosquito, the host species for the malaria parasite, and malaria was endemic. The small inventory of quinine, used as both a preventative and treatment for malaria, was quickly set aside for treatment only. By late February most of the command had been infected. By early March there were 300 new cases of malaria per day; by the end of the month, 1,000 per day. Attacks brought chills and fever that were totally debilitating. Another medical condition was amoebic dysentery, a nasty disease that is associated with bad sanitary conditions, and so did not become a severe problem until the surrender. The early cases could be treated with sulfadiazine, which was available. This powder was also used to treat skin infections, which were almost impossible to cure; Dr. Poweleit attributed this to the lack of protein in the men's diet.

General Weaver wrote up the lessons learned in the campaign with respect to tactics and equipment and sent them to USFIP, which forwarded them to Washington. The use of light tanks in jungle fighting was a totally novel concept, and Weaver stressed the importance of the tank-infantry team. Communication was important and needed to be improved; the infantry needed to stay close to the tanks; and armor was most effective in limited, slow attacks enabling either tanks or infantry to destroy enemy forces that had been flushed by the other arm. Tanks should never be used as pillboxes or left alone without infantry protection. All of these tenets were used by the armored units that succeeded the PTG in the Pacific war.

For the most part the men liked their M3 light tanks, and their design defects, such as riveted construction and a high profile, were known in Washington and either being addressed on the production line or would have to wait for new designs. Its 37mm main gun was already obsolete against the Afrika Korps in North Africa but was perfectly adequate on Luzon. One unanticipated problem was early failure of the suspension; the 17th Ordnance Company found that the volute springs were freezing up from corrosion due to the saline atmosphere. The chief of the Ordnance Department in Washington was so advised, and the springs, which were used on all American armor models until 1945, were redesigned.

The M2 and M3 half-tracks in the PTG were seeing combat for the first time. Forty-six were assigned, primarily in the headquarters and reconnaissance platoons. The M2 was intended as a prime mover and was slightly shorter than the M3, which was a personnel carrier with easier access than the M2 and bench seating for a squad of ten men. They were typical late 1930s designs with the same reliable vertical volute suspension as the M3 light tank. The M3 half-track eventually furnished transportation for every armored infantry regiment, and M2s and M3s were popular in utility roles for the entire war. It was understood by everyone that they were not designed for the jungle and were as road-bound in the Philippines as the tanks. General Weaver took great pains to evaluate them for the Ordnance Department. Here are the problems Weaver reported to Washington, and their brief response in caps:

1. front leaf springs too fragile—FIXED

2. tendency to throw tracks—IMPROPER TENSIONING, NEED BETTER TRAINING

3. failure of power train—IMPROPER TENSIONING & WHEEL ALIGNMENT

4. thin armor—NEVER ADDRESSED

5. no overhead cover—PROTOTYPE BUILT BUT NOT PURSUED

While the tank crews found themselves with little to do during the lull but hunt for food, the 17th Ordnance Company stayed very busy. The PTG was fortunate in having a good inventory of spare parts, and the company brought the mechanical condition of all vehicles up as close to standard as possible. The company's other major project was the production of high-explosive shells for the tanks' 37mm guns. As mentioned, these did not come to the Philippines with the tanks, and were needed to fight enemy infantry, especially in the jungle. The 37mm high-explosive shells available for the antiaircraft guns would not fit the M3's gun—the size and rifling were incorrect—but the projectiles themselves would work and were fit into the casings of disassembled AP rounds; additional gunpowder was added to these to compensate for the smaller HE projectile. About 1,000 rounds were modified and used with great success in the final week of the campaign, killing many Japanese infantrymen and enraging the rest to the extent that American prisoners were careful not to identify themselves as tankers.

At the end of February, the 14th Army's reinforcements reached the Lingayen Gulf from Shanghai. The major unit was L/Gen. Kenzo Kitano's 4th Division, which was up to strength with 11,000 men. Other components were the Nagano Detachment of the 21st Division and the 22nd Air Brigade. The 65th Brigade and the 16th Division received 7,000 replacements for their dead, missing, and disabled. Homma's chief of staff and most of his staff officers had already been relieved and returned to Japan; his new staff had a month to plan an offensive. They underestimated the number of defenders but overestimated their strength. They failed to identify the Fil-American lines of resistance—Japanese aerial reconnaissance even under conditions of total air supremacy was incredibly poor—but in the end that didn't matter. The 4th Division and the Nagano Detachment would make the main attack against II Corps in the east, while the 65th Brigade and the 16th Division made diversionary attacks in the west to pin I Corps in place. Air and artillery attacks began ramping up in late March, and American intelligence was well aware of Japanese plans. On March 30 Japanese air made an apparently deliberate attack on Bataan's well-marked Hospital 1, killing twenty-three, injuring seventy-eight, and severely damaging the facilities. Wainwright reported the raid to Washington, and the Japanese issued an apology over Manila radio.

THE FINAL OFFENSIVE

April 3 was set as the date of the attack. This was the anniversary of the death of the legendary Emperor Jimmu, the first ruler to sit on the imperial Japanese throne. It was coincidentally Good Friday on the Christian calendar. The Japanese began their most devastating artillery barrage of the campaign at 10 a.m.; it continued with only one brief pause until 3 p.m. The 22nd Air Brigade flew 150 sorties and dropped more than sixty tons of bombs, mostly on the western half of the II Corps lines. The air-artillery bombardment smashed the carefully constructed front-line defenses. Burning cane fields and bamboo groves raised great clouds of smoke that prevented American artillery observers from directing return fire. Japanese infantry began their advance at 3 p.m. and broke through the western end of the line, quickly threatening to roll up II Corps from west to east. Maj. John Morley, the PTG intelligence officer (S-2), visited II Corps headquarters and the affected division headquarters to see what the tanks could do. General Parker at II Corps was still preoccupied with defending the beaches and wanted to keep the 194th Battalion there, but General Weaver talked to General King that night, and King ordered two companies of Lieutenant Colonel Miller's 194th and all SPMs to the front, to be replaced on the beaches by B/192TB from the reserve; the rest of the 192nd was ordered to remain with I Corps.

The next morning the Japanese 7th Tank Regiment made its first appearance en masse since the beginning of the Bataan campaign, proceeding unimpeded down the Pilar-Bagac road. Weaver had suggested in March that trees be felled to block this road, but this had not been done. Most of the few Filipino antitank gunners were ill, and the only effective weapons against armor were now the 37mms on Miller's tanks and the 75mms on the SPMs, but these were late getting into position; traveling to the front over the narrow, torn-up jungle trails was made difficult by the troops pouring the other way, and no example of tank-versus-tank combat on the 4th or 5th is known.

On the 6th General Parker refused his left flank (doubled it back) and attempted to form some semblance of a defense along the San Vincent River, which ran diagonally through the region. An attempted counterattack by part of the Philippine Division failed. Two tiny probes, one led by Captain Moffitt of C/194TB and containing 1st Sgt. Ben Saccone's four tanks and a half-track—Saccone was C Company's first sergeant, which was an administrative position, but he was now commanding a platoon, albeit in a half-track instead of a tank—and the other led by Lieutenant Colonel Miller himself, gained some ground but had to retreat due to losses and lack of infantry and flank support. Capt. Moffitt led his small group's single-file attack in the scout tank, one hundred yards ahead of the rest. Sgt. Frank Muther was Moffitt's radioman, and recalled that as they came around a bend in the trail a white ball of fire from an antitank gun flew over the tank. Moffitt returned fire, hitting the Japanese gun a glancing blow that peeled back its shield. The gunners ran for cover and were mowed down by the tank's sponson guns. Moffitt ordered retreat, and the driver spun a track and managed to turn around on the narrow trail and head back, pursued by small-arms fire. Muther attempted to warn the other tanks by radio but was unsuccessful; the other operators couldn't read Morse code, and the tanks lacked voice radios. Moffitt hand-signaled the withdrawal as he squeezed by, and the other vehicles attempted to turn around, only to be caught in a 200-yard-long ambush the Japanese had set up on both sides of the trail. Three of the tanks shed their tracks, and their crews evacuated under the cover of Moffitt's tank and Saccone's half-track. The half-track was hit by an antitank round that took off one gunner's foot and injured a second man in the shoulder. The men pulled back, but the man with the shoulder injury contracted fatal gas gangrene before he could reach an aid station. Moffitt's tank developed engine trouble and had to be abandoned temporarily before it could be towed to Cabcaben.

Moffitt's advance had been observed by Col. Richard Mallonée of the 21st Field Artillery Regiment (PA), who reported in his memoir:

Our . . . tanks were sent westward . . . to form strong points upon which the infantry could rally. [They] did fine work, [but] were eventually sacrificed. Without organized infantry support to protect them from the flanks and rear, and in the middle of a jungle, the vehicles were too vulnerable. One by one I saw these units leave the beach road and go up the trails to the destruction they knew awaited them. None came back.

Lieutenant Colonel Miller was to make a probing attack with the rest of C/194TB in support of the 45th Infantry Regiment (PS). An attack in this terrain meant a single-file reconnaissance along a jungle trail. Miller asked the infantry commander if he had any mortars and was told that there was one, with ten shells. Five were allotted for this attack. The mortar was set up, direct observation of the Japanese positions along the single trail was obtained, and the five shells were fired off, with dramatic results. The Japanese were taken completely by surprise and ran. The Scouts made a quick attack, killing Japanese on both sides of the trail. Miller followed up on foot, as the tanks had not yet come up the trail. He found the trail and surrounding jungle were strewn profusely with Japanese pie plate antitank mines. There were no engineers available to neutralize these; no other Fil-American attack was succeeding, leaving the flanks of the 45th completely open; and its attack was called off.

The 6th proved to be the decisive day in the brief campaign. The Japanese had taken all of the important north–south trails in the western part of the II Corps zone, as well as Mount Samat, had split I Corps from II Corps, and were heading for the east coast. The Fil-American counterattack had failed miserably, and the Bataan defenders were in a desperate situation. The Philippine Division was cut off from the rest of II Corps, and on April 7 Miller and C/194TB were ordered to probe eastward with the 45th Regiment Scouts. On this day the 2nd Platoon led with two tanks. They were ambushed at a sharp bend in the trail, and Lt. Frank Riley's lead tank was hit by an antitank gun. Riley suffered a severe concussion, but Pvt. Ray Peeples took command and the two tanks backed to safety around the bend, knocking out a Japanese tank shortly thereafter. Peeples and Captain Moffitt were both put in for Silver Stars for this combat. Meanwhile, 1st Sgt. Saccone's 3rd Platoon made a grandiosely titled enveloping maneuver with two M3s and two half-tracks but were stopped at a roadblock. They suffered no casualties in a fierce battle but were out of radio contact with headquarters and retreated to the southwest coast, where they joined the 192nd Tank Battalion.

These two combats were the last for PTG armor and C/194TB. The Philippine Division joined the rest of II Corps in its headlong flight to the south. Weaver and Morley tried without success to obtain orders from King or Parker for the employment of the rest of the tanks. Weaver did send Smyth, his executive officer, north on the coast road in Jim Bashleben's half-track to find dispersal sites for fourteen tanks in case a renewed offensive was ordered. Forrest Knox recalled that A/192TB spent a day on the highway as the only unit bucking the steady stream heading south. The rest of the 192nd Tank Battalion stayed put in the I Corps rear, awaiting orders.

During the crisis Wainwright made the only positive response available to him—he ordered an increase in the rice ration. He also passed on to King an order he had received from MacArthur forbidding surrender (Wainwright had already warned MacArthur that the end was near) and instructing King to prepare and execute a sudden mass attack on Olangapo to capture Japanese supplies, led by the tanks and all available artillery. (Olangapo is only 49 kilometers [30 miles] from Mariveles as an airplane flies, but 98.9 kilometers [61.5 miles] by road.) King calmly asked Jones, whose intact I Corps would have made the attack, for his opinion, was told it was "impossible," so without telling Wainwright King proceeded with his own plan—to surrender the next day, April 9.

Organized II Corps defenses comprised only a thin line of New Mexico National Guardsmen from the 200th Coast Artillery Regiment (AA) that partially surrounded Cabcaben. The open-air hospital that it protected now contained 24,000 sick and injured soldiers who would be massacred in the next Japanese attack. King began an evacuation of key personnel and nurses to Corregidor; 2,000 made it, including several dozen tankers, who were not ordered directly to leave their units, although some insisted that their officers told them it was "every man for himself," and were definitely not welcomed on Corregidor. King ordered demolitions readied and told his higher-level commanders to prepare to destroy all records and combat weapons upon receipt of the code word "BLAST" on the radio or from a messenger. Not knowing these plans, Weaver sent Morley west to 192nd Tank Battalion headquarters to prepare an attack northeast by its three companies, apparently to reestablish contact with some part of II Corps. Plans were drawn up and distributed, but unsupported by infantry or artillery, it would have been a suicide mission. The message "BLAST" was received at 5:35 a.m. on the 9th after the tanks were on the trail, and they returned to battalion headquarters to destroy their tanks and await the arrival of the Japanese.

At 9 p.m. on the 8th, nature preempted King's demolition orders with a rare earthquake that was felt by everyone on Bataan but did little damage. At 3:30 a.m. on the 9th, King sent two unmarried officers through the lines under a white flag with orders to negotiate a surrender with General Homma. This well-known event has two connections to the tankers: The white flag, a sheet, was from a double issue of bed linen that A/192TB had received accidentally at Fort Knox and had kept clean since then; and second, after their scout car was blocked by oncoming traffic, the officers were loaned a PTG headquarters jeep driven by Cpl. William Burns, who received a Bronze Star for the day's events. After two SPMs helped the jeep pass through the lines, the two men met a Japanese officer who insisted on the presence of the American commander. The men returned after a massive Japanese air raid and got King, who reached the Japanese headquarters at 11 a.m. When Homma learned that King was surrendering only his own Bataan command and not the entire Philippine theater, he refused to see him. Out of options, King offered the unconditional surrender of 12,000 Americans and 64,000 Filipinos to Homma's operations officer at 12:30 p.m. The Japanese accepted, but without a signed agreement, and interpreted the surrender as that of units and individuals, and those surrendering as captives and not as prisoners of war.

Bill Gentry recalled that two companies, C/192TB and C/194TB, voted not to surrender but to head north to the mountains. They had gone three or four miles when an officer arrived in a jeep and told them that King's surrender applied to everyone, and that they would either surrender or be court-martialed. The men were furious and humiliated but returned to battalion headquarters on the coast to await the pleasure of the Japanese. The men filled their shrunken stomachs with carefully hoarded food. They destroyed their tanks and other vehicles either by driving them off cliffs or by draining the recoil oil from the 37mms, plugging the barrels with rags and cleaning rods, setting the tanks on fire, and firing the guns with long lanyards. The battalion destroyed its sidearms by holding them down on an anvil and beating them with sledgehammers.

Lieutenant Colonel Wickord received an order to proceed a few miles down the road to surrender. He directed the officers to board the few trucks that had been kept serviceable for this purpose and ordered the enlisted men to march under the command of the unit's sergeant major, who according to Al Allen was ignored completely, in a foretaste of the anarchy that would overwhelm the prisoners in the weeks to come. Most men expected that they would eventually be driven to whatever camps would be set up for them; a few even thought they would be released. Each man's experience on his first encounter with the victorious Japanese was unique, but any optimistic expectations were quickly dashed. When marching out to the main road, Maj. Morley of Headquarters passed several formations of marching Japanese troops, many of whom were obviously fatigued. Some collapsed in view of the Americans. If after repeated kicks in the belly and beatings over the head with rifle butts they failed to get up, their exhaustion was ruled genuine and they were left to recover on their own. This was how the Japanese Army normally treated its enlisted men but was a total shock to the Americans, who did not suspect that they would soon be facing the same treatment.

The battle for the Luzon mainland, including Bataan, had lasted four months, and the siege of Corregidor would continue for another month. Five months was twice the original Japanese estimate. Was the delay imposed by the Americans and Filipinos militarily significant? No. The Japanese always considered the Philippines a secondary theater. Its nominal strategic asset, Manila Bay, had lost its significance for either offense or defense in the aviation age. The Philippines was too isolated to be of any use as an American base once the Japanese had surrounded it, which they did very quickly. Many Bataan veterans believed to their dying day that their sacrifice had saved Australia, but this isn't true. No

Japanese planner originally suggested the invasion of Australia. The idea was broached when the Indies campaign ended early with the Japanese in complete control of the air and sea in the region. The Philippines were not relevant to this thinking, which ended after the United States decided to make Australia its major Pacific base. The defense of Bataan did serve to boost civilian morale in the United States during a period in early 1942 when the Japanese were running rampant in the Pacific, and Bataan's self-sacrificing defenders were exploited for the rest of the war by America's war propagandists, who were careful not to blame America's war leaders (especially not MacArthur) for the islands' unpreparedness and poor initial response; rather, unnamed prewar isolationists took the hit.

In this author's opinion, the Provisional Tank Group should be judged one of the most successful units in the campaign. The tanks, SPMs, and (very early) the cavalry were the only weapons MacArthur had that could hold the Japanese back, if only briefly, and allow the retreat of the rest of his army to Bataan. That Bataan itself was a trap was not the fault of the tankers, who helped MacArthur successfully execute the tactical plan he was forced to adopt. The effectiveness of the tanks on Bataan was hampered by the terrain and the lack of doctrine, but they were the key to defeating the Japanese in the Points and Pockets, persuading Homma to pull back and call for reinforcements. The tank-infantry doctrine that was worked out in combat on Bataan was used for the rest of the Pacific war.

Wainwright's low opinion of tanks has been belittled by Weaver and other armor aficionados. But his view of the PTG's tanks as infantry support weapons, as in World War I, was far more realistic in the Philippines than the gauzy vision of MacArthur and Weaver. The Armored Force intended its Reserve GHQ Tank Battalions to be attached to other units involved in far-distant operations—that is, for infantry support. Their role was to supply tanks where tanks were needed. These units lacked the ancillary formations such as armored infantry and armored artillery that were supposed to be used in all combined arms offensive operations. MacArthur probably felt that he could take the infantry and artillery necessary to support tank offensives from his beloved Philippine Army, which proved inadequate even in its conventional role. Weaver's independence allowed him to keep many of his tanks operational for the entire Bataan campaign—though in the end to no avail. But MacArthur's last-minute order that the tanks lead an attack on Olangapo to capture supplies was preposterous, and months too late. There was not enough gasoline left to make such a long-distance attack, and many of Weaver's men lacked the strength to operate their manual-transmission tanks.

CHAPTER 8

Captives of the Japanese

GENERAL KING'S SURRENDER OF HIS BATAAN FORCES WAS NOT THE TRIumph General Homma would have obtained three months previously. Homma now had to end the Philippine campaign as quickly as possible. His next step was the capture of Corregidor, prior to which King's men had to be removed from the Bataan Peninsula. Plans had been made to march the captives north to Camp O'Donnell, an unfinished Philippine Army camp a few miles north of Bataan, but the Japanese were totally unprepared for the number of captives (12,000 Americans and 60,000 to 70,000 Filipinos) and their poor physical condition. More time, more food, more vehicles, and more medical facilities were needed, but none were requested. The Imperial Japanese Army was never willing to admit that a plan was flawed; it was a matter of prestige. The captives were to be force-marched up the East Road sixty-six miles from Mariveles to San Fernando, shipped thirteen miles by boxcar to Capas, and trekked a final eight miles to Camp O'Donnell. This was an easy three-day march for the Japanese Army, which was apparently the time requirement assumed by the Japanese planners. This assumption, invalidated by the weakened condition of the captives, racial animosity, and the Japanese contempt for captives and hatred for the enemy, resulted in the two-week atrocity known later in the United States as the Bataan Death March, and to the men at the time as "The Hike."

THE HIKE
The exodus from Bataan took place in the hottest, driest time of the year, the season of drought. The unclouded sun seared the earth; by afternoon

the air was an oven and the ground was rock-hard. The East Road was a typical provincial highway, twenty feet wide, originally rock covered with crushed stone and sand. The four-month campaign had left the road a mix of potholes, soft sand, rocks, and loose gravel. Convoys of trucks carrying Japanese infantrymen south kept the air above the road stirred up in a swirling dust cloud; the normally green foliage along the shoulders was covered with a heavy coat of chalk.

The plan called for the men to be formed up in units of about a hundred with individual guards in the front, rear, and sides of each group. The guards were to be changed at regular intervals, nominally every four hours, but whatever plan existed for feeding and resting the prisoners broke down very quickly. Some early units made it to O'Donnell in three days; others took two weeks. Some days the men marched for five miles, or not at all; at other times they were double-timed, or even forced to turn around and march south. The progress of the stream of men resembled an accordion; it is probable that most of the delays resulted from the need to build, fill, and empty holding pens for the unanticipated mass of men.

As many as fifty tankers escaped to Corregidor on April 9–10, in violation of orders. The rest formed up west of Mariveles (192nd Tank Battalion) or near Cabcaben (194th Tank Battalion) on the 10th or 11th to begin The Hike. They walked the sixty-six miles in stages. For those who started at the tip of the peninsula, stage one was a stretch of road that ran east for nine miles to Cabcaben. There the road turned north and proceeded along Bataan's east coast for twenty-seven miles, passing through the town squares of Lamao, Limay, Orion, Pilar, Balanga, Abucay, Samal, Orani, and Hermosa. At Hermosa the Old National Road turned west toward Layac Junction, then northeast eleven miles across a torrid, sandy plain to Lubao, then continued northeast to San Fernando.

Initially the men were herded onward with blows and shouts, but no sign of organization or plan. The first assembly point was Balanga, about twenty miles from Mariveles. The Japanese made no plan to feed the prisoners prior to Balanga; they assumed that the men would be carrying their own provisions. Most of the half-starved men carried no food at all. The countryside had been stripped mostly bare, but since guards were scarce on the first stage, the men could sometimes break free to forage. Small turnips and sugarcane provided just enough energy for many to make it to Balanga. Thirst was not a problem at first but became the cause of many men's deaths later in the march.

On their last night of freedom, the D/192TB tankers were treated to a "last supper" of pineapple juice and light bread and a brief speech by their commander, Capt. Jack Altman from Texas, who dismissed the Harrodsburg men with, "From now on, boys, it's every man for himself." Some took this literally and tried to make their own way to Corregidor. Others thought about heading north into the jungle, but most thought better of it; they were just too weak and were hoping their surrender would mean food.

It's true that the loners stayed loners on The Hike, but many men, especially in the PTG, survived with the aid of one or two friends. They helped each other over rough passages and shared their meager possessions. T/Sgt. Mel Madero of C/194TB recorded,

> I was very fortunate in that I had a buddy. We helped each other. I managed throughout the lootings to keep a bottle of iodine. Now, my buddy had some solvent coffee—you know, the old K rations had biscuits, a little piece of chocolate, and some coffee. So, between us we had a combination that kept us going. Occasionally on the march, when we were crossing a stream and the guards were not near, I managed to get some water in my canteen. Then we'd slip in my iodine to purify it, and my buddy would slip in his coffee to make it palatable. That way we avoided any dysentery. For the rest of the guys, however, it was murder.

The PTG was quick to lose a man. The early marchers were caught in a crossfire between Corregidor and Japanese artillery. Some A/192TB tankers hot-wired a truck to cross a two-mile gap. The company commander, Lt. Kenneth Bloomfield, collapsed while chasing the truck and died. Bloomfield was apparently buried by the side of the road, but his body was not found after the war.

According to Forrest Knox,

His lard ass was too much to carry. He collapsed of heat prostration before he reached the end of the field. Sure, the men in our company could have picked him up and carried him, but you only did that for your friends. Somehow we were indifferent about him.

None of the prisoners knew where they were going—some were told Manila—or why the Japanese were in such a hurry, but it was obvious from the start that their treatment would be far from humane. An English-speaking guard told Capt. Harold Collier the Japanese words for rest, march, and water, and advised him to obey any command from any Japanese instantly. Most guards assumed that the Americans understood Japanese, and that failure to respond to an order implied disobedience warranting punishment. There is no evidence that the march was a planned atrocity; it was rather the inevitable result of poor planning and haste, exacerbated by racism and the cruel and callous behavior of many Japanese Army soldiers. The Japanese treated their own men little better than they did their enemies. Early in the march one man saw an exhausted Japanese guard shot to death by his countrymen for failure to keep up. Another saw a hundred contorted and bloated bodies off the road near the small compound the Americans had set up for Japanese POWs, and word came back that the Japanese had machine-gunned their own countrymen who had surrendered. 2nd Lt. Russell Swearingen saw two Japanese soldiers open cans of Sterno with their bayonets and eat the contents. They got roaring drunk. At guard change, a sergeant and two guards took the two men into the woods. Swearingen heard screams; the guards returned from the woods wiping blood from their bayonets.

Mistreatment of the prisoners began immediately. No two PTG men had exactly the same experience, but ghastly scenes were seared into their memories for the rest of their lives. Poweleit and Tenney witnessed beheadings carried out apparently for sport. A sailor marching near Gentry had an American flag tattooed on his left forearm. The Japanese pulled him from the line, put his arm over a post, and chopped it off just above the elbow. He was shoved back into the line, bleeding badly. Nearby medics, without stopping, stanched the bleeding with a tourniquet and saved the man—Gentry saw the sailor later at Camp O'Donnell. Gentry also saw prisoners forced to dig graves into which they were thrown after being shot. A few wounded men tried to climb out of the graves and were either shot again, bayoneted by the guards, or beaten back into the graves by the entrenching tools of other prisoners. Some prisoners committed suicide by bolting from the line of march into the fields, prompting immediate shooting or bayoneting by the guards. One tanker's marching companion, an unidentified major, jumped from a bridge into a muddy creek, sinking immediately up to his shoulders in the ooze, and was left behind. Bashleben felt that the worst part of The Hike was having to step over men calling for help. Bayoneting was a common punishment for men holding out their canteens for water or breaking from line in desperate attempts to get water from the many free-flowing artesian wells or even the stinking, death-ridden carabao wallows. But the guards showed no consistency in their behavior. Al Allen was given goat's milk by a guard. It stank, but he drank it greedily. Some guards allowed canteens to be filled and even permitted civilians to throw food to the marching men.

The first men to reach Balanga remembered it as a source of food. This was typically only a ball of sticky rice and a pinch of salt, but it was the first evidence that the Japanese did not intend to starve them to death. But within a few days, Balanga, at which the prisoners were held outdoors for at least a day, became noticeable for its horrible smell, detectable for miles. There had been no planning for the sanitary disposal of human waste. Many of the prisoners had dysentery or at least diarrhea, and sick men who could not control their bowels defecated at will in the area. The town quickly became a quagmire of corruption, overarched by a fetid mist. The men who died lay where they fell, in their own excrement. Their bodies soon began to putrefy in the heat and turned into fertile breeding places for maggots. The Japanese had no medical facilities for their prisoners. American doctors set up aid stations, but had little medicine, and thus had no effect. They were out of quinine, which had kept malaria under control during the siege, and this disease recurred; its symptoms, raging fevers followed by debilitating chills, further weakened the men.

The Japanese were very rank-conscious and afforded many perquisites to generals and full colonels. General Weaver was the only member of the PTG in this category, and he was allowed to drive all the way to Camp O'Donnell with his trunk of personal belongings. Al Allen surmised that his favored treatment was at least partially attributable to the Japanese respect for the PTG. The Japanese believed that the Americans had had 500 or 600 tanks. They did not believe Weaver's word that he had begun the campaign with 104 tanks and entered Bataan with only 40 to 50 until they had completed their salvage of Bataan. Battalion commanders Wickord and Miller were lieutenant colonels and began the march with their men. Both were still in fairly good physical condition. Miller's 194th Battalion was concentrated near Cabcaben at the surrender, left on the march early, was blessed with "good guards" (in Miller's words), and reached Camp O'Donnell on April 13. Miller did not mention it in his memoir, but according to a diary kept by Capt. Clinton Quinlen of HQ/194TB, the two men spent the last day on a bus, Miller suffering from fallen arches. (We are very fortunate that Quinlen's diary, which included a 194th Battalion roster, survived, buried at a camp—Quinlen himself died on a prison ship en route to Japan.)

The 192nd Battalion had farther to go and was slowed by the overcrowding and chaos that took over the march. Wickord did not arrive until the 18th, but still on his own feet. Wickord was large-framed and could have been called "portly" when the siege began. He had obviously lost weight but showed fewer signs of malnourishment than most of his men. I have concluded that field-grade officers often ate better than their men, not only during the siege but later in the camps. This minor scandal was overlooked in the bigger tragedy, but there is ample evidence that discipline began breaking down with the surrender. Col. Irvin Alexander (not a tanker) noted, "If an officer spoke to a soldier the natural response was, 'Go to hell!' No officer could expect any assistance whatever except from another officer." Company-grade officers in the combat units were more likely to have shared their men's diets and remained as well-respected as they had been before the surrender. Bill Gentry weakened rapidly. He recalled eating one rice ball and two stalks of sugarcane and drinking seven canteens of water during his eleven days on the road. He became delirious with malaria, lost consciousness for two days, and was carried by comrades for the last three days. Many other PTG survivors recalled getting lifesaving assistance from fellow prisoners at some point during the march.

Maj. Richard Kadel, commander of the 17th Ordnance Company, was beaten so severely by interrogators before joining The Hike that he remained crippled for the rest of his life; he had refused to disclose any details of the maintenance of M3 light tanks and was thrown into the stream of shuffling men. He escaped by rolling into a culvert and survived the war with the guerillas. Five more men from his unit escaped either during the march or shortly thereafter, probably the greatest number from any American unit of its size, but Kadel never took credit for any joint effort, always claiming to have escaped alone.

The march became better organized at Balanga, most men starting out in units of one hundred Americans or Filipinos walking four abreast with a half-dozen guards. But the road became crowded, the guards became less patient, and deaths became more frequent. These could come arbitrarily, from bayoneting or shooting, but most deaths were the result of illness and exhaustion. Men fell, struggled to rise, crawled forward groaning, and either managed to get up and back into column, often prodded or supported by their comrades, or fell again, faces pressed to the ground, dying or already dead. The dying tended to be either the youngest, weakened the most by Bataan's low-calorie diet and dispirited by the lies told them by their superiors, or the oldest—the Philippines had been very desirable peacetime duty and sought out for final tours by senior officers and NCOs. The seniors on the march were much older than their counterparts elsewhere in the army, with more of the debilities of age.

The lucky survivors had one thing in common, a strong desire to live, and most came up with tricks to avoid the guards and keep their minds engaged. Forrest Knox stayed away from the outside of the rows and tried to start each leg near the front of his column. As he tired, he could drop back in the column safely; anyone who fell out all the way to the rear was killed by the "buzzard squads." Harold "Snuff" Kurvers was always ready to change columns. He would spot a hiding point, drop out completely to rest, and join a later column. He kept up his strength with sugarcane and soup extract from a friend and was never struck during the entire march. Les Tenney needed short-term goals; he would keep moving to the next carabao herd, the next bend in the road, and so on. Zoeth Skinner counted bodies on the side of the road but found this was no way to keep his spirits up and quit at 1,000.

Most men suffered mutely in this week or more of misery. Only one act of revenge is known to this author. Early one morning Dr. Alvin Poweleit and a sergeant heard water dripping from a spigot, snuck over to it, and were filling canteens and Poweleit's musette bag when a guard saw them, hit the sergeant with his gun butt and struck Poweleit in the face. The ex-boxer Poweleit had had all he could stand. He surveyed the column closely, turned back, and cracked the guard on the jaw. The man dropped; the doctor struck him a few more times until he went limp. Poweleit and the sergeant dragged the man into the thicket and the doctor returned to the column. The sergeant rejoined him a few minutes later and told him that he had stabbed the Japanese in the heart with his bayonet and then hid the rifle separately from the body. Both men moved forward in the column as quickly as they could; they could hear the Japanese calling for the missing guard until the next town.

San Fernando, the largest town on the trek, was the next major stop. It was the capital of Pampanga province and had not been damaged greatly by the war. The Japanese had prepared for this stop and provided food. Enclosed areas were filled quickly with the arriving prisoners—a cock-fighting pit was remembered by many—and men were pushed into them until they could not sit comfortably and were often wedged between bodies. Again, no latrines or medical facilities were provided. Dysentery was still rampant; excrement soon slickened the ground and thickened the air with its foul odor.

Most men stayed in San Fernando several days; they did not know it, but they were waiting for transportation for the next leg of the trip, which would be a train ride for the thirteen miles to Capas. The Japanese chose to use sealed boxcars rather than coaches for this task. Boxcars for the narrow-gauge Philippine railroad came in two sizes: steel cars about thirty-three feet by eight feet by seven feet, and wooden cars about half as long, just as wide, but only six feet high. These contained a single door and were tight enough to ship loose wheat and rice. As many as one hundred men were shoved into each car with kicks and rifle butts, and many doors were bolted shut. The cars were so crowded than the men were pinned into whatever position, sitting or standing, they had been in when the shoving stopped. The cars soon became unbearably hot. The only ventilation came from the door at one end. In some cars the men attempted a system of rotation to give each some fresh air; in others men did not move jointly and began to pass out and die from heat exhaustion and asphyxiation. Dysentery took its toll, and men retched from the resulting foul odor, the heat, and the jerking ride. Floors became slick from feces and vomit. At the frequent stops Filipinos attempted to throw food in through the doors, and were met with varied responses from the guards. The trip took an average of four hours of stopping and starting; many survivors felt that these were the worst four hours of the trek. When the trains reached their Capas destination, the men tumbled from the boxcars as quickly as they could without prompting from the guards. The dead remained on the cars; some had been wedged upright by the men on either side and did not fall until the cars began to empty.

Most of the inhabitants of the small barrio were on hand to greet the prisoners and tried to press food, water, and even head coverings on them. The guards, who were almost as exhausted as the prisoners, allowed most of these interactions, which were remembered fondly by the Americans. The men were formed up into columns and ordered to march. Their destination was Camp O'Donnell, the first permanent POW camp the Japanese established in the Philippines. An estimated 650 Americans died on the march; of these, only a dozen were from the PTG. The enlisted Guardsmen were on average more mature and better educated than the regular army men marching with them, and it's possible that this allowed them to better withstand mistreatment from the Japanese, at least initially. However, they were so weak and ill that their death rate accelerated in the first camp they reached.

CAMP O'DONNELL

The columns of men stumbled west from Capas along a tree-lined jungle road that had been untouched by the fighting. Filipinos emerged from the foliage to again press water and food on them. After seven miles the jungle ended and the road crested a small rise to overlook a broad, hot, dusty, cogon grass plain. A prison camp could be seen in the distance. This was Camp O'Donnell, a never-completed Philippine Army training base that the Japanese converted to house the prisoners from Bataan until Corregidor was subdued. Closer inspection showed it to be a totally uninviting array of unfinished nipa-roofed bamboo-stilted barracks surrounded by rusty barbed-wire fencing punctuated by guard towers. There were no trees, but grass was everywhere, even in the wide-open huts. The rat- and insect-infested dwellings reeked of decay. Forty men were to be crowded into each hut, which had been intended to house sixteen. The road split the camp into a smaller northern section for the Americans and a larger southern section for the Filipinos. During the retreat in December, the Fil-American Army had attempted to destroy the camp's water supply. When the American prisoners arrived four months later, there were, in their section of the camp, only two partially functioning water pumps.

The Japanese put all the arriving prisoners through the same procedure. They were searched once more; this time the emphasis was on Japanese souvenirs and money. To the Japanese these could only have been taken from dead soldiers and warranted an immediate death sentence. Most of the Americans were warned in time and could swallow any contraband, bury it in the soft soil with their feet, or at least stand over it. Maj. Havelock Nelson of HQ/192TB was caught with either a Japanese coin or a battle flag (accounts vary) and was shot and buried alive during a rainstorm. He dug himself out, escaped the still weakly guarded camp, and joined Lt. James Hart (ex-A/194TB) as a guerilla in the mountains, but succumbed to his injuries in June.

After the search the men waited in the hot sun to hear a welcoming speech by the commandant. Capt. Yoshio Tsuneyoshi was a caricature of a bombastic prison warden. A short, bowlegged man with a Hitler mustache, he wore baggy pants and riding boots with spurs. A large samurai sword dangled at his side. "He was one of the ugliest mortals I have ever seen," one prisoner later wrote. "He breathed the very essence of hate." Tsuneyoshi was obviously not a bright man. "The loose-lipped vacuity of his expression was that of an idiot," one prisoner observed. His speech varied little, and all survivors could recall it in some detail. After climbing onto a wooden platform, the commandant began a screaming, spittle-punctuated harangue emphasizing that the men were captives, not prisoners, and that the penalty for any rules infringement would be death. The men were finally released, split up, and ordered to the barracks.

One of the barracks was taken over for a hospital, but no medicines were provided. It was soon named "St. Peter's Ward"; men carried to it very rarely left alive. There were no sanitary facilities, and slit trenches were quickly dug for latrines, and just as quickly filled with fecal matter by men with dysentery. Many ill men could not reach the latrines and fouled themselves where they lay. The stench was almost unbearable at first, but the men became accustomed to it. Dozens of men were dying every day. The Japanese wanted to cremate the bodies, as was their custom, but American chaplains insisted that their men be buried, and the Japanese consented to this. The American cemetery was set up outside the main gate heading north, and men were drafted into work details to carry the bodies for burial, which took place in mass graves with little or no ceremony. With luck the dead men had retained their dog tags, which allowed their burial plots to be recorded properly.

The Japanese restricted water to a single trickling spigot; men lined up at daybreak to fill their canteens. Men were not allowed to bathe themselves or wash their clothing for three weeks, although Generals King and Weaver, who were driven to the camp with their footlockers and bedrolls, were always well groomed. Meals were more regular than back in Bataan and were based on either steamed rice or *lugao*, a thin rice gruel. For the first two weeks, rice was the only food obtainable. Then it was supplemented by about two to four ounces of camotes (native sweet potatoes) per day. Mongo beans, or dried peas, which were very vitamin rich, were received a few times. About once a week carabao meat was issued, based on less than one-fourth ounce per man. As an example, Miller's mess was feeding 900 men. One weekly meat ration for these 900 men comprised eighteen pounds of carabao ribs. There was ample food available, but the Japanese deliberately withheld it.

The leaves and bark from guava trees proved to be an aid for the lesser cases of dysentery. These were boiled and brewed into a tea. Diseases common during Miller's two-month stay at Camp O'Donnell were malaria, dengue fever, dysentery, diarrhea, malnutrition, beriberi, yaws or tropical ulcers, Guam blisters, and yellow jaundice. Many men, especially those with dysentery, found the food repulsive, refused to eat despite the entreaties of their friends, and starved. Most men who made it home believed that a will to live was a key ingredient in their survival.

The American field commanders and staff officers continued with their paperwork as long as their strength permitted, attempting to summarize the failed campaign. A few reports were smuggled out, and others were buried and recovered after the war. Most were edited to standard military blandness, while a few managed to convey the men's bitterness with brutal honesty. From Gen. W. E. Brougher's 11th Division Operations Report to General Wainwright, written from O'Donnell in May:

Who had the right to say that 20,000 Americans should be sentenced without their consent and for no fault of their own to an enterprise that would involve for them endless suffering, cruel handicap, death, or a hopeless future that could end only in a Japanese prisoner-of-war camp? Who took the responsibility for saying that some other possibility was in prospect? And whoever did, was he not an arch-deceiver, traitor and criminal rather than a great soldier? Didn't he know that he was sentencing all his comrades to sure failure, defeat, death or rotting in a prison camp? A foul trick of deception has been played on a large group of Americans by a commander in chief and small staff who are now eating steak and eggs in Australia. God damn them!

The Japanese began selecting men for work details, and men with initiative and relative good health clamored to join these. This reduced the head count in the camp, which peaked at about 6,000 Americans and possibly 50,000 Filipinos. On May 10 most generals and full colonels were sent from O'Donnell to Tarlac. Colonel Sage of the 200th Coast Artillery Regiment (AA) took command of the Americans in the camp. According to Miller, Weaver attempted to leave Lieutenant Colonel Smyth, his executive officer, in command of the PTG POWs, but Miller persuaded Sage of his seniority and Miller was given the position, which brought some space for an office but little authority. Conditions in the camp continued to worsen. The odor of putrefaction spread to the entire plain, irritating the fastidious Japanese, and on May 16 the camp was ordered closed, with the survivors to be moved to other camps, but this took time, and fifty Americans died on May 29, the deadliest single day in O'Donnell's history. When Camp O'Donnell finally closed on January 20, 1943, 1,547 Americans had died there. After the war, Captain Tsuneyoshi was convicted of war crimes and sentenced to life imprisonment. He spent six years in Sugano Prison, but was then released under the terms of the 1951 Peace Treaty.

CORREGIDOR

The Japanese could not end the Philippine campaign victoriously until the island fortress of Corregidor, "The Rock," was taken. Corregidor and three smaller fortified islands blocked the entrance to Manila Bay. This no longer had its previous strategic value—the Japanese had bypassed the Philippines and were now in control of Malaysia and the Netherlands East Indies—but was of immense propaganda value to both the Americans and the Japanese. Corregidor was only two miles south of the Bataan coast. The Japanese rush to clear Bataan of its Fil-American prisoners to make room for its Corregidor assault forces helps explain the Bataan Death March and the fatal inadequacies of the first camp to which these prisoners were sent.

Corregidor's main batteries had been in place since 1914 and were very inadequate for the present war. The 12-inch guns in two batteries dated from 1885, and the 12-inch mortars in two other batteries were older still. There was a total of twenty-three batteries, with fifty-six different guns and mortars. Their efficient use required that the enemy attack from the sea, not from the Bataan heights—from which the interiors of the gun pits could be seen—and not use aircraft. Corregidor was doomed on December 8, 1941, when the Japanese took control of the air. Its anti-aircraft defenses were as poor as those of Bataan. The dominant feature of the Corregidor defenses was the Malinta complex. Its main artery was a reinforced concrete tunnel 1,400 feet long, 30 feet wide, and forming a 20-foot-high arch, passing from one side of the island to the other. It was completed in 1932 and was originally meant for storage. It was damp and poorly ventilated and, except for the hospital, was never intended for human habitation. But Japanese air supremacy forced the men out of their barracks and into the tunnels to live. All aboveground structures were damaged by air attack and, after Bataan's fall, artillery shells. Disease resulting from heat, humidity, and psychological factors became rampant, but raw hunger and vitamin deficiency diseases were never a problem. Corregidor was the principal supply base for all American forces in the Philippines, and although stringent rationing was imposed in January, the men always ate relatively well from the army's and navy's stocks of canned meat, vegetables, and fruit. They also had access to clean drinking water, showers, and laundries, and the swarms of malarial mosquitoes that infested Bataan were lacking. The Rock was an irresistible urge for 2,000 men who fled Bataan for Corregidor on April 9–10, many of them against orders.

About fifty tankers made it to Corregidor. Lt. John Hummel of A/194TB decided to swim for it, invited three men to join him, and set out with the aid of a five-gallon water can. He drifted east, was rescued by a patrol boat, and was assigned to command a new MP platoon. Hummel was a tank platoon leader but had left his men, and was always considered a deserter by Colonel Miller, his battalion commander. More 192nd Battalion men decided to continue their fight on Corregidor and found at least three motor ships and one rowboat hidden beneath the Mariveles cliffs. Pvt. Kenneth Hourigan of Company D had to moor the rowboat to a buoy but was rescued and put ashore at a beach. He found the Malinta tunnel; there he and his men encountered a ghost-pale colonel with shoes shined and trousers pressed, who asked the filthy, scrawny, bedraggled group, "Where in the hell are you boys from?" Hourigan said, "Bataan, sir! We thought it was better to come over here and fight rather than surrender to those yellow-bellies [sic]." The colonel replied, "You should have stayed with your organization rather than come over here to eat the fighting man's chow" and directed the men to a tunnel to sign up for beach defense, which is where most of the tankers wound up.

2nd Lt. Matthew MacDowell and his entire twenty-man B/192TB platoon reached The Rock on an old tugboat. Bud Bardowski and his friends always called it "Bardowski's platoon," but Bud was a sergeant, and this was MacDowell's unit. They were kept together as a provisional company in the marine regiment. Bud thought this was his best time in the armed forces and considered himself an "honorary Marine" until his death. T/4 Frank Goldstein and a few other B/192TB men found a water tender whose captain was persuaded to go to Corregidor by Goldstein's pistol. Radioman Goldstein helped the ship navigate through the minefield by flashing Morse code to a signalman on the island with a flashlight. Once ashore Goldstein was split from the other tankers and put on beach defense with complete strangers. Three 192nd Battalion noncoms including Arnold Lawson led separate groups of tankers down the cliff and found a large boat owned by two Czech nationals who had a plan and supplies to escape to Cebu, but their boat would not run. A tank mechanic fixed the boat, and the tankers voted to leave for Cebu that night but were overruled by a pistol-wielding New Mexico National Guard officer, who directed them to Corregidor, where a few men including Sergeant Lawson were assigned to the marines, but the rest were sent to Fort Drum, a smaller island fortress in Manila Bay.

The marines had commanded the Corregidor beach defenses since shortly after the war began. The 4th U.S. Marine Regiment had been based in the Shanghai International Settlement for many years and was evacuated to the Philippines in November. They disembarked at the naval base at Olangopo, Subic Bay, Luzon, where they drilled intensively for several weeks to toughen up after their soft duty in China. Just before Admiral Hart evacuated from the Philippines, he ordered the regiment to transfer to Corregidor, under command of the army. The marines hated having to report to the army, and especially to MacArthur, but quickly moved to the island, where they were immediately placed on beach defense. They were the first and only organized infantry to be based on the island, which was top-heavy with supply forces and coast artillery, and there was apparently no thought of leaving them on the Luzon mainland to bolster the inexperienced Filipinos and the single U.S. infantry regiment there. They spent the next several months digging defenses along the beach, especially that portion facing Bataan. The 4th Marines began April with 1,500 men and ended it with 229 officers and 3,770 enlisted men. They apparently welcomed the reinforcements from Bataan, despite their wretched physical condition, if they were combat soldiers, which applied to the tankers.

Conditions on Corregidor became progressively worse as the Japanese were able to supplement their daily air raids with Bataan-based artillery. The emperor's birthday on April 29 initiated six days of round-the-clock shelling. The 240mm mortars were especially dangerous; their shells were able to penetrate several feet of concrete and exploded several ordnance magazines. The electrical system—which was already operating on backup generators—water supply, and buried communications lines were all shredded by the shelling. By May 2 the bombardment, guided by an observation balloon, had destroyed all aboveground structures and vegetation. The continuous shelling harmed morale, and the tunnels began to fill with both the injured and malingerers.

At 10:40 p.m. on May 5 the Japanese began the pre-invasion bombardment of the invasion beaches. Landings began at 11 p.m., shortly before moonrise. The defenders had very few operational artillery pieces, but two guns on the eastern beaches had not been detected and were able to cause frightful damage to the invasion fleet, most of which had drifted to the east. Col. Gempachi Sato, the commander of the invasion force, lost 60 percent of his gunboats and landing craft. Of 2,000 Japanese in the spearhead battalions, only 800 made it to shore, but they secured a beachhead.

Several 7th Tank Regiment tanks set out from Bataan. All of the Type 95 Ha-Go light tanks were sunk in the channel, but three tanks made it to shore—two new Type 97 Kai medium tanks and one captured M3 light tank—and remained masked for much of the morning behind a cliff. They bogged down, but the M3 towed the other two free, and they began a slow, circuitous route up the cliff in the direction of Malinta Hill. The infantry fighting was by now hand-to-hand, and the marines requested reinforcements, which were difficult to pry out of the tunnels.

Both Bardowski and Goldstein were injured during this period. Bud was bayoneted and shot in the leg by a Japanese who jumped into his foxhole and was then shot by Bud's foxhole mate. Bud waded into the ocean after the surrender and worked the bullet out of his leg when the flesh softened. He felt that the salt water prevented infection but had problems with that leg for the rest of his life. He was eventually awarded his fourth Purple Heart for this wound. He later lost his front teeth to a guard's rifle butt at POW camp but received no recognition for this last injury. Goldy was badly injured by machine gun fire while getting water and ammunition for his ad-hoc unit. He made it into the naval tunnel before the surrender and was well treated by the Japanese, for whom he read food can labels. He spent thirteen months at Bilibid Hospital in Manila before his shattered leg was declared healed and he was sent to Cabanatuan.

The Japanese were running low on ammunition, and General Homma had made no provision for resupply, but there was no way for General Wainwright to know this. The marines were falling back to the unventilated tunnel, which was growing more fetid and crowded. The three tanks continued to creep up the hill, and the marines passed the word to bring up antitank guns. It is not known whether these even existed; at any rate, they never came forward. Wainwright decided that he had no option other than surrender. To quote Wainwright:

> *It was the terror vested in the tank that was the deciding factor. I thought of the havoc that even one of these beasts would wreak if it nosed into the tunnel, where lay our helpless wounded and brave nurses.*

He ordered a white flag to be run up the main flagpole at noon, at which time Wainwright left the tunnel to find Homma, who was still on the mainland. Wainwright did meet Colonel Sato and tried to convince him to accept the surrender of only Corregidor and the other three fortified islands. Sato would have none of this, but had Wainwright escorted to meet Homma. While he was on the mainland, the Japanese tanks lined up abreast ten yards from the east entrance to the Malinta tunnel. Eight Japanese stood in front with flamethrowers, fully outfitted and hooded in asbestos suits. Colonel Sato gave the 4,000 able men plus 1,000 wounded in the tunnel complex ten minutes to come out. General Drake, the senior American present, bargained for "as soon as possible," which was agreed to. To save the men on Corregidor, Wainwright was forced to surrender all of the Philippine Islands, which Homma knew full well he commanded, and returned to The Rock to find the Japanese in complete control. Bardowski, who always claimed that he recognized the M3 tank as his own, was convinced that the tanks had won the battle for the Japanese and found it highly ironic that Wainwright had never before seen any use for these weapons.

The new POWs were held for several days without food or water in a barren area on the eastern end of the island known as the 92nd Garage, and were then subjected to what the Japanese considered perfect humiliation. The prisoners were taken in barges across Manila Bay to the foot of Dewey Boulevard and then ordered off the barges into water over their heads. Arnold Lawson could not swim and saw a man ahead of him plead the same with a guard, who beat him with his sword and threw him overboard. Lawson whispered his problem to the man behind him, who helped him into the water and held his head up until their feet touched the ground. The soaking wet men were formed up in fours and marched down Dewey Boulevard accompanied by the screaming and slapping of their guards. This was intended as a further demonstration of the superiority of Asians to the Americans, but the Filipinos, who were the intended audience, stayed inside. The POWs were marched to Bilibid Prison north of town, where they stayed until the next permanent camp, Cabanatuan #3, was completed. The men did not as yet recognize their relative good fortune. The odds of Corregidor prisoners surviving the war were one in three; the odds of Bataan prisoners surviving the war were one in five.

PHILIPPINE WORK CAMPS

Prisoners reaching Camp O'Donnell in April could tell immediately that it was a death camp. Men with initiative and relative good health sought any way out of the camp that presented itself. Only four or five days after PFC. Roy Diaz arrived, the Japanese called for mechanics, and Diaz immediately volunteered. The next day he was on his way back to Bataan. The task of this detail was to rehabilitate the hundreds of vehicles the Americans had abandoned, and Diaz and his crew were soon putting an average of a dozen trucks per day in working order. The Bataan detail's task was soon broadened to the salvage of all equipment; metal parts were consolidated at San Fernando, driven to Manila, and shipped to Japan for re-use. More men were needed, and Les Tenney volunteered for a work party of one hundred. Although city boy Les lacked any of the skills requested, he felt he could learn on the job and became a blowtorch operator. He joined a group of seven men who looked out for each other; they tried to do just enough work to avoid most beatings by the guards, which couldn't always be avoided. The work was difficult, and all the men were ill and malnourished. Tenney and his group lasted for three months and were then taken to Cabanatuan, the new and largest Philippine POW camp.

Men were shuffled from O'Donnell and Cabanatuan to Bataan throughout the summer, often without "volunteering." Sgt. John Rowland was one of these, although he was quite sick with beriberi. He didn't last long before being returned to camp but recalled the first act of kindness ever shown him by a guard; one gave him a handful of vitamin B1 tablets for his illness. Turnover of men on the Bataan detail was high because many of them suffered the return of their malaria, which was endemic on the peninsula. There was no quinine available for treatment, and the weakened men were quick to die—probably one-third of the men on the Bataan detail died on Bataan or soon after their return to camp. Although the salvage task ended, the need for mechanics was constant, and Roy Diaz was chosen to join a group in Manila. While being trucked there, the men passed through barrios whose inhabitants tried to throw them food and give them signs of encouragement. At one stop a twelve-year-old boy flashed them a V sign. A Japanese officer saw this, walked up to the boy, and cut the boy's two fingers off with a bayonet. At the next stop the guards went into a store and returned with armloads of food. Some of this they shared with the prisoners, and Roy never forgot what it was—jars of strawberry jam. The jarring irrationality of Japanese behavior preyed on the minds of American survivors then, and long after the war.

The next contingent of prisoners taken from O'Donnell was assigned to rebuild the central Luzon bridges destroyed by Filipino and American engineers on the retreat. On May 7, 300 men reached Calauan, a town forty miles southeast of Manila, and were deposited outside the *cabildo*, or town hall, where they would be lodged. Captain Wakamori, commander of the area's Japanese engineers, made a brief speech that contrasted strikingly with Captain Tsuneyoshi's harangue at Camp O'Donnell. Wakamori explained what the men would be doing and the need for discipline but was visibly shocked at the prisoners' poor physical condition. The men were all malnourished and most were ill. He had requested men with specific skills, such as carpenters and mechanics; many PTG men fit the requirements, and 250 of the men on the detachment were tankers. One of the tankers, Bernard FitzPatrick, had a special skill. A college graduate who sold insurance prior to mobilization, he had minored in education and marked "teacher" on the questionnaire, and when asked what he taught, he replied "singing," one of his hobbies. He did not know that teacher was one of the most honored professions in Japan. Becoming a "sensei, teacher of singing" eased his path from that day forward.

L/Col. Ted Wickord was the detachment's senior American. Captain Wakamori and his men paid him the deference owed his rank, but he had less real authority than the lowest Japanese private. When Wickord met Bill Gentry in Chicago after the war, he told Gentry that he had answered to Gentry's name when roll was taken before the detachment left. He was extremely anxious to leave the camp before the answers he had written down for the Japanese interrogators could be checked out and found to be false. Gentry did not hold Wickord's subterfuge against him, as he had seen him under interrogation—his hands tied, his head on a block with a sword held over it—and agreed that it was good for him to get away. Wickord's men had widely different opinions on his value to the detachment. Wickord was a firm believer that rank had its privileges. Frank Goldstein recalled his obsession over his private toilet seat, which was carried everywhere for him.

Wickord should have been responsible for minor discipline, taking care of problems before they reached the Japanese. His ability to schmooze with the senior Japanese officers is unquestioned, but as it happened Wakamori was the most sympathetic Japanese officer any PTG member ever encountered, and on his own did much to improve their physical condition. He allowed the Filipinos to slip them food and invite them to religious festivals—some of them invented for the Americans—which ended in feasts and often sing-alongs led by Bernard FitzPatrick. A favorite with the Japanese was "My Old Kentucky Home."

One of the bridge-building unit's sub-detachments was the sawmill detail, based at nearby Lumban. Guerillas raided Lumban, killed several guards, and tried to persuade the entire POW contingent to flee to the hills. The prisoners' weakness made this impossible, but one man did accompany them. This triggered the Japanese "ten-for-one" principle, of which the prisoners had already been informed. Ten prisoners were to be executed in retribution for anyone escaping. Ten men from the detail were selected at random and executed by firing squad. It is not known if Wickord witnessed the execution, but he was shown the grave site and told to warn his men. Later all prisoners were divided into permanent groups of ten, known as "blood brothers," all of whom would be executed if any one of them attempted to escape. This proved to be very effective dissuasion. The American commanders and men stayed alert for anyone showing signs of being a potential escaper—usually they were "crazy" in other ways—and got them moved out of their groups, often into whatever passed as a hospital.

The Japanese Army built bridges without power equipment, using hand tools only. This was impressive enough that at least two survivors, including Al Allen, described the procedure in their postwar interviews. The beams were solid mahogany with tongue-in-groove connections. The beam shore ends were typically given Japanese inscriptions and decorations by Japanese cabinetmakers at the sawmill. Concrete was mixed on sheets of steel about four feet by eight feet, and lifted and poured by hand—there were no mixers. The hardest part was hand-driving piles into the center of the streams. This took a great deal of teamwork—ichi, ni, san (one, two, three)—as the piles were lifted vertically and pushed onto those below it. This work was given to the Americans, whose height should have helped them but whose weakness slowed them so much that senior Japanese engineers came from Manila to speed them up. After stops to repair several other small bridges, the work was finally finished, and in September 1942 Wickord's detachment was taken to Cabanatuan, which most of his men had never seen. FitzPatrick observed that conditions were terrible, with walking skeletons eerily like those he had left at

O'Donnell, but that the PTG men were still sticking together, which he attributed to the discipline imposed by his old boss Lieutenant Colonel Miller, the senior tanker present.

Work details were drawn from Cabanatuan for other projects, not only on Luzon but on other islands, such as Palawan and Mindanao. Some of those on Luzon, such as the garage, truck driving, and the Manila port details, were considered cushy; others, such as those building runways in southern Luzon, were considered death details. Not only was the work extremely hard—leveling rice paddy dikes at one field by pick and shovel took over a year—but the Japanese at these locations were more vicious than elsewhere. The airfields belonged to the Japanese Navy, whose officers knew full well how badly the war was going. The guards were enlisted men from garrison units and had either been wounded in action or disqualified from front-line units owing to other disabilities, primarily mental. Glenn Oliver summarized this group as "small, mean, unpredictable, irrational, perverts." This work was never completed, and Oliver was transferred to Bilibid in September 1944 for transfer to Japan. Cabanatuan itself was emptying out, as the Japanese attempted to move all mobile American prisoners out of the Philippines prior to the arrival of the Americans.

Camp Cabanatuan

The city of Cabanatuan is located one hundred miles north of Manila in Luzon's central plain. The camp given its name was built just before the war for one of the Philippine Army's reserve divisions. It comprised three sites, one for each regiment. Each contained several wooden buildings and some sixty-foot-long, nipa-thatched, sawali-sided barracks that would accommodate 120 POWs. The Japanese surrounded each site with a hard-packed dirt road, eight-foot-high barbed-wire fencing, and four-story-high guard towers. Camp #1 began receiving Camp O'Donnell's American wretches on June 1, and soon had them all—the Filipinos stayed at O'Donnell until they were released in late 1942. Prisoners from Corregidor and Bataan's hospitals began arriving at Cabanatuan in late May and were first placed in Camp #3 before being moved into Camp #1. Camp #2, which had no water supply, became the Japanese headquarters and guard barracks.

Camp #1, soon called simply "Camp Cabanatuan," became the largest POW camp in the Philippines. It at first offered no improvement over O'Donnell other than its sheer size (600 by 800 yards), a regular water supply, and somewhat better food, which could be prepared in permanent messes. A hospital was established in one of the wooden buildings, separated into dysentery, communicable disease, and "St. Peter's" or "Zero" wards, the latter for those about to die. The Japanese would not supply lifesaving medications such as quinine, emetine, and sulfa tablets, and their policy seemed to be one of "malign neglect," in author Hampton Sides's words, until the value of the prisoners as slave labor became evident. Some medication was smuggled in, and more was obtained from the medics from Corregidor, who had not undergone the extensive shakedowns of the Death March. Most men were ill; the main problem was their inadequate diet. Some new vitamin deficiency diseases made their appearance at Cabanatuan. Ernie Miller recorded in his diary that the most serious medical problems at the time were pellagra, scurvy, blindness, eye ulcers, pneumonia, tuberculosis, genital itch, worms, and diphtheria. The death rate continued high—503 died in June, 786 in July—before peaking and dropping off. The doctors noted a frequent cause of death as inanition, defined as a lack of mental vigor and enthusiasm. December 1, 1942, was the first day with no deaths, and was celebrated in the hospital.

Camp Cabanatuan was large enough to separate the enlisted men's berthing areas from those of the officers. The ratio of enlisted men to officers was five to one, much smaller than that of the army as a whole. There were eventually 3,000 officers. Many had been former commanders of Philippine Scouts units and advisors to Philippine Army units. The Japanese normally did not require commissioned POWs to work, and a daily walk around the camp boundaries was the only exercise many of them got. This caused much tension, which was exacerbated when in a slight bow toward the Geneva Conventions the Japanese began paying the prisoners. Lieutenant colonels such as Ernie Miller received 220 pesos per month; lieutenants received 85; and privates received 3 if they were working, but nothing if they were not. Food was always available for money, but enlisted men could not survive on what they were paid. Welfare funds to which the officers donated were set up for the enlisted men, but there was never an even distribution of money and thus food, and an officer's chance of surviving the camp was much greater than that of an enlisted man.

The enlisted men grumbled about the favored treatment their officers received, but this did not lead to the revolt that might have taken place in Vietnam's fragging era. The Depression generation had been reared to respect the upper classes, and muttering was as far as their opposition went. Some officers did maintain a high reputation for leadership. Ernie Miller tried to buck up the tankers' spirits, even though he was isolated in the colonels' barracks and had no direct responsibility for the men. He was shipped to Japan as early as November 1942, and Bernard FitzPatrick recorded that the men of his battalion lined up to shake his hand. One of them pressed a can of sardines into Miller's hand and died of starvation a few weeks later. Respect was also shown to three West Point engineers who with no help from the Japanese designed, dug, and built a complete sanitation system to replace the open, festering latrines serving 6,000 men. FitzPatrick noted seeing these officers grinning broadly while up to their necks in shit. The system was completed in mid-December and contributed greatly to the decreased death rate.

Forrest Knox seems to have been the most introspective of all the surviving tankers. By Cabanatuan he had given much thought into what it would take to survive, in addition to blind luck. Self-pity was always fatal. Most important was a strong philosophy, a reason to live. This was not necessarily religion. To Forrest, an atheist, "hatred" was sufficient. Next, native intelligence was important, but not sufficient, as was physical strength. He tried not to attract attention to himself, to plan carefully, and to conserve his energy. Consideration of others was good, but not at the expense of one's own chances of survival. Al Allen included a sense of humor on his own list, as he felt that no one without one survived. This may sound strange, but it was healthful to see the antics of the guards as humorous, even if painful, rather than wasting energy trying to assign a rational purpose to them.

Men with a will to live tended to group together for self-protection in what Forrest called sub-tribes. He felt three to five men worked best. When men left on work details, at least one had to be available to guard their belongings, the most valuable of which was *quan*, their joint pot containing anything edible that could supplement the Japanese ration. Protein was highly prized, and quan frequently included rats. Sometimes lives were saved by one-on-one friendship. Bud Bardowski had lived with the officers since Corregidor—the reason why is lost to history. He caught an officer rifling his belongings, beat him up, and was thrown into the nut ward by the barracks commander, an American colonel. There he would have died but for a 192nd Battalion medic in the ward who recognized him and talked an American psychiatrist into declaring him cured and releasing him to the enlisted men's barracks. Bardowski never forgot this entirely, although the details became hazy with time. He returned the favor when he found Jim Bashleben in the Zero ward, where he had been placed after returning from the bridge detail very weak with dysentery. Bud offered Jim two sulfa pills from an unknown source. Bashleben did not ingest them, but returned them to Bardowski, who gave them to someone else. Bashleben credited Bud with saving his life simply by improving his mood with the unselfish gift; the two Maywood Company men remained friends for life.

Ben Morin arrived at the camp from Tarlac on June 12 with his tank crew and several other early POWs. Morin, who had been taken prisoner on December 22, had missed the entire Bataan campaign, the subsequent Death March, and Camp O'Donnell. He was shocked not only by the physical condition of the Bataan survivors, but by the general breakdown of authority. He noted mistrust, selfishness, whining, and complaining by the American soldiers "and some of the officers," but welcomed the gift of a blanket. Since his capture his only kit had been the clothes on his back, his cavalry boots, a rag for a towel, and a burlap bag.

All enlisted men were expected to work—if they didn't, their rations were cut in half and their pay was cut entirely. They were assigned to work details at morning roll call. Some were within the camp—burial detail, building cleanup, cooking and KP, and so forth—and some were outside, such as the bridge building, driving, and airfield construction (discussed earlier). The detail needing the most labor was the farm, 300 acres of garden requiring as many as 2,500 men. It grew beans, carrots, peppers, corn, onions, radishes, eggplant, okra, cassava, sweet potatoes, and squash, in quantities adequate to maintain the prisoners' health. But the Japanese took the produce for themselves, for their own mess, to feed their animals, and to trade with the Filipinos. All that the Americans got were the tops of the root vegetables, which went into their daily soup. Most prisoners felt that the farm detail was the worst of any, and turnover was very high. Workdays under the tropical sun were long and enervating. All work was by hand, with Filipino-size tools. The men were required to remain stooped over with their heads lower than their rear ends, and anyone raising his head was beaten; the farm guards, who were assigned permanently, were the most sadistic and slow-witted of all those at Cabanatuan. Their tempers were probably shortened by the same constant tropical sun that weakened the prisoners. Forrest Knox felt that the only decent job on the farm was pollinating, which he called "flower fucking." The Cabanatuan area lacked bees, and the prisoners were required to crawl among the vegetable plants pressing the flowers' pistils into the stamens of adjacent plants before moving along. The pollination guards chose not to carry clubs, which Forrest appreciated.

The Japanese made some minor, low-cost gestures toward keeping the morale of the prisoners up. A small glee club was allowed. Bernard FitzPatrick heard it sing soon after his arrival at Cabanatuan, joined it, and on October 1, 1942, took it over. He found a way to arrange and copy sheet music and obtained musical instruments from the nearby city with the aid of a priest. Musical groups soon flourished; these included the Dysentery Quartet and the Cabanatuan Cats, a big band. Before Bernard left in July 1944, he had produced Shakespeare plays, Broadway shows, and Christmas mass.

At the end of 1942, the Japanese allowed the distribution of one Red Cross package per prisoner. These were eight-pound boxes of condensed food and sweets that had been rifled by the Japanese but were essentially complete. There were British Christmas boxes and Canadian New Year's boxes, whose contents varied somewhat, giving the men trading material for weeks. These packages were lifesaving, not only for their nutritional content but for their effect on morale. This was the first indication that anyone else in the world knew or cared of their existence, and it did not matter that these people were British and Canadian instead of American.

Cabanatuan was always intended as a source of labor for other camps. These were primarily on Luzon, but contingents were also shipped to the large southern islands of Mindanao and Palawan. Beginning in July, 1,942 men were sent from Manila to Davao on Mindanao by interisland steamer. Tankers included Maj. John Morley from the PTG HQ, Maj. Charles Canby from the 194th Battalion HQ, Capt. Bill Gentry of C/192TB, and Pvt. Roy Diaz of C/194TB. The men were sent to the Davao Penal Colony, which had been the main Philippine civilian prison. The 2,200 men already there included those who had surrendered on Mindanao. The farm was intended to supply the Japanese Army with lumber, hemp, coffee, and rice. It is not known if Morley and Canby had supervisory roles, but Bill Gentry was given command of the rice plantation. Although he had grown up on a Harrodsburg farm, rice was not a Kentucky crop, and Bill knew nothing about it. He had written "agriculture—general" on his interrogation form, and the Japanese assumed that meant he was a high-level supervisor. He succeeded at this job well enough to keep it and was proud that while his men met all production quotas, they sabotaged every shipment, as well as every spool of hemp rope, which also wound up under Gentry's supervision.

Gentry was USAAF Maj. Ed Dyess's bunkmate and was offered a chance to join him on his famous escape, but turned him down owing to his other responsibilities. Dyess and nine other Americans escaped on April 4, 1943. Everyone knew of the Japanese ten-for-one policy, and Gentry expected one hundred of his men to be executed, but all that the men lost were their privileges. Dyess reached the United States and described for the first time what immediately became known as the Bataan Death March, giving the PTG families who had heard nothing from their tankers one more thing to worry about. The farm was shut down in June 1944, and the men were sent back to Luzon. Gentry suffered his first attack of dysentery at this time and remained at Cabanatuan while the rest of the men went to Bilibid for further shipment to Japan. Gentry's illness could well have saved his life. Although Roy Diaz survived his trip to Japan, Morley, Canby, and many of the enlisted men from Davao died on Japanese prison ships.

In 1943 a number of prisoners were brought from Cabanatuan to Palawan Island to build an airfield. This was slave labor at its worst—pick and shovel work under brutal guards who disciplined the men with pick handles. B-24s bombed the field on October 19 and 28, 1944, after which the men were ordered to build what was described as air raid shelters—three covered trenches five feet deep, four feet wide, and long enough for fifty men. These were to have only one entrance until an American officer insisted on two, one at each end. At this time there were 150 men in the camp, including five tankers. The senior American was Capt. Fred Bruni, who had commanded the 192nd Battalion Headquarters Company. He had the impossible job of enforcing the orders of one of the most irrational Japanese camp commanders. His technique of placating his captors could be questioned. The survivors recalled that when the prisoners finally received Red Cross packages, Bruni shared them with the Japanese.

On December 13 an American convoy entered the Sulu Sea, headed for Mindoro. Captain Kojima, the Japanese commander, believed an invasion of Palawan was imminent. He had received a written "Kill-All" order that no prisoners were to be retaken alive:

When the battle situation becomes urgent the POWs will be concentrated and confined in their location and kept under heavy guard until preparations for the final disposition will be made. Although the basic aim is to operate under superior orders, individual disposition may be made in certain circumstances. Whether they are destroyed individually or in groups, and whether it is accomplished by means of mass bombing, poisonous smoke, poisons, drowning, or decapitation, dispose of them as the situation dictates. It is the aim not to allow the escape of a single man, to annihilate them all, and not to leave any traces.

Captain Kojima ordered the POWs to be awakened at 2 a.m. They were told work would start at dawn and stop at noon. After two small P-38 overflights, a large incoming raid was reported and the men were ordered into the shelters. Fifty or sixty Japanese arrived with light machine guns, rifles, and gasoline. They threw lighted torches into the shelters, followed by gasoline. Men running in flames from the shelters were shot down by the machine guns or bayoneted. Incredibly, eleven survived (none from the PTG) and were rescued by guerillas. Word of the massacre quickly reached MacArthur, who immediately ordered that an attempt be made to rescue the prisoners known to be at Cabanatuan and Bilibid.

On January 27, 1945, General Krueger ordered Col. Henry Mucci to lead part of the 6th Ranger Battalion thirty miles behind the Japanese lines to rescue the Cabanatuan POWs. Details are beyond the scope of this book, but this was the war's most successful Ranger raid. Five hundred fifty-two POWs, including twenty-one tankers, were rescued on January 30 at a cost of two Rangers and two POWs KIA and four Rangers and twenty-one Filipinos WIA. Bill Gentry, one of the men freed, had been told by a guard on the previous day that the massacre of the prisoners was only days away. The similar but less well-known raid on Manila's Bilibid Prison on February 4 rescued Fred Moffitt, the former commander of C/194TB, and twenty more tankers.

CHAPTER 9

The Home Front

THE AMERICAN CIVILIAN POPULATION RESPONDED DURING WORLD WAR II as it never has to any emergency before or since. Everyone participated in the war effort. The first economy-related civilian sacrifice came on December 11, 1941, when tire sales were stopped. Rationing began on January 5, 1942, under the control of the Office of Price Administration (OPA) and its unpaid three-man volunteer boards. The OPA was subordinated to the War Production Board (WPB) when this was established on January 16. Under chairman Donald M. Nelson it comprised the Secretaries of War, the Navy, and Agriculture; the lieutenant general in charge of War Department procurement; the OPA director, the federal loan administrator, and others, and by all accounts was one of the most efficient government agencies in history. Its main task was converting civilian industry to war production by assigning priorities and finding raw materials. New car sales were stopped on January 1, 1942, typewriters in March, and bicycles in May. No metal civilian goods were produced after June. Food ration books were ready by May, and gasoline cards later that month, issued only to those certifying need. During the war the WPB supervised the purchase of $183 billion in weapons and supplies, 40 percent of the world's output of munitions.

Citizens of the six towns that had sent their men to the Philippines participated in the rationing program, planted victory gardens, and bought war bonds, as did all their neighboring towns, but they saw their sacrifices as far greater. They could get very little information on the fates of their tankers and the course of the war in the Philippines. A few family members received brief radiograms postmarked Fort Stotsenburg—possibly from Bill Gentry's radio shack—but these ended when the fort was abandoned to the Japanese on Christmas Day 1941. The parents of Pvt. Elmer Blonien of the Janesville Company received a cablegram on December 22 stating that he was "fine," and that the weather was "fine except for the constant hail," a clever way of evading the censors with a reference to Japanese air raids. In August 1942 families in Janesville received surface mail letters written in March. That same month some Brainerd families got mail posted shortly before the surrender and found floating in a mailbag from a sunken ship. The men attempted to remain optimistic in their letters while hinting at the drastic lack of supplies, especially food. The communiqués from USAFFE kept everyone informed of MacArthur's activities, but rarely mentioned the fighting men themselves. Reports from war correspondents varied in quality, but tended to parrot the official jingoistic line, and most of these men left Bataan for Corregidor and then exited the war zone before the campaign ended. Frank Hewlett of the AP was an exception; he stayed on Bataan until just before the surrender, and his colorful articles named names. His interview of Bill Gentry and description of the battle of Baliuag, the PTG's greatest victory, brought great cheer to the tankers' families, but news most often came in the form of government telegrams and was not pleasant. Herbert Strobel's family got word of his death, the first in the Brainerd Tank Company, on December 26. The wife of the Janesville Company commander, Walter Write, received news of his death on January 21 at a baby shower for John Bushaw's wife.

Such official communications were rare—PTG combat deaths were in fact relatively few—but the tank company women could not assume that no news was, in fact, good news. They began meeting as early as January 1942 to bolster one another's spirits, trade news and rumors, and do whatever they could for their men in the Philippines. This was little enough, but the women scheduled regular meetings and began doing useful work such as donating blood; sewing, knitting, and packing relief boxes for the Red Cross; and carrying on child welfare work. The groups originally took various names: Janesville's was the Tank Company Auxiliary; Port Clinton's the Service Mothers Club; Salinas's the Bataan Mothers Club. Maywood's group took a formal turn early; on March 29 the American Bataan Clan (ABC) was established with Sgt. Roger Heilig's mother Viola as president. In April it was chartered as a charitable organization under the laws of Illinois. Membership was limited at first to female relatives of B/192TB members, but was broadened to men, and after the surrender, to the relatives of everyone on Bataan. Its best-known activity was selling war bonds at the Lido Theater. Other fund-raisers fed a savings account to be given the veterans on their return.

The only National Guard unit in the Philippines other than the PTG was the 200th Coast Artillery Regiment (AA), which contained most of the New Mexico National Guard, 1,800 men. The Bataan Relief Organization (BRO) was formed in New Mexico in March to demand action in the Pacific and incorporated in April just after the surrender on Bataan "to obtain immediate relief for all Americans held as Japanese POWs, their release as soon as possible, and their safe delivery home—we will not let them down." From the beginning it was more a pressure group than a service group, sending lobbyists to Washington to talk to Congress and the War Department. The highly organized Maywood ABC absorbed the other three midwestern tanker's mothers' groups and, as the war went on, joined the BRO in its pressure on Washington, with no obvious result.

Salinas differed from the other five tank company towns in that it was in a war zone. A Japanese air raid was reported on San Francisco on December 8, 1941, and although this was a false alarm, as were many to follow, the commanding general of the Western Defense Command began arguing for the complete expulsion of all Japanese and Japanese Americans from the three West Coast states. The War Department agreed, and on February 19 President Roosevelt signed Executive Order 9066 authorizing the Secretary of War to designate certain areas as military zones, from which any and all persons could be excluded. Public Law 503 quickly followed; this made violation of military orders civilian misdemeanors punishable by $5,000 in fines and one year in prison. Evacuation of the Japanese began immediately.

Salinas and Monterey County paid important roles in the expulsion. The first raid on suspected aliens was conducted on February 10, 1942. The San Francisco FBI agent in charge led fifty-two agents and seventy-two highway patrolmen, sheriff's officers, and policemen in raids on five

Monterey County towns, including Salinas. They took thirty-seven people into custody, including the "Emperor of Chuilar," a foreman on the Spiegel lettuce ranch whose workers were called by the FBI agent the "mystery colony of the West Coast." Three Buddhist priests were arrested, including a former Tokyo police chief. The contraband seized included radios, knives, cameras, binoculars, guns and ammunition, and one bow and seven arrows. This raid received massive nation-wide media coverage, but there were no repeat raids in Monterey County. The rest of the area's Japanese and Japanese Americans went into custody peacefully, beginning on February 20, when a field agent of the wartime farm adjustment program began duties in Salinas to assist in the voluntary evacuation of Japanese farmers in the area.

On April 27 the Salinas Assembly Center opened on the site of the Salinas Rodeo Grounds, one of seventeen such centers on the West Coast. Eventually 3,608 people were held there, mostly from Monterey County. The center closed on July 4, after most of its evacuees were sent to the Poston concentration camp in Arizona. After serving as the site of an overflow barracks for Fort Ord, the rodeo grounds returned to its earlier use after the war and is now the Salinas Sports Complex.

For the most part the tank company towns shared in the general prosperity brought by the war. Companies in the industrial North and Midwest were quick to convert to military production under the guidance of the War Production Board, and new factories sprang up to join them. Workers left to join the armed forces just as requirements for skilled labor increased sharply, but labor was supplied by trainable women, including relatives of tank company men, and by African Americans, who were hired by companies in the North while still barred from those in the South.

Janesville had its old General Motors plant and its world-scale Parker Pen Company, which produced a number of small military items in its own factory and volunteered to lease an empty building and manufacture artillery fuses there around the clock, selling them to the government at cost. Several members of the Tank Company Auxiliary went to work in war plants, and the patriotism of some went farther. Five joined the WACs, and a sixth the WAVEs.

Maywood was now a suburb of Chicago, surrounded by other suburbs, but had its own American Can Company plant, which produced containers in the millions for the government, and a new company that took over the old armory to build medical devices for the U.S. Army. The town was also well served by public transportation to other plants in the Chicago area, including the 125-acre Buick factory in adjacent Melrose Park, which built nearly 75,000 Pratt & Whitney aircraft engines, primarily for B-24 bombers under construction at Ford's Willow Run Plant.

Port Clinton was a small town, but its Matthews Boat Company, an important part of the local economy from 1906 to 1974 for its high-end pleasure boats, built patrol boats during the war. The Standard Products Company converted from making automobile window trim moldings to M1 carbines, and employed as many as fourteen Bataan relatives at one point.

Brainerd remained a railroad town, and the Northern Pacific built a factory 916 feet long to manufacture freight cars and enlarged a shop to preserve railroad ties with oil and creosote. This latter shop closed in 1986 and is now a Superfund site.

Prosperity was harder to come by in Harrodsburg and Mercer County. Mercer is an agricultural county in an agricultural state, and although farm income more than doubled in the South during the war, this success was the result of consolidation and mechanization, neither of which came easy in Mercer County, which saw the size of its farms actually decrease. Local farming still used nineteenth-century technology requiring large families. As young men left the farms for the service, their places were taken in part by tankers' wives, who moved in with their parents or in-laws. The only other farm workers available were a few German POWs furloughed from the nearby Darnell General Hospital, which also hired a few of the tankers' wives. Very few of the tankers' wives and sweethearts left town to find factory work or join the military; this was too detrimental to their reputations as Southern women. Only two are known to have found war production jobs in Louisville, and these were only temporary. Harrodsburg's largest employer was Sportleigh Hall, for which 450 workers manufactured women's sport coats. The town did not attract any military plants. Kentucky had WPB-authorized war production plants in only 39 of its 120 counties, none in Mercer County.

Salinas boomed during the war, which saw Monterey County agriculture burgeon into a multi-million-dollar business. Its political strength gave it incentives unavailable to Harrodsburg. When the Spreckels Sugar Company was forced to shut down its Salinas sugar (beet) mill—America's largest—temporarily in August 1942 owing to a shortage of harvest labor, the U.S. government responded quickly with the bracero program, which allowed millions of Mexican migrants into the country for agricultural labor under decent, guaranteed living conditions. The program ended in 1964, but the problems of undocumented migrant labor that it generated continue well into the twenty-first century.

In March 1943 Ellis Spiegel, a prominent Salinas grower and shipper, announced plans for a mammoth half-million-dollar food dehydrating plant to process cabbages and carrots. This was to be self-financed and employ 900. The plant—double the size of anything similar in the world—was in full production by the end of August and reduced 700,000 pounds of carrots per day to 70,000 pounds of concentrated food for the military. It is not known if any members of tankers' families found jobs on the production line, but work to benefit the war effort was widely available in Salinas.

The surrender of Bataan (April 8, 1942, in the United States) hit the tank company towns hard. The six towns lost more men missing in action in a single day than any other cities of their size in the country, a distinction that lasted for the rest of the war. News of the tankers' fates was agonizingly slow to arrive. On April 17 the War Department announced the loss of sixteen top-ranking officers, including General Weaver. His parents got the news on their fifty-fifth wedding anniversary. On April 22 Washington stated that Weaver's men were all prisoners, although there was no confirmation of this from the Japanese, and they were officially "missing in action." The towns assuaged their grief to some extent with a quick increase in patriotic activities. Maywood's American Bataan Clan showed a film, *Remember Manila*, at Proviso High School, with benefits going to the International Red Cross in Geneva. The town's "Proviso Day" on April 30 registered 116 donors at the American Red Cross blood center. Port Clinton held a misnamed "Get 'Em Out of Bataan" bond rally and parade on May 1.

On May 18 General Marshall, the U.S. Army Chief of Staff, wrote the governor of Ohio,

> *I regret to advise that it now appears certain that the officers and enlisted men of Company C, 192nd Tank Battalion are prisoners of war. Under the Geneva Convention lists of prisoners are exchanged by belligerents and as soon as such a list is received, it will be made public with other available information.*
>
> *The National Guard unit of your state served as part of a provisional tank group throughout the Philippine campaign. The citizen-soldiers of this company manned some of the small force of tanks which contributed so much to our prolonged resistance on Bataan. The skill, heroism and devotion of these men will be a source of pride to every American, and a great morale force for our new Army.*
>
> *The War Department has felt that probably the most convincing evidence of the determination of our people has been the courage and fortitude with which the relatives of these men have endured the tragic uncertainty as to the fate of their sons and husbands on Bataan.*
>
> *The inspiring example of these citizen-soldiers will hasten the day when peace will be won, and then we can all unite in welcoming back to the country these men who have done so much to make us proud of them.*

The governors of the other five tank company states undoubtedly received similar letters.

The largest commemoration in the period immediately after the Bataan surrender was in Harrodsburg, which on June 16 recognized the sacrifice of sixty-six D/192TB men on Bataan while simultaneously celebrating the town's 168th anniversary and the 150th anniversary of Kentucky statehood with a parade and luncheon. M/Gen. Jacob L. Devers, commander of the Armored Force, arrived from nearby Fort Knox with seventeen tanks, ignoring protests that this was a frivolous use of military resources. A speech by the governor, which praised "Billy" Gentry by name and mistakenly attributed his victory to Harrodsburg tanks, went well, but that of General Devers did not. The newspaper reporter stated bluntly, "The crowd listened grimly to his remarks and did not applaud. Their heroes are 8,000 miles away, and their fate is unknown." The citizens of Harrodsburg apparently felt that the War Department and generals such as Devers bore the blame for their loss.

LIFE magazine put a patriotic gloss on this Harrodsburg ceremony in a seven-page article, "Missing in Action," timed for its July 6 American flag–cover edition. Photographs of many of D Company's families and missing men appeared; one father was posed next to Devers's tanks. *LIFE* exhorted the citizens of America to prepare to make the sacrifices already exhibited by the National Guard towns. These citizens understood this and early in the war were predisposed toward sympathy. Support extended to popular culture; the popular song "We're Going Back, Back to Bataan" was published in 1943 with a dedication to "The American Bataan Clan, Maywood, Illinois."

Maywood made big plans for its own Bataan Day. The all-day ceremony featured a drum and bugle corps contest, the unveiling of a huge B/192TB photomural in the Lido Theater lobby, and a war bond rally. A three-hour parade containing twenty-five floats was organized by the Veterans Council, a joint American Legion–Veterans of Foreign Wars group. The reviewing stands contained families of the captured men, the Illinois governor, one senator, and Lt. Emmett Gibson, who had become a Chicago celebrity since his return from the Philippines. Bataan Day was held on September 12, a date of no special relevance for its tank company, but the earliest that the town could prepare the ceremony. Bataan Day has been held in Illinois ever since on the second Sunday in September and was declared a holiday by an act of Congress. Janesville and Port Clinton chose dates in late October for their own Bataan Days, commemorating the date in 1941 on which the 192nd Tank Battalion left San Francisco for the Philippines.

On July 20 the Salinas Chamber of Commerce joined the San Francisco press club in a campaign to send a shipload of relief supplies to the Bataan prisoners. The American Red Cross chartered the Swedish cargo ship *Kanangoora* to carry useful loads of relief supplies on a shuttle service to Manila. The Red Cross stated that they would give this a high priority, "over aid to starving countries." The ship was to be painted white with red crosses. A carload of Salinas lettuce was auctioned off by New York mayor Fiorello LaGuardia, raising $3,000 for non-perishable supplies. The *Kanangoora* made it as far as San Francisco, where it sat awaiting a safe-conduct pass from the Japanese, which was denied. The ship was downloaded in September.

The Japanese were agreeable to an exchange of diplomats and other foreign nationals, and the United States chartered the Swedish motor ship *Gripsholm*, a 1925 luxury cruise ship, for this purpose. The *Gripsholm* arrived in New York to load Japanese diplomats and 300 tons of food, clothing, tobacco, and medicines. Its departure was delayed until September 1943 by the Allied invasion of North Africa and an obvious lack of priority given the operation by the United States, which meant last-minute changes could be made to the relief packages to include more meat, clothing, and drugs, based on escapee reports. The *Gripsholm* made two trips to the Far East, and other shipments of Red Cross packages reached Japan via Vladivostok. Distribution of these parcels was wildly uneven. Most prisoners saw at least parts of one, and others received several; all considered them lifesavers and high points of their time in captivity.

Japan began releasing lists of prisoners in September 1942, and the names of several hundred tankers had been dribbled out by December, when they stopped. Their resumption the next June included the first indication of deaths in the POW camps but was shortly followed by communications from the survivors themselves. Most were standard Red Cross postcards with a handful of items to be ticked off (e.g., my health is excellent, good, fair). The cards were uninformative except for the men's signatures, which were genuine and recognizable. In August 1943 Ann Miller got an actual letter from her husband in Zentsuji, Japan, informing her of the health of several of his officers. This was the first firsthand prisoner news to reach Brainerd.

Before the end of 1943, several men in Japan and Formosa were allowed to make shortwave radio broadcasts to the United States. Most were high-ranking officers—Molly Weaver got word from thirty-seven people who had heard her husband's—but did include some privates. These were scripted, of course, but were nevertheless highly informative. A ham operator told Pernina Burke, Ed Burke's wife, that the messages were recorded in the camps on a portable recorder, and the records were taken to Tokyo for broadcast by transcription. By the end of the war, the tank company families had received anywhere from a dozen messages from their men to none. A few men in the latter category showed up unexpectedly at home, or telephoned from the West Coast, but most were carried missing until the government had enough information to declare them dead.

In April 1943 the army pursuit pilot Capt. Ed Dyess escaped from the Davao, Mindanao, prison farm with nine other American POWs. They eventually reached Australia and were debriefed by the USAFFE staff. Dyess had survived the Death March and Camp O'Donnell, was already famous in the United States for his exploits in the campaign, and was personally chosen by MacArthur to reveal the horrible details of Japanese treatment of POWs to Washington and the American people. Dyess's fourteen-page official report stunned the War Department, but FDR forbade its release; some members of his administration feared that this would enrage the Japanese and they would retaliate by increasing their abuse of the remaining POWs. A frustrated Dyess negotiated a contract with the *Chicago Tribune* for a serialized memoir without revealing all the bloody details. There must have been leaks, however. Dyess was killed on December 22 while taking off on a fighter test flight, and three days later Albert C. MacArthur Sr., whose namesake had died at Cabanatuan the previous autumn and who was now president of Maywood's American Bataan Clan, told the Associated Press that the full story of Bataan should be told to the nation, that "someone in Washington made a costly mistake and wants to forget all about it." He declared that there existed a policy that demanded silence from those returned from the Philippines, and that Dyess, instead of being treated as a hero, had received a "strange reception" in Washington, being told that he "knew too much," and was cautioned against telling his story for publication.

Albert MacArthur was undoubtedly alluding to errors made by the War Department before and during the campaign, and not Japanese atrocities, but Washington bowed to the inevitable and cleared the story. On Sunday, January 28, 1944, the first chapter of "The Dyess Story" appeared on page one of the *Chicago Tribune* and one hundred associated newspapers, and the nation exploded. The tank company towns were furious not only at the Japanese but at their own government, which had withheld the story of their men's terrible mistreatment for a year and a half while the families were crying out for any kind of news. Maywood by now knew of thirteen B/192TB deaths in the prison camps, but not the details, and the father of S/Sgt. Robert Peterson was quoted: "The Japs should be exterminated to the last man."

The mayor of Salinas said, "The news of the inhuman treatment of Bataan and Corregidor prisoners confirms our worst fears. . . . The sufferings of our men must be avenged in the only manner that such savages understand." The president of the Salinas Bataan Club was too stunned to comment. Her predecessor, Mrs. S. A. Dolk, was ready, and declared,

We have been crucified anew. Many of us heard these things from Gripsholm repatriates and our only comfort is that conditions are believed to be better now. But the Japanese must never be permitted to return to California. Our men could not live on the same soil with these people.

Mrs. Agnes Below, the sister of Sgt. Elmer Smith and president of the Port Clinton Bataan Clan, was incensed enough to write Roosevelt and Stimson:

We . . . protest the withholding of information concerning Jap atrocities until this late date. It has been a grievous error to wait for a "psychological moment" before unloosening the screws on the lid of censorship. We gave our boys, and we had a right to know what was happening to them then, not twenty-one months later.

The letter added a demand for reinforcements for MacArthur "to free our boys as soon as possible" and is not known to have received a formal reply.

Harrodsburg took a more nuanced view of Japanese atrocities than the other towns. The mayor and the president of the Mercer County Board of Trade made a conventional reply: "The spirit of our people has not been crushed; our determination has only been increased." But the editor of the local weekly newspaper countered with: "They [the citizens] just don't believe a lot of it. They think the stories are just a lot of propaganda to help sell War Bonds." He felt that people were being made to suffer unnecessarily; the atrocity stories were old news, and letters had been received from many of the sixty-two known to be prisoners from the sixty-six who had left Harrodsburg.

However, the Harrodsburg families were moved enough by the Dyess revelations to establish the Mercer County Bataan Relief Organization, two years after the other tank company towns started their own clans. Mrs. Edwin Rue was elected president by acclamation. The group voted to model itself after New Mexico's Bataan Relief Organization (BRO) rather than the clans of the nearby 192nd Tank Battalion towns. This appears to be a snub, and one wonders if the Fort Knox barracks battles of the D/192TB "hillbillies" with the "town boys" of the other three 192nd Battalion companies had left some bad blood.

In February 1944 the founder and president of the BRO in New Mexico called for a conference in Washington, D.C., of thirty-seven organizations from fourteen states to demand aid for the men captured in the Philippines and more men and equipment for MacArthur. It is known that the Maywood, Port Clinton, and Salinas Bataan Clubs were represented at this meeting, at which the BRO claimed that the Senate and House committees on prisoner relief had never even held meetings. Any positive results from this conference are unknown. Roosevelt was asked to declare April 9, which was Easter Sunday, "National Bataan Day." He refused, but the governor of New Mexico did, and it was observed in churches nationwide.

By mid-1943 the question of when the Japanese Americans could be returned from concentration camps to their civilian homes was being debated coast to coast. Salinas had had more Japanese residents in proportion to population than any other U.S. city, most employed in lettuce field labor. The Salinas Chamber of Commerce voted 802 to 1 against permitting their return during the war. But in December 1944 the commanding general of the Western War Command announced that the incarceration centers would be closed down within a year and the internees returned home. The anti-Japanese hysteria of the war's early days returned, and the chairman of the California Committee on Japanese Problems stated that the return of Japanese would allow enemy aliens to be smuggled in by submarines from Tokyo and mingle with the natives. The chairman of the California Legislature's joint immigration committee noted, "It is the height of folly to move the Japanese back to a place like Salinas and expect the people to feel kindly toward them." Mrs. C. F. Lang, the president of the Bataan Mothers Club of Salinas, said resignedly, "What can we say when a hundred of our boys are still in the hands of the Japanese?"

The internees began returning to what was left of their homes in early 1945. A barrage of newspaper ads crossed over their heads. Four hundred and forty Monterey artists and intellectuals called for a welcoming attitude to the internees, while a committee headed by the president of the Salinas Grower Shipper Vegetable Association took out grim, anonymous ads predicting violence. It is possible that this was all part of a longstanding Monterey-Salinas feud. The Japanese return was for the most part quiet, although John Steinbeck, who belonged to the artist clique, moved to Mexico before the war's end, stating, "This isn't my country anymore."

News of MacArthur's return to the Philippines in October 1944 was greeted with joy in the tank company towns, who expected that the Bataan prisoners would soon be freed. News that the Japanese had evacuated the men from the Philippines had not been declassified. Family members had begun to receive messages with return addresses in Manchuria or Japan, but those who got no news had no way of knowing about the high casualties on this journey. U.S. Army raids on POW camps in the Philippines did free forty-two ill tankers; ten more were rescued by Filipino guerillas; and one enterprising escapee made it to China. These men began returning to the United States in late 1944. Sergeant McComas and PFC Lamkin, the first to reach Brainerd, slipped into town quietly, not knowing the reception they would receive. Those whose health and mental state would permit it were treated as heroes. Captain Gentry was greatly in demand for war bond drives. He was also a speaker on the Blue (radio) Network's coast-to-coast Memorial Day program from Harrodsburg, which was one of the media's favorite small Southern towns. The program also featured Maj. Bacon Moore (the first commander of the 192nd Tank Battalion), families of the dead and missing, the head of the local Red Cross chapter, a Western Union messenger, and "a small choir that had been organized to sing patriotic songs." The low-cost nature of the program speaks to the budget of either Harrodsburg or the Blue Network.

News of the atomic bombs made the end of the war seem inevitable. Mrs. Agnes Below, president of the Port Clinton Bataan Clan, wrote President Truman and the State Department in one of her last official tasks, requesting that before accepting the Japanese surrender they must demand that POWs be placed in the hands of the Swiss or the International Red Cross to avoid exposing them to the debris from atomic bombs. She had no way of knowing that there were POW camps in the proximity of both Hiroshima and Nagasaki, but the letter was extraordinarily well-informed. It was ignored; events were moving too rapidly to react, even if the U.S. government had assigned a high priority to the treatment of POWs.

August 15, 1945, brought the ceasefire. V-J Day would come soon and was expected to bring still more nationwide revelry. Harrodsburg still had forty-two men in POW camps. A newspaper reporter asked Mrs. Edwin Rue what she thought the town would do when the war came to an official end. Rue said, "Harrodsburg has suffered too much and too long to celebrate on V-J Day."

CHAPTER 10

Hell in the North

THE HELL SHIPS

The large number of men who surrendered during the first six months of the war—American, Australian, British, Canadian, Dutch, Filipino, Indian, Javanese—took the Japanese completely by surprise. It was soon decided to release the Asians and bring the rest north to Formosa, Manchuria, Korea, and Japan to labor in heavy industries and mines as soon as camps were prepared to receive them. The POWs were not assigned priority shipping value over any other kind of war material, but when ready for transfer were forced into the holds of any available ship, whatever its previous cargo. If the POWs were lucky, their ship had been used to transport Japanese troops, who had berthed on shelves built around the sides of the holds. The spacing was too narrow for Americans, but squeezing into these shelves was far better than curling up on the floor with animal feces, scrap metal, or coal or flour dust. The holds were always overcrowded as voyages began, with no room for the men to stretch or, in some cases, even to lie down, until removal of dead bodies made space. The only ventilation was through the overhead hatch, which could be closed at any time at the whim of the guards. The smell in the hold was unimaginably foul, and it was difficult even to breathe—low oxygen drove men on some ships insane. Food varied with the ship but was typically steamed rice lowered into the hold in buckets. Water was also lowered in buckets, and typically measured less than a cup per man per day. The sanitary facilities were the same buckets, which quickly overflowed with the men's feces and urine.

Men making the trip in 1942 could consider themselves fortunate if on a fast ship traveling alone; the trip from Manila to Takao, Formosa, took only two days. But by 1944 ships had to travel in convoy at the speed of the slowest ship and were subject to attack by both aircraft and submarines. The Japanese refused to identify the ships carrying POWs, known then and now as "Hell Ships," which were as vulnerable as any of the others in the convoy. Twenty-five of these ships, carrying 18,901 POWs, were sunk by the Allies; 10,853 prisoners, including 3,632 Americans, died when they went down. In addition 1,635 Americans died on the ships themselves or shortly after their arrival at a northern port, in many cases dressed only in g-strings. The tankers of the PTG, who had long before been split into small groups, began the journey on twenty-two ships, four of which were sunk en route.

The first ship to leave Manila with northbound prisoners was the *Nagara Maru*, a clean, new freighter that took Wainwright, King, and 200 other high-ranking Americans from Tarlac to Takao and then to Karenko, Formosa, arriving on August 15, 1942. It is possible that the senior officers were the first moved from the Philippines because the Japanese feared their influence on their juniors. Wainwright and King shared a cabin on the main deck. The other men, including General Weaver, shared the hold. Weaver did not record his impressions of this trip. The only member of the PTG that he would see for the next three years was his orderly, Cpl. Daniel Nugent. Karenko was a model camp, known as the "generals' camp," which the Japanese apparently intended to milk for its propaganda value, although images of an emaciated Wainwright tending to his garden could not have helped much.

Two months later an old coal-burning tramp steamer, the *Tottori Maru*, was loaded in Manila with prisoners for the northern labor camps; 1,961 men were shoved into the two holds—500 in the front, 1,461 in the rear. Many were National Guard enlisted men: New Mexicans from the 200th Coast Artillery Regiment (AA) and tankers from the PTG. The latter included Al Allen, Walter Cigoi, and John Rowland. The ship left on October 8, 1942, and arrived in Formosa three days later. Several ill men were put ashore, including Cigoi, who died there. After plowing through a typhoon and evading submarine torpedoes, the *Tottori Maru* eventually reached Pusan, Korea, where the men were allowed to bathe, and half were put on a train for Mukden, Manchuria. The rest were deposited in Osaka, Japan, on November 11. Eleven men are believed to have died on the voyage, among them three tankers.

On November 1, 1942, an announcement was made in Cabanatuan that a detachment of 1,500 skilled men was being formed for transfer to an undisclosed location. Some officers, such as Miller and Wickord, were assigned. Men with specific skills were identified from their questionnaires, and volunteers were also accepted; Arnold Lawson recalled that several D/192TB men who had stuck together decided that Cabanatuan was not going to get any better and signed up. An all-day trip was made in the tiny closed Philippine boxcars; Ben Morin, who had missed the rail trip that ended the Death March, recalled this day as one of his worst as a POW. The men reached Manila, were marched to Pier 7 (where they had arrived from the United States the previous year), and were told that they would be going to Japan. Eighteen hundred men were loaded into the holds of an old freighter, the *Nagato Maru*. The ship already held scrap metal in the forward and rear holds. The most recent cargo in the middle hold had been horses, and the residual straw and horse manure made it the most comfortable of the three; its smell was quickly overpowered by that of the men's own vomit and excrement, while the sharp metal pieces in the other two made it impossible for the men to get comfortable for the entire trip. The ship left Manila on November 7, docked twice in Formosa, leaving Richard Danca there to die, and reached Moji, Japan, in freezing weather on November 24. The shivering men in their cotton clothing remnants were split up; Miller's group went to Tanagawa, and Wickord's to Osaka. Apparently only seven men died en route, which Lawson attributed to the speed of the trip, but some of the ill men froze on the docks and were never seen again. Miller's group did not receive winter clothing and overcoats until December 11 and were not allowed to bathe their lousy bodies until December 26.

The next two Hell Ships left Manila in the summer of 1943. Lester Tenney was among 500 prisoners on the *Clyde Maru*; this is known from the surviving roster. The men nicknamed the skipper "Big Speedo" and were apparently fed and treated well. The ship was laid out as were the others, but according to Tenney the hold was spacious and well-lit enough for a continuous craps game, for which he served as the house until a skilled gambler won all the money. This may or may not be true, as much of what Tenney said after the war fails to check out (for example, the name and sailing date of the Hell Ship that he names in his memoir are incorrect). The POWs suffered no casualties. This can't be said of the other 1943 Hell Ship, the *Taga Maru*, which carried 850 men, including some tankers, to Moji. The ship arrived safely, but seventy POWs died, primarily for lack of water. The submarine USS *Sargo* sank the *Taga Maru* with a full load of prisoners on its next trip.

Shipments of American POWs to Japan accelerated as U.S. forces approached the Philippines in late 1944. The Japanese took extreme measures to prevent their prisoners from being liberated. Between September and December too many men were put on too few ships. Convoys were now necessary to make the best use of the weak Japanese anti-submarine forces, and the unmarked Hell Ships had to join them. But there were few major shipping lanes between the Philippines, Formosa, and Japan, and the American submarines lay in wait there, with disastrous results for the POWs.

The next freighter to leave Manila with tankers among its load of POWs was the *Canadian Inventor*. At 8,100 tons it was the largest ship in the Japanese merchant marine, with a nominal top speed of 13 knots, but it was a mechanical wreck. It left Manila on July 2, 1944, with a load of 1,100 POWs, including tankers Jim Bashleben and Roy Diaz, but was forced to return on July 4 with boiler problems and did not leave again until July 16. The ship stopped twice in Formosa with mechanical issues and did not reach Moji until September 1, where the POWs were split up and sent to three Japanese camps. Only six prisoners died on the trip, none tankers. The reason for this high survival rate is not clear from the survivors' interviews, but it could have been simply good ventilation from the ship's shoddy construction, or an unusually compassionate set of guards.

Next was the *Nissyo Maru*, a 6,527-ton passenger-cargo steam ship with a top speed of 15 knots. Built in 1939, it was practically new, but the POWs called it a "dilapidated, rusty hulk." On July 17, 1,600 prisoners, including tankers Bud Bardowski and Bernard FitzPatrick, were crammed aboard the ship, which pulled out into Manila Bay and dropped anchor for a week. The hold thus became unbearably hot before the journey even began. The food on this ship, steamed barley, was better than average, but the heat, thirst, and shortage of oxygen drove men insane. One case of vampirism was recorded, and men drank each other's urine. The men were crammed on the deck of the hold, with little room to lie down, and Preston Hubbard of the Signal Corps had nightmares for forty years of the coating of semi-solid waste on the deck, "a mix of bloody, dysentery-induced diarrhea, urine, vomit, and rainwater covering everything like a thick beige soup." Several ships in its convoy were sunk by submarines, but the *Nissyo Maru* survived and docked at Moji on August 3. The tankers were then split up among at least seven camps. Twelve men, but no tankers, died on the trip.

The *Noto Maru* was a large (7,191 tons), fast (16 knots), army-controlled cargo ship that loaded 1,035 POWs in Manila, including Frank Goldstein, and left for Japan on August 25. The trip was fast and apparently uneventful, and reached Moji on September 6 with the loss of one non-tanker. The men were split up, and Goldy went to a copper mine, but was so ill with pneumonia that he spent the rest of the war making nails from copper wire.

The *Shinyō Maru* was a very small freighter (2,634 tons) that had been built in Scotland in 1894 and captured in Shanghai in 1941. It brought 750 prisoners who had been working on an airfield at Lasang, Mindanao, from Zamboanga to Manila on September 3. The ship's previous cargo had been cement, leaving white residue that coated the men's parched lips and throats, but this misery did not last long. The ship found a convoy waiting and left Manila Bay on September 5, right into a waiting ambush. This late in the war, all U.S. submarine skippers were informed of the routes and makeup of all Japanese convoys by the ULTRA codebreaking organization. The presence of POWs in the convoy was thus known, but since the ships they were on were not marked, this knowledge did not play a role in target selection. The USS *Paddle* put torpedoes into the *Shinyō Maru*, which quickly began to sink. Guards opened fire on the POWs to keep them in the holds. However, a hundred or more fought up through the hatches with clubs and improvised weapons and jumped over the side. About thirty were picked up by boats engaged in rescuing Japanese *Shinyō Maru* survivors and were immediately shot. Six hundred sixty-eight prisoners, including fifteen tankers, died. Eighty-two men reached shore on Mindanao and contacted friendly guerillas, who asked USAFFE to evacuate them. The submarine USS *Narwhal* answered the call and took all the men to Australia, from where they were quickly returned to the United States. James McComas and Joe Lamkin of A/194TB, Willard Hall of HQ/194TB, and William Biddle of the 17th Ordnance Company were among the men rescued.

Eleven hundred American POWs still at Cabanatuan were issued overcoats and shoes and taken to Manila on October 1. Forrest Knox and Dr. Alvin Poweleit were among them. They found the *Hokusen Maru*, a small, rusty freighter, waiting for them at Pier 7, and were crammed aboard by screaming, club-swinging guards. Seven hundred men were forced into the rear hold, which had previously contained coal, and 400 men went into the forward hold, which still held horse manure from earlier occupants. Conditions soon became intolerable. Most men had drunk their canteens dry on the dock, and no more water was provided for a day. When the eighteen-ship convoy got underway on the 3rd, the water ration lowered into the holds daily amounted to three tablespoons per man. The daily food ration, about one-half canteen cup of *lugao*, was also inadequate, but it was the lack of water that drove men to murder. Arthur van Pelt of B/192TB was beaten to death with a canteen in a fight over water. Men drank sea water left in the latrine buckets. They would go insane, leaping around like animals, and would belch an eerie blue phosphorescence. A few slashed their wrists and drank their own blood; these men usually bled to death. In one or two cases, a deranged man tried to bite someone's throat.

Men were affected by the lack of oxygen as well as water and began to die of suffocation. Forrest Knox recalled that others went mad, charging at the bulkhead, trying to smash their own skulls. They would cower, but then they would run some more, crashing into other men, howling like dogs. A colonel safe on deck shouted down the hatch that the Japanese were not going to put up with the howling; if it did not stop they were going to cover the hold, suffocating everyone. Knox had no intention of dying because of some howling madmen. His appeal to the officers in the hold brought only blank stares, in his opinion probably from drugs brought aboard by the doctors. He decided to take matters into his own hands. Knox had only three personal items: an engraved canteen cup, his toothbrush, and a neck towel that he had used for the entire war, first to protect him from hot shell casings within his tank, and then as a head scarf protecting him from heat stroke on the Death March. He now used it to strangle screaming men. When the hold became quiet, he was sick to his stomach. The experience haunted him for the rest of his life.

In the mornings the Japanese lowered ropes to haul up the dead. In the roll of the ship they swung slowly back and forth, eyes bulging, lips drawn back in a hellish death smile. Naked except for g-strings, they danced a ghoulish dance. The bodies were thrown over the side, to be churned up by the ship's screws. The convoy was diverted to Hong Kong before eventually reaching Takao, where the holds remained closed for thirteen days. The Japanese then opened them, wearing face masks against the stench. They prodded the prisoners ashore with rifle butts and boathooks, sprayed them with disinfectant, broke them into small groups, and trucked them off to various Formosan prison farms to await a more propitious time to try for Japan. Thirty-nine men died on the *Hokusen Maru*, of whom Van Arsdall was the only tanker. The survivors, by now walking skeletons, continued to die on Formosa.

The next Hell Ship to leave Manila was the *Arisan Maru*, which survivors remembered as a "dirty, smelly little freighter." It had three cargo holds, of which one had small shelves in tiers of three, implying that it had previously been used to transport Japanese troops. Eighteen hundred prisoners from Bilibid were crammed aboard. About 1,000 of these, including many tankers, had come from Cabanatuan. The ship was scheduled to depart on October 11 but did not join a convoy and leave until October 21. Five men died in the first forty-eight hours aboard. Men were too cramped to reach the eight five-gallon latrines, and the floors were awash in fecal matter; the shelves were crawling with bedbugs and roaches. After a day 600 men were moved to the coal hold to relieve the crowding but found a new misery; they were forced to lie on the loose coal.

A submarine wolf pack awaited the *Arisan Maru's* convoy when it reached the South China Sea, and on October 24, about 225 miles off Hong Kong, the USS *Snook* torpedoed the freighter. The Japanese cut the rope to the coal hold, slammed shut the hatches to the cargo holds, and abandoned ship. Many of the POWs were killed by the torpedo explosion. The living made pyramids of the dead, climbed them to open the hatches, which had not been battened down, and tried to leave the ship. Most of the few men to make it into the water were machine-gunned by the escorts. Five men, including Anton Cichy of HQ/194TB, avoided the escorts, found lifeboat components, built a sailboat, and sailed to the China coast, where they were rescued by Chinese guerillas. Four men, including Glenn Oliver of A/194TB, floated in the wreckage for several days and were eventually pulled from the water by Japanese sailors who let them live. One later died, but three survived the war as POWs. The 1,791 men who died in the sinking itself included ninety-eight tankers, among them Maj. Charles Canby, Capt. Jack Altman, and 2nd Lt. Arthur Holland.

By December 1944, 90 percent of the enlisted Americans taken prisoner in the Philippines had been taken north; only a third of the officers had gone. In 1942 the enlisted men were younger and/or had skills better suited for the labor the Japanese had in mind than the officers, so had been picked first. The officers at Cabanatuan were better treated than the enlisted men, especially after they started getting paid, and few had volunteered to leave. By 1945 all of the prisoners were underweight, and most were ill. Their labor was now of little value, but the Japanese did not want them to fall into the hands of the U.S. Army, and one more Hell Ship was scheduled. This was the *Ōryoku Maru*, a 7,365-ton passenger/cargo ship built during the war and used primarily as a troop transport. Early in the morning of December 13, 1,634 POWs in the unusual ratio of two officers to one enlisted man were fed at Bilibid Prison and marched through Manila to Pier 7, where they were forced into the three cargo holds while about 1,900 Japanese civilians and military personnel moved into the above-deck cabins. Loading was completed by 6:30 p.m., and the ship got underway at three the next morning. The hatches to the holds were closed and battened down—according to the Japanese interpreter this was to prevent the noise and smell from bothering the Japanese passengers—and men soon began to pass out. These men were pulled beneath the hatches to get them as much air as possible, but according to one source fifty men died the first night and were lifted to the main deck the next morning. Scouting aircraft from the USS *Hornet* spotted the ship, which pulled into Subic Bay and anchored. Bombers attacked the ship throughout the day and didn't hit it, but near misses started leaks. Between attacks the civilians were off-loaded and taken back to Manila, while the prisoners remained locked in the holds. Conditions became even less bearable—a doctor's thermometer read 120 degrees F—and by the night of the 14th men began to go mad. A colonel wrote in his official report:

Many men lost their minds and crawled about in the absolute darkness armed with knives, attempting to kill people to drink their blood, or armed with canteens filled with urine and swinging them in the dark. The hold was so crowded and everyone so interlocked with one another that movement was only possible over the heads and bodies of others.

The *Hornet* aircraft returned on the 15th and struck the *Ōryoku Maru* with at least six air-to-surface rockets. When it became obvious that the ship was going to sink, the interpreter opened the hatches and shouted that the men could come up in groups of twenty-five, jump overboard, and swim to shore. The men jumping in the correct direction and reaching shore without attracting the attention of the armed guards were herded onto a tennis court that had been strung quickly with barbed wire. They were on Olangapo Point, a prewar U.S. Naval Station. A roll call showed 1,331 shivering survivors, of whom nine died on the court. Fifteen of the worst injured were driven off in a truck and executed. The rest survived five days on the court with plenty of water but only two tablespoons of raw rice per day. The rice was not cooked because "fires were not permitted," although the guards staying nearby not only cooked their rice but ate from Red Cross parcels meant for the POWs.

On December 20 the men were loaded into trucks and driven to San Fernando–Pampanga on the Bataan Peninsula. There they were fed rice balls and put on trains for San Fernando–La Union. After waiting on the beach at Lingayen Gulf for two days, they were loaded on two old freighters to continue their journey—1,070 went aboard the *Enoura Maru* and 236 boarded the *Brazil Maru*. The ships reached Takao in six days. The POWs from the *Brazil Maru* were then moved to the *Enoura Maru*, where men continued to die. Both ships remained anchored at Takao.

On January 9 carrier aircraft raided the harbor, and the *Enoura Maru* was badly damaged by bombs and strafing. The Japanese on the upper decks were slaughtered. At least 350 prisoners were killed below, many by a falling hatch cover; others were badly injured and died from lack of treatment. On January 13 the 900-plus survivors were moved from the *Enoura Maru*, now considered unseaworthy, to the *Brazil Maru*, which in the meantime had been loaded with sugar and thus became extremely crowded. This ship joined a four-ship convoy that included the *Melbourne Maru*, which was taking 500 POWs from Formosa, primarily off the *Hokusen Maru* and including Forrest Knox and Alvin Poweleit, to Moji. The convoy left Takao on January 14 and got split up, apparently by bad weather. The *Melbourne Maru* reached Moji on January 23 with only one recorded death. The *Brazil Maru* did not arrive until January 29 and had lost more than 450 men; only 450 could walk down the gangplank into the bitter Japanese winter. These were the only survivors of the 1,634 men who had originally boarded the *Ōryoku Maru*. The *Brazil Maru*'s trip from Formosa had been one of incredible misery. Men died at a rate of fifty per day; the corpses were piled up on deck, stripped of clothing, and thrown overboard. Cause of death was listed as "malnutrition, dehydration, and exposure."

The PTG officer cadre was especially hard hit in the *Ōryoku Maru*-*Enoura Maru*-*Brazil Maru* incident. Four of the majors who had survived to date (John Morley, Thaddeus Smyth, Maynard Snell, and Robert Pettit) died, as did fifteen other officers, including captains Arthur Burholt, Harold Collins, Clinton Quinlen, and Russell Thorman. Nineteen PTG officers were lost on these three ships, 37 percent of the fifty-one lost during the war. Fifteen enlisted tankers were also lost on the three ships. A total of 152 PTG officers and men were lost on the Hell Ships, a quarter of those lost during the war, and 13.5 percent of the tankers who had arrived in the Philippines in 1941.

THE NORTHERN CAMPS

The prisoners headed north starting in the spring of 1942 were destined for Japan's heavy industries. The 1929 Geneva Convention allowed enlisted prisoners to be used for labor such as farm and road work, but stated explicitly, "Work . . . shall have no direct connection with the operations of the war." Japan never ratified the Convention but followed it when it chose to. However, virtually all POW work sites in Japan and its northern occupied territories (Formosa, Korea, and Manchuria) were directly related to war production. Japanese corporations were clamoring for forced laborers very early in the war, and it was obvious that the companies themselves would be responsible for how they were treated. A cache of charred documents was found in 1946 on the site of a Formosan copper mine. In one of these, dated April 29, 1942 (before the fall of Corregidor), the chief of the [Japanese] POW Management Bureau wrote, "The Army will take responsibility for control and supply, but the POW camp facilities with the exception of repairs . . . will be the responsibility . . . of the companies which use the POWs." Allied Intelligence learned of the POWs' northern exodus in a top-secret message from Japan's transportation and communications chief to the Shipping Transport Command on September 8, 1942, which stated, "Due to a serious shortage of labor power in Japan, the use of white POW is earnestly desired. Therefore it is required to . . . send some white POW to Japan by every returning ship. . . . It is desired to send as many personnel as possible by every means such as loading them on decks."

More than sixty Japanese companies used slave POW labor during the war, paying the army for the men and using company employees as supplemental guards and jailers. These POWs included about 450 from the PTG, who were taken to 139 camps: 129 in Japan, 3 in Manchuria, 3 in Korea, and 4 in Formosa. Thirty-five tankers died in these camps. Although the Japanese first wanted men with specific mechanical skills, they soon put prisoners to work in every heavy Japanese industry:

shoveling coal, pushing dump cars, chipping paint, feeding and cleaning blast furnaces, unloading and loading ships, laboring in rolling mills, foundries, and steel plants, manufacturing graphite, digging out harbors (by hand) for dry docks, and mining coal, lead, nickel, copper, and manganese. Mining was a low-status occupation in Japan, often carried out by Koreans who were treated little better than slaves, and before the war the accident rate in Japanese mines was the highest in the world. Ironically, this rate seems to have dropped during the war; the prisoners either successfully resisted the most hazardous Japanese practices and/or improved them.

Moji, a city on the northern coast of Kyushu, the southernmost Japanese island, was the main port of entry for prisoners arriving in Japan from the south. The stories told by the surviving tankers were very similar: They were herded up from the dank, airless Hell Ship holds onto the Moji docks. In the autumn or winter it would be sleeting or snowing. The dead bodies would be trucked away with the immobile ill, while the rest would be shaken down one more time, stripped naked, probed with glass rods inserted in their rectums (supposedly for later medical examination; the Japanese were deathly afraid of epidemics), hosed with cold salt water, sprayed with disinfectant, ordered to dress—sometimes in new, cheap Japanese work uniforms—counted off, split into new groups, and marched through the streets to be transported to their assigned work camps. To their constant hunger was added a new misery—the cold. Their thin clothing and flimsy, inadequate blankets were never enough to keep them warm, and none of the barracks in the POW camps was heated.

The Japanese civilians the men passed on their way out of Moji looked as miserable as they were. All were in war issue uniforms. Food was scarce, and the daily civilian ration was less than 2,000 calories. The fish supply was still adequate, but other meat was almost entirely gone; even the zoo animals had been eaten. Rice was the staple of their diet, but the rest of what the Japanese were eating was just as disgusting as boiled rice to the prisoners—seaweed, vegetable tops, roots, pastes, and odd gelatinous soybean-based substances that the POWs nicknamed "snotty gobbles" and "elephant semen." The prisoners scavenged for what they could find: Fish scraps discarded by the Japanese, slaughterhouse bones, trapped dogs, and dead horses were valuable sources of protein, supplemented in the inevitable soups by weeds and vegetable tops.

The first Hell Ship that headed north in 1942 had carried only two PTG men, General Weaver and his orderly, and off-loaded in Formosa. The next carried a full load of skilled men—of whom tankers formed a large percentage—to Formosa, Korea, and then, when a camp was ready for them, many to Mukden, Manchuria. The destination of every Hell Ship leaving the Philippines for the rest of the war was Moji, where the POWs were split according to the needs of the various industries. The next ship to arrive carried a large number of PTG "volunteers" to Moji, where they were split into three groups. One, led by Lieutenant Colonel Miller, went to Tanegawa. Another, with Lieutenant Colonel Wickord as the senior officer, went to Umeda outside Osaka. Prisoner officers as a class were treated better than enlisted men, but the experiences of all ranks had much in common: inadequate food, inadequate medical care, inadequate heat for much of the year, and mistreatment by the guards. The guards in the camps were mostly crippled war veterans, while those on the work sites were civilians unfit for military service; neither had any love for Americans, especially after the B-29 raids started.

TANEGAWA, ZENTSUJI, AND ROKUROSHI CAMPS

The tankers were split among so many camps and moved so frequently during the war as needs changed and the American armed forces approached that it is impossible to cover their individual histories in detail in this book. Several good books have been written on the camps, and many surviving tankers wrote memoirs; readers are referred to these for more information. I'll concentrate on a few camps, those which contained the greatest number of tankers. One of the first work camps in Japan to take in prisoners as slave labor was Tanegawa, near Osaka. Ernie Miller led 178 officers and 322 enlisted men into the camp on November 26, 1942. Ben Morin recorded this description:

> *There were five new barracks very flimsily constructed with dirt floors and paper-thin walls coming to six inches off the floor. The barracks were very cold. There were two decks of bunks with a ladder going*

*up every twenty feet to the second deck which was eight to ten feet off
the ground. . . . At the foot of each bunk were five synthetic blankets
made out of peanut shell fiber and a rigid pillow in the shape of a small
cylinder filled with rice husks. The barracks had no heat, and with
temperatures falling below freezing, the conditions were very tough.*

If things were tough for the officers, they were even worse for the
enlisted men, because their job at Tanegawa was to manually tear down a
mountainside to build a breakwater for a primitive dry dock and submarine base. This camp was noted for severe malnutrition and a high death
rate. The dock was never completed, and the camp was closed in April
1945. Ernie Miller became American commandant briefly and spent his
time complaining about conditions to his Japanese superior. These com-
plaints were not all what one might believe, however. Miller thought one
letter was important enough that he buried it with the notes that he wrote
up at Zentsuji, a later camp, and it survives today in the Library of Congress. One of its eleven points reads,

*[O]fficers were used to carry food to the enlisted men working details,
and also . . . officers have been used on several details to perform manual labor. It was understood that officers would not be used for this type
of work, especially when it would humiliate them or lower them in the
eyes of enlisted men.*

The class structure persisted in the American army throughout the
war, even in POW camp. The Japanese would typically reply to com-
plaints like this that hard work was good for everyone and that the Japanese could use whomever they wanted for labor, as they had never ratified
the Geneva Accords. Nevertheless, officers were never employed on the
harder tasks, such as mining and smelting, and the Japanese quickly
reduced the number of officers at camps associated with work sites to
the minimum needed for administration and moved the rest, especially
obstreperous ones such as Miller, to Zentsuji Camp on Shikoku Island,
known as the officers' camp, which was shown off to International Red
Cross (IRC) representatives. This was the first POW camp built in Japan,

was not associated with any work site, and is frequently called a "model camp," although this is probably a misnomer. Conditions in the camp itself were no better than those at any other camp, but the absence of any nearby work sites certainly helped to disguise the nature of the POW slave labor-industry connection from the inspectors.

When Miller and his group of 130 officers, which included Eddie Johnson and Ben Morin, arrived at Zentsuji on January 16, 1943, they were in such bad physical condition that they were quarantined for a month before they could join the 350 Americans plus Royal Navy, Australian, and Dutch officers who were already there. Miller became leader of the 3rd and 4th Divisions in the camp. Most of the surviving PTG officers eventually came to Zentsuji. Ted Wickord arrived from Umeda and became Ben Morin's roommate. The two of them spent part of each day reciting Catholic prayers and rosaries. Morin said Wickord helped persuade him to enter the priesthood after their return home. Most of the officers had little to do to kill the time, although Zentsuji's status as an IRC inspection camp put it on top of the list to get recreation equipment, books, and Red Cross packages. Since prisoners who worked got twice the ration of those who didn't, a rule that the Japanese enforced rigidly, even for officers, many worked in the camp's vegetable garden.

In June 1945 Zentsuji was shut down, and the prisoners were moved from Shikoku Island to Honshu, the main island, apparently in an attempt by the Japanese to keep the prisoners ahead of the advancing American armed forces. The American POWs were split from the other nationalities and 335 were sent to Rokuroshi, a tiny, isolated camp high in the mountains that appeared to the more suspicious POWs to be an ideal execution site. The camp was in disrepair, and in Miller's words, "food, treatment, and fleas" were worse than before. A farm was cleared and planted. Its produce would be required for the men's subsistence if the war lasted until the coming winter. The rice ration was reduced, wild greens were sought out for soup, the few snakes and wasp larvae seen were caught and roasted, and any root that could be chewed was eaten. Treatment got slightly better with the August 15 ceasefire, but the men remained in the dark until the 22nd, when Lieutenant Colonel Miller returned to the barracks with the announcement: "Gentlemen, the war is over!" Crowd voices: "Who won?" One man jumped on a chair: "When do we eat?" B-29s with supplies did not find the camp until V-J Day, September 2, and the rescue party arrived on September 8. The men were soon on their way to Manila for debriefing (and to fatten up) and headed for the States in October.

FUKUOKA CAMP #17

The Fukuoka POW camp complex comprised some two dozen work sites in western Kyushu. Ninety-nine enlisted and one officer tanker survived Fukuoka, and eleven enlisted and four officer tankers died there. The largest sub-camp was Camp #17, near a coal mine owned by Baron Mitsui. The barracks were originally the laborers' quarters. The mine was nearly played out, and Mitsui requested slave labor to extract the coal that was left. The POW camp opened on August 7, 1943, with the arrival of 500 Americans from the *Clyde Maru*. It measured 200 yards by 1,000 yards and was surrounded by a twelve-foot-high wooden fence topped with heavy-gauge wire. There were thirty-three barracks, each with ten rooms built of wood with tar paper roofs and glass windows. There was no heating, a serious problem in the winter for the undernourished prisoners, and one 15-watt lightbulb per room. The two meals daily were usually a cup of rice and some radish soup, with little or no protein.

Prisoners continued to arrive until June 1945 and eventually totaled about 1,735. Americans, Australians, and Dutch worked in the coal mine, while the British worked in the nearby Mitsui zinc foundry. Shifts were twelve hours, with one day off every ten days. The mine as originally dug had tunnels sixteen feet wide with lateral supports of unmined coal, also sixteen feet wide, between them. The men replaced these supports with rock and then dug out the ore from the coal-laden supports. This work was very difficult and dangerous, but the Americans persuaded the shift foremen that as "weak white men" their goals had to be reduced, and taught the Japanese miners sharing the work the great American custom of goldbricking, which made the workload bearable.

The Americans, to a greater extent than their Allies also working the mine, took great delight in sabotage. This was as simple as derailing the mine cars, but quickly got more complex. According to his memoir, Les

Tenney discovered that the entire mine was powered by a single fifty-horsepower engine, which was halfway down the main shaft. He made a plan for his team of eight. The first two opened the lubricant fill cap, the next four dropped in as much dirt and coal as the reservoir would hold, and the last two replaced the cap. They were digging in their tunnel when the lights went out and all the machinery ground to a halt. The engine had of course stalled, and the men enjoyed the rest of their shift relaxing in the dark. The Japanese never learned the truth, and in fact never caught on that the American POWs were doing their best to hinder the war effort.

Aching hunger was ever present; the vitamin deficiency diseases such as beriberi that the prisoners brought with them got ever worse; and the men continued to lose weight and weaken. Some mutilated themselves to obtain at least temporary respite from the mines. Open sores were easy to infect with battery acid from the mine, lye from the latrines, or caustic soda from the zinc smelter. Men could be paid to crush arms or legs with jackhammers or drills. Self-mutilation did take place at other camps, but apparently nowhere was bone crushing as common as at Camp #17.

According to numerous sources American collaborators controlled the Camp #17 food supply. These officers and senior enlisted men were known as "the Mafia." The Japanese paid the prisoners as in other camps, but the money was soon concentrated in the hands of the Mafia, either from trading or gambling. Geoffrey Adams, an English officer taken prisoner at Singapore, arrived at Camp #17 in late June 1944 and was shocked at the corruption. Quoting Adams:

> [B]y the time we arrived, half the cash in the camp was in the hands of one big-time gambler, Lester Tannenberg [sic—Les Tenney], who ran a blackjack and poker school—with the backing of the "Mafia," of course. When the Japanese discovered this, they withdrew all money, and we merely signed that we had had it!

According to the American survivors, Adams's book overemphasized the significance of gambling, which was an innocent way to pass the time. Their overarching concerns were their constant hunger and the resulting illnesses. The stronger men found two ways to improve their diet, and Les Tenney profited from both of them. Although the Japanese civilian diet was poor and getting worse, the civilians in the mine did have food to trade, and the Dutchmen, who had managed to keep their luggage, had trade material such as toothpaste and shoes in their original boxes. Les Tenney managed these trades, for a cut, until he was ratted on and sentenced to death, which, according to his own account, Tenney avoided by making an impromptu plea for mercy that brought tears to the eyes of the Japanese commandant. Tenney does not mention his camp gambling activities in his book, and it is entirely possible that the death sentence he received from the Japanese and talked his way out of was for the school Adams described and not for trading with civilians in the mine.

Tenney was also noted for futures trading with his fellow prisoners. Cigarettes were rationed out at about five per man per day, which was not enough for some addicts who were willing to trade their food, a bowl of rice or soup, for cigarettes. Some would trade the next day's ration for a single cigarette. The trader's cry, "Nicotine for protein," while inaccurate, was catchy, and was remembered by survivors from many Japanese camps. Apparently only in Camp #17 were the "hard traders" such as Tenney allowed to get up to ten rations ahead of their weaker fellow prisoners, effectively sentencing them to death. The Allied camp commanders were apparently inept or corrupt enough to allow this to happen.

A solution to futures trading was eventually found by setting up a bankruptcy court. Any man owing more than three meals had to sign up and list his creditors. The creditors had to waive interest payments and were issued postdated IOUs for the rice principal. A Dutch chaplain was chosen as trustee of the court, although all debtors and creditors were American, and saw the debtors through the chow line to ensure that the men ate. He eventually had fifty men under his watch but was unable to keep some of them from starvation.

The daily grind continued for the rest of the war. In late April 1945 nearly all of the Australian, British, and Dutch officers were told they would be transferred to a safer camp. "Safer" meant for the Japanese, and Adams speculated that the Japanese wanted to move them out of the way of the anticipated American invasion of Kyushu. He implied that the

Japanese considered that these Allies would be more dangerous in their rear than the American officers. His new camp turned out to be Mukden, and Adams was thrilled to find that the American commanders there ran a competent and empathetic organization.

The end of the war came to Camp #17 as it did to most POW camps: with the guards locking up and departing, B-29 supply drops, the arrival of a war correspondent—in this case George Weller of the *Chicago Tribune*—and the eventual arrival of American troops. There were also events unique to Camp #17: Some of the American collaborators got beaten up, and Lieutenant Commander Little, the American mess officer, was locked up for his own protection.

MUKDEN, MANCHURIA

Most men in the first wave of prisoners shipped north in 1942 had been selected as skilled and were destined for the Manchukuo Machine Tool Manufacturing Company (MKK) in Mukden, Manchuria. The 1,200 Americans reaching Pusan, Korea, on the *Tottori Maru* left 181 men in the hospital to rejoin later, were supplemented by one hundred Singapore survivors, and headed to Mukden (called Hoten in Japanese and Shenyang in Chinese) by train. They arrived at the freight yard on November 11, 1942, in mud, rain, and cold and were quartered in a temporary camp comprising nineteen barracks, two hospitals, two bathhouses, and two kitchen buildings. None but the bathhouses were heated. The barracks were as flimsily built as chicken coops, and cold air leaked in constantly. Work uniforms and thick blankets were issued, but the men were painfully cold both in the barracks and in the factories. Their diet was bread and cabbage soup, occasionally fortified with pork and dog. This was different from the food in the Philippines, but no more nutritious; their vitamin deficiency diseases did not heal, and a new one, dry beriberi, became common. The emaciated men continued to die, but the rest were too weak to bury them in the rock-hard soil in minus fifty-degree F. cold, and 152 corpses piled up to be buried the following spring.

The main factory in the MKK complex was to use new American machinery, probably imported into Japan in 1940–1941, to build machine tools. Although the complex eventually contained a manufacturing plant for small electrical cranes, a canvas manufacturing plant, an ironworks, and a lumberyard, the tool plant was the most significant for the Japanese war effort and was the target for American sabotage on the first December day that the prisoners entered the plant. They had to finish the factory's construction, which required pouring concrete and setting the machinery. Parts, including one complete lathe, according to many accounts, were immersed in the setting concrete; the machines were set up off level, resulting in parts that looked OK but were off spec; and sand was put in the lubricating oil. Replacement parts for the American machinery had to be reverse-engineered from scratch. Many prisoners said that no finished, operational tool was ever exported from MKK. The Japanese could not accept that American POWs were capable of direct disobedience and blamed the plant problems on American stupidity rather than sabotage. Their solutions—beating the Americans, cutting their rations, and locking them up in the guard house—were accepted readily by the POWs as their payment for helping the Allied war effort.

The first B-29 raid on Mukden on December 7, 1944, was a complete surprise and not only killed nineteen POWs but infuriated the Japanese, who punished the prisoners for it. News of the war reached the Mukden camp periodically from friendly guards and new cohorts of prisoners reaching Manchuria from Korea and Japan. One group contained survivors from the *Ōryoku Maru*, including PTG junior officers Jacques Merrifield and Frank Riley, and were notable for their terrible physical condition. Another group of 320 American, British, and Dutch generals, colonels, and their orderlies arrived from a camp 150 miles north of Mukden. The senior Allied officers of this group and now the camp were Major General Parker and Air Vice Marshal Maltby. Generals Wainwright and Percival were kept in a small camp elsewhere. The number of prisoners at Mukden peaked at 1,600 in 1945. About fifty survivors were tankers; five more tankers died in camp.

The USSR declared war on Japan on August 8, and the Red Army immediately crossed the Manchurian border. With the ceasefire on the 15th, the Office of Strategic Services (OSS) headquarters in China planned the drop of a team of specialists on the camp to facilitate the rescue of the men, especially Wainwright, who was believed to be there. They were to be preceded by a drop of pamphlets announcing the ceasefire, but the team of six parachutists arrived on the 16th and the pamphlets on the 22nd. The Japanese had heard of the ceasefire from their own sources and so did not imprison the OSS team, who took over the camp and sent a couple of men to fetch Wainwright and his men. American cargo planes began landing on the Mukden airstrip with rations; B-29s also dropped them from the air, destroying several buildings.

The Red Army arrived on the 20th, disarmed the Japanese, killing some, and allowed the POWs to form a camp guard. The American idea of revenge was to seat the worst of the guards in the middle of the parade ground and pour the contents of #10 fruit cans over them, which was supposedly the worst humiliation of the guards' lives to date. American POWs began driving into town and returning so drunk (and infected with gonorrhea) that this practice had to be stopped. The OSS commander, Colonel Donovan, arrived by plane on the 29th and took control of the evacuation of the former POWs, while the Russians were rounding up the Japanese to go to Siberian prison camps and loading factory machinery onto rail cars for shipment to Russia. Most Allied hospital patients and high-ranking officers were evacuated by air. Wainwright and Percival reached Tokyo in time for the surrender ceremony on the USS *Missouri* on September 2. The rest, including Weaver, flew west, to China, India, Egypt, Dakar, Brazil, and Miami. Weaver got off a letter to his parents in which he warned against giving any "consideration" to Japan. His peculiar vocabulary did not serve the PTG's interests well in the history wars to come.

Colonel Donovan arranged for the evacuation of the lower-ranking men and returned to China. On September 10, 750 men were evacuated by train to Dairen on the coast, followed by the remaining 638 the next day. Al Allen recalled being on the last train car to Dairen, where he was deloused and boarded a U.S. naval ship for Okinawa, from where he quickly left for the Philippines and then home. His experience was a little smoother than that of most, but all of the tankers in the northern camps eventually took the same route: Okinawa, Philippines, United

States, home. A few made the trans-Pacific leg on an aircraft, but most took U.S. Navy or U.S. Army troopships, where they were allowed to eat anything they wanted at all hours, and many arrived in the states in an unhealthy bloated state and were sent to hospitals for physical conditioning as well as treatment for their panoply of vitamin deficiency, jungle, and other diseases.

CHAPTER 11

Return Home

EMPEROR HIROHITO'S SPEECH TO THE JAPANESE PEOPLE JUST AFTER noon on August 15 (Japanese time) ended the fighting in the Pacific, and President Truman's nationwide radio broadcast the evening of the 14th (U.S. time) announcing the surrender led to enthusiastic celebrations verging on orgies in the major American cities, which were only slightly more subdued in the heartland. Brainerd may be considered typical of the tank company towns. The whistle in the Northern Pacific Railroad yards announced the news, followed by a chorus of hundreds of automobile horns as an unbroken line of honking cars paraded through town, led by the hastily assembled Brainerd Ladies' Drum and Bugle Corps. Downtown was littered with toilet paper streamers and homemade confetti. Celebrants crowded the downtown streets, but their joy was not unrestrained. Too many families had suffered too much. The editor of the *Brainerd Daily Dispatch* wrote, "We came down town for a while and watched the folks celebrate . . . but we didn't stay long. We got to thinking about the families who have loved ones who won't be coming back from the war—friends of ours and neighbors of ours—and, well, to make a long story short, we just went home."

More messages from the prisoners had been reaching home, and families who had gotten them recently could feel some reassurance, but some were worried all over again by the news of the atomic bombings of Hiroshima and Nagasaki on August 6 and 9. POW camps containing tankers were known to be near both cities. It was not until September 19 that the families learned that the camps were fifty and thirty-five miles, respectively, from the two cities and were undamaged by the bombing.

The armed forces trivialized the danger from radiation exposure, however, and freed POWs in Japan were allowed to wander through the flattened cities as tourists. Radiation damage was not one of the many infirmities diagnosed among the returning tankers, but Nicholas Fryziuk of B/192TB did father a disabled child before he died young from leukemia, which was attributed by his family to radiation.

On August 6 the tankers in camps in Japan figured something big was about to happen when guards began acting strangely and those POWs working with civilians heard mutterings of a "big bomb." On August 9 men in the camp nearest Nagasaki felt the ground rumble and could see a reddish cloud rising from the area of the city, and the camps in Formosa and Manchuria heard of the "big bombs" through the Japanese grapevine. Treatment became more lenient, and several camps declared holidays from work.

After Hirohito's speech on August 15, guards, especially the bad ones, began disappearing from the camps, and several camp commanders assembled the POWs to declare that the war was over. It was up to the men to decide what to do next. Their first thought was food, and the Japanese storerooms were rifled; undistributed Red Cross packages were found in several. The next steps were virtually the same for all camps. A fighter from an aircraft carrier or Okinawa would fly over the camp at low altitude, recognize the frantically waving white men, waggle its wings, and fly off, frequently to return with the rest of its flight and drop duffle bags full of the pilots' own clothing, cigarettes, and food. Soon another drop would contain a message to paint "PW" in large white letters on the barracks roof. Then would come B-29s dropping tons of food, medicine, and clothing, a total of five tons of crates and bales and barrels per plane. These had parachutes, but many failed, especially at the beginning; other packages broke open in flight, and prisoners and civilians were killed by falling canned goods. In less than a month, 1,006 planes flew 900 effective sorties to more than 150 camps in Japan, Manchuria, Formosa, China, Hainan, and Korea. Leaflets with the food read, "DO NOT OVEREAT," but these were ignored by the men, who started to gain a pound or two per day. This was water weight, but the men started to look and feel human again, rather than walking skeletons weighing in most cases one hundred pounds or less.

Some enterprising prisoners felt that the occupying American forces were taking too long to reach the camps and walked out the gates to meet them, violating the orders of their officers. Civilians treated them with indifference or the grudging respect due their new conquerors. Men such as Arnold Larson on Honshu boarded trains, made it clear to the conductors that they wanted to go to Tokyo or Yokohama, and got there without problems, even before September 2, when MacArthur conducted his elaborately choreographed surrender ceremony on the USS *Missouri*. Jim Bashleben and Les Tenney had similar experiences on Kyushu before reaching Kanoya. Bud Bardowski walked through the radioactive rubble of Nagasaki to reach a temporary naval base he heard had been set up outside that city. All ex-prisoners were greeted with open arms by the American troops, who were following MacArthur's orders to spare no expense to get the POWs, now known as RAMP, or Recovered Allied Military Personnel, in shape to go home. This meant feeding them at all hours, and the men continued to stuff themselves.

The tankers got back to the States in several stages. Those leaving from Manchuria were discussed in chapter 10. Those in Japan first went to Okinawa for physical examination and treatment, and then by airplane or hospital ship to Luzon for debriefing and, the men suspected, for further fattening up to make them presentable to their families. The trip back to the States was by airplane or passenger ship, frequently at the choice of the men. The return process went incredibly smoothly, and less than six weeks after the emperor's address there were no prisoners left in Japan or the rest of northeast Asia, and 32,624 RAMP were on their way home.

The tank company families had to wait a while longer before seeing their men, if they ever did. The names from the camps were announced quickly, but there were many MIA (missing), most of whom were buried in the Philippines or had been lost at sea. The death rate for Westerners in the German POW camps was known to have been 4 percent. The death rate in Japanese captivity was expected to be roughly the same but turned out to be 27 percent.

The RAMP were in worse physical condition than expected. The average life expectancy of men returning from Japanese POW camps was shortened by fifteen years. Most RAMP returning to the United States were put immediately into the hospital nearest their port of entry. If this was San Francisco, they were admitted to Letterman General Hospital. There they were given cursory mental exams in the form of more debriefings, and checked for gastrointestinal problems and infectious, treatable diseases such as tuberculosis. In most cases the men were given home leave after a week to a month, after which, if needed, they were to report to the Veterans Administration (VA) hospital nearest their home. Many men tried for years to get adequate compensation for their disabilities, only to give up in frustration. The VA doctors had no experience with the long-term effects of vitamin deficiency diseases such as beriberi and could not diagnose them properly, but the VA's biggest insult was telling the men that they had to prove that their diseases and injuries were service-related. Japanese POW camp medical records were, of course, unavailable.

One condition common to most of the Bataan RAMP was post-traumatic stress disorder (PTSD), which at the time was neither diagnosed nor treated. Many returnees had vivid nightmares and difficulty sleeping for the rest of their lives. Divorces were common, and suicides took place. One PTG veteran served a prison sentence for killing his mother and was then shot and killed by his wife. A few men remained in or returned to the service and had successful military careers. John Hummel of A/194TB stayed in the army and retired as a lieutenant colonel; he then became a supervisor at Johns-Manville. Ted Spaulding of HQ/194TB became a brigadier general in the South Dakota National Guard and a South Dakota state senator. Charles Jensen of B/192TB left the service, got a degree with the GI Bill and became a vice president of Darling & Co., managing five feed and fertilizer plants. Most men, who had left the country young and with very little education, retired from either low-level manufacturing or service jobs or else early, on disability. Some could never hold a job, such as A/192TB's Snuffy Schmidt, who never married and died in a VA hospital suffering paranoid delusions. In 1997 Phyllis Wallisch told a plaintive, bitter tale to a *Janesville Daily Gazette* reporter looking for stories for Veterans Day. Her husband Lewis (A/192TB) took a job at the GM plant but felt that people were talking about him behind his back. A doctor prescribed an evening beer to unwind, and Lewis became an alcoholic. It took three sobriety programs to dry him out, while Phyllis was raising ten children alone. His children fortunately remained supportive, but Lewis withdrew from his family and refused to leave the house. He had never been in Phyllis's four-year-old car at the time she was interviewed, and spent all day watching the History Channel, to make up for the news he had missed in POW camp.

The MIA lists were quickly winnowed with the recovery of rosters from the Hell Ships and death lists from Camps O'Donnell and Cabanatuan. Men who died on the ships had been thrown overboard, and those who were lost when ships sank had similarly been given up to the sea. Those who had died in the Luzon camps were buried in mass graves, some with some type of identification and some not. The Cabanatuan Project was initiated to disinter the remains for identification and proper burial, either on Luzon or in the United States, according to the wishes of the next-of-kin. Some could be buried alone; other bodies had to be combined with other remains, depending on the ambiguity of the identifications. The caskets coming to the United States with comingled remains were buried in the military cemetery nearest to the homes of the next-of-kin. The Cabanatuan Project ended in 1951, and the remains that were still unidentified were interred as "unknowns" in the Manila American Cemetery. The Joint POW/MIA Accounting Command is now responsible for the men missing from all U.S. wars and still works on these unknowns from existing medical records.

SGT. ALBERT ALLEN JR., C/192TB

Al Allen reached San Francisco on October 28, 1945, four years and one day after leaving. Back in Mansfield, Ohio, he married his fiancée Nancy when she was discharged from the WAVEs and raised a son and daughter. He was discharged in 1946 and enlisted in the reserves, having enough college credits for an immediate commission. He returned to college and got his degree. In 1952, in one of the last World War II medal distributions, he was awarded a Silver Star for "being chased on a motorcycle by a Zero," a decoration in which he took great pride. He led numerous campaigns for the rights of POWs and retired from the reserves with the rank of lieutenant colonel. He suffered no long-term physical deficits from his imprisonment, but the nightmares continued for the rest of his life. These usually involved explosions from which he was trying to escape; he was looking for his shoes, motorcycle, or jeep. He was also highly sensitive to bad odors, which would bring back never-forgotten war experiences. Allen died in 2004 and is buried in the Mansfield cemetery.

SGT. ZENON ROLAND "BUD" BARDOWSKI, B/192TB

Bud Bardowski's trip to San Francisco and a brief stay at Letterman Hospital were routine, and he was quickly released to go home to Gary. He may have talked his way out of the hospital too soon, for he left with many undocumented physical problems. He wanted to work. He certainly did not want to return to his parents' grocery store and could not immediately get back into auto racing, his true love. He was discharged from the army on April 12, 1946, after he was rejected for reenlistment owing to his poor physical condition. A neighbor, Rae Bandanish, had had her eyes on Bud since she had served him soda in her parents' drugstore before the war. On her sixteenth birthday she asked him to marry her. "Sure, why not?" the good-natured Bardowski replied. They married on May 2, and her parents did not speak to him for five years, although he seemed to be the innocent party—Rae just wanted out of her parents' house. Bud spent his army savings on a semi-stock race car, named it the "Army Recruiting Special," and took it to Indianapolis for the Memorial Day race. His trial runs made him a crowd favorite, although he was not in physical condition to qualify, and he hired an experienced driver. The driver's qualifying time was only good enough for "first alternate starter," and he did not race. Bud returned to Indianapolis in 1947 but did not qualify.

Bardowski raced cars on dirt tracks until he flipped three times in Atlanta and broke most of his bones. He then quit racing, and the couple had to find ways to make a living. They sold recapped tires and then used cars, but Bud was a sucker for anyone with a "ruptured duck" (veteran's insignia) in his lapel, and they lost money. He then became a distributor for an oil additive, but the company switched to mass marketing, and Bud lost that job. He was commander of the local VFW chapter, Rae was president of the women's auxiliary, and the pair were in the American Legion. They were both precinct chairmen—apparently in different parties—but none of these positions paid anything. Finally, in 1955 Bud used his political connections and was hired as Gary's Civil Defense director.

Bud's and Rae's lives were outwardly stable for the next twenty years, during which they had a son, but Bud woke up screaming and sweating most nights and was in a continuous fight with the VA, which would approve only 10 percent disability despite phlebitis in the black and bloated leg that had been bayoneted and shot on Corregidor, bad eyesight from pellagra, missing front teeth that a Japanese guard had knocked out to help him with his head count, malaria, and beriberi. In 1974 Gary's city administration changed, and Bud again lost his job. It was now time for Rae to use her own contacts. She called a friend who was the wife of the head of the VA and asked for help. They found a job for Bud in Temple, Texas. The family moved to nearby Belton, and Bardowski became assistant director of Canteen Services in the Temple Veterans Center. He found a doctor who agreed that he was 100 percent disabled and called friends from around the country who had VA problems, boarding them at his home until they could see this single doctor. Bud had a heart attack while working at the hospital, regained consciousness to see a Chinese doctor poring over him, and went into cardiac arrest at the sight of a "Jap" in his face, mute evidence of the permanent effects of PTSD. He finally got his 100 percent disability rating and retired to his home in Belton in the mid-1980s. He died in 2000, and his ashes were taken to Arlington National Cemetery.

SGT. JAMES P. BASHLEBEN, B/192TB

Jim Bashleben was one of the few tankers who was honored on his return with a full-throated celebration. He got a brief furlough from Mayo Hospital to come home to Park Ridge, was met at a service station by his father, and found a reception waiting along the highway. He was hoisted on men's shoulders to cross the banner-decorated road to his home and was praised in a young girl's speech. He returned to Mayo; while there Bud Bardowski introduced him to Joyce Peyron, a USO worker whom he later married. She had walked past Jim's Harley-Davidson war bond poster every day during the war. After his discharge on June 19, 1946, he returned to work at a public utility company and fathered two sons.

Bashleben died in 2009, and his ashes are interred in Arlington Heights, Illinois.

PFC ROY L. DIAZ, C/194TB

Roy Diaz did not learn of the ceasefire until two weeks after the A-bomb explosions. He was put on a ship for the Philippines and then on another to Seattle, from where he was taken to Fort Lewis and Madigan General Hospital. He weighed ninety-eight pounds on rescue and was fed continuously until he reached the United States. He suffered from stomach and other health problems for the rest of his life, which his wife attributed to this overfeeding. When well enough Roy went to work on his family's vegetable farm (still called a "ranch"). In 1955 Roy met Lorraine Sayers, who was eighteen years his junior, at the Salinas Rodeo. They hit it off and married the next year. Roy always joked that he had robbed the cradle; Lorraine said that their fifty-seven-year marriage was "a lot of fun." Roy became a successful salesman for Spreckels Sugar and Glazer Bros. Wholesalers. After he was mentally ready, he became very active in veterans' organizations and was a popular speaker. The couple traveled to POW conventions in Miami and elsewhere. According to Lorraine the upbeat Roy "loved everybody," and a newspaper reporter called him "the best-known veteran in Salinas." In 1972 he and another survivor attended the seventieth anniversary luncheon of the Salinas Tank Company, which attracted a number of family members and notables and prompted a letter of appreciation from the couple in the local newspaper. Roy died on May 25, 2013, at age ninety-six, and is buried in the Garden of Memories cemetery in Salinas. He was the last C/194TB veteran living in Salinas. The last overall, Manuel Nevarez of Sparks, Nevada, with whom Diaz had been in regular telephone contact, outlived him by exactly one month.

T/5 BERNARD T. FITZPATRICK, A/194TB

Bernard FitzPatrick, the "music sensei," returned to Brainerd in reasonably good health and resumed his prewar occupation as an insurance salesman and his hobby as a choral singer. He married Corinne and fathered eight children. He made the Brainerd newspaper in 1947 when he wrote Charlie Wilson, the president of GM, in an attempt to get a car; these were very scarce at the time. He was calling on his insurance customers by streetcar and bus. After two letters he got his car. He served as president of the University of St. Thomas Alumni Association, and in 1993 published his excellent memoir, *The Hike into the Sun*, which won the Minnesota Book Award. He died in 2004 and is buried in the Fort Snelling National Cemetery in Minneapolis.

1ST LT. WILLIAM H. GENTRY, D + C/192TB

Bill Gentry was treated as a celebrity in Harrodsburg after his rescue from Cabanatuan and his early return from the war. He had been promoted to captain before he reached home, and his eventual medal count—two Silver Stars for bravery, one Bronze Star, and a Purple Heart, plus the PTG's three Distinguished Unit Citations, was one of the highest in the unit. A *LIFE* photographer and Brooks Atkinson from the *New York Times* were waiting for him at his parents' home and stayed for at least a day. The photographer asked Gentry to take him to his old hangout downtown, a drugstore, but they could not reach it. After parking they were surrounded by well-wishers emerging from nearby stores. Gentry became a popular public speaker at bond rallies and elsewhere, but the army had warned him that he could not say anything about men still missing, forcing him to lie about men whose fates he had personal knowledge of and about the Hell Ships, which he had not experienced but knew about. Some families never forgave him for lying to them, and he regretted this experience for the rest of his life. He remained in the reserves as a captain until he was discharged in 1953. Bill married Katherine Poor, fathered three children, and worked at Corning Glass for twenty-five years, retiring from the Vienna, West Virginia, plant. Bill moved to Blacksburg to be near his son, died there in 2000, and is buried in Harrodsburg.

T/4 FRANK A. GOLDSTEIN, B/192TB

Frank Goldstein weighed ninety-seven pounds on his release from the Hanawa copper mine, and in his words rated fast transportation to Luzon on a destroyer to fatten up. He returned to Chicago, married, fathered two children, and worked in the radio industry until retirement. He took part in only one postwar POW activity, dedicating the B/192TB memorial in

Maywood in 1947. Goldstein heard that much of the money raised had been pocketed by the organizers, became disillusioned, and never again met with the POWs. Frank died in 2010 and is buried in Skokie.

Capt. Lyman E. "Eddie" Johnson, C/194TB + HQ/194TB

Eddie Johnson was released from Rokuroshi and returned to San Francisco in fairly good shape apart from weight loss (down from 180 to 110 pounds) and was held only briefly at Letterman General Hospital. He returned to Salinas and resumed his career at the Dayton-Johnson Company, an insurance/real estate brokerage. The senior partner, Eugene Dayton, had saved Johnson's share of the profits for him; this provided a substantial nest egg for Eddie and his wife, Irma. Eugene Dayton was a very prominent figure in Salinas, having served as mayor and president of the Salinas Rodeo, and with his contacts had made the company very successful. Dayton died in the 1950s; Johnson bought his widow's share and operated independently until he sold the firm in the 1970s.

In 1947 Johnson founded the "4047 Club" for the forty Salinas Tank Company survivors and kept it going for years as a drinking group. He remained in the Guard and in 1947 was given command in Salinas of the Headquarters Company of the new 1st Battalion, 199th Armored Regiment, as a lieutenant colonel. He was joined by two noncommissioned tank company survivors and Maj. Frank Heple, who had commanded the company long before the war. The battalion contained tank companies based in towns in the Salinas Valley and Monterey Peninsula. Johnson retired in 1952 as a colonel in a ceremony at the National Guard Armory in which he was awarded the California National Guard Medal of Merit and the two noncoms received commendation ribbons. Johnson contracted Parkinson's Disease in his late seventies and died of it in 1994, at age ninety-three. He is buried in Salinas.

L/Col. Richard C. Kadel, CO 17 Ord. Co.

Richard Kadel, the 17th Ordnance Company's only commander, had escaped from the Bataan Death March and survived as a guerilla for three years before his wife Kathryn learned he was alive. He entrusted a letter to a U.S. Navy pilot who had crashed and was attempting to escape Luzon by submarine. His letter was dated November 6, 1944, and was delivered the next January 19 in Cave City, Kentucky. A few days later he was one of a party of three guerillas to meet the 6th Army landing at Zambales to assure them that the landing would be unopposed. He was soon on his way back to the United States. He arrived in March and was amazed to hear that he was now a lieutenant colonel—he had never learned of his promotion to major early in the Philippines campaign. He was first held at Letterman General Hospital and then Nichols General Hospital, not being released to return to Cave City until June. He had back problems resulting from beatings on the first three days of the Death March, which he said he received because he refused to divulge the secrets of the M3 light tank, and he was forced to walk with a cane for the rest of his life. In 1946 he underwent treatment at Walter Reed Hospital in Washington, D.C. He returned to Cave City where he did some architectural consulting work and swore out an affidavit against two of the Japanese officers on the Death March. In late 1946 he retired as a lieutenant colonel and moved to a Lake Worth, Florida, retirement community on 100 percent disability. In 1947 he was awarded the Legion of Merit for his Philippine exploits in a Fort Knox ceremony attended by several members of his company. He was a member of the Disabled American Veterans of Kentucky and continued his life in retirement in Lake Worth until his death in 1983, after which his body was taken to Cave City for burial.

SGT. FORREST K. KNOX, A/192TB

Forrest Knox made the Okinawa-Philippines-San Francisco-Letterman trip and reached Janesville around Thanksgiving 1945. His parents had moved, and he did not have their telephone number, so he spent his first night back in his hometown in a bar. He soon entered the Battle Creek army hospital, where he stayed for a year being treated for hookworm, which the staff at least understood. Other problems included vitamin-related eyesight loss and a hole in an eardrum that doctors could not find. His PTSD was severe; he suffered from nightmares and sleepwalking, and when he returned to Janesville and went to town he would see tank company comrades approaching him. They were dead men and would disappear when they got close; this so spooked Forrest that he quit going downtown alone. He also had flashbacks to the killing and madness in the dark hold of the *Hokusen Maru.*

He made it a point to attend every Janesville POW funeral, frequently as a pallbearer, and accompanied his brother Henry on condolence visits to the families of men declared dead. Henry was a lieutenant, the only A/192TB officer who survived, and his visits were official. Forrest went along because he thought he could help, but his inability to tell the grieving families the truth about the deaths that he had witnessed only worsened his mental condition. In 1948 the VA sent him to what was called a mental hygiene hospital. When he came home he was hired as a mechanic by the Cardinal Bus Company in a program subsidized by the government. When this expired he got a job with the W. R. Arthur Company, found his fellow mechanics congenial, and stayed for twenty-six years, until forced to retire by bad vision and bad legs. He married and quickly divorced, but got lucky with his second wife, Adeline Yost, with whom he had six children.

Talking helped Forrest's mental state, and he talked to anyone who would listen. He was a principal interviewee for many books on the Bataan campaign and the POW experience. The sharp and insightful comments for which he had been known in Company A never left him, salted now with his bitterness at anything and everything—corrupt, self-serving authority; an incompetent, stupid military; and, especially, the Veterans Administration, which continued to stamp his every claim "denied." He would give lists of his Company A friends to interviewers; the list grew ever shorter as the prematurely old men died. One man was deaf, blind in one eye, and diabetic, with one bad leg; he was awarded 40 percent disability. Others were alcoholic; two were dying from emphysema. One had two dead legs from beriberi and fell down a lot, whether he was drunk, which was most of the time, or sober. None of these men could persuade the VA that they had come home from POW camp with these problems. Another had gone blind in camp from vitamin deficiency. He was given a sign to wear around his neck to keep the Japanese guards from hitting him for not bowing. According to Forrest, it took the VA twenty-five years to translate the sign and declare his residual blindness service-related.

Forrest loved to speak to schoolchildren. In 1983 he and a fellow Company A tanker discussed their experiences at a Janesville high school assembly. A reporter wrote, "Knox is almost blind and deaf, has dental problems and limbs that go numb, stemming from his treatment in the camps." Asked how they survived, Forrest's companion gave a conventional response—he had had "God and luck on my side." Forrest took the provocative tone that he loved. He had survived, he told the class, because he was an atheist who believed only in himself and his "bull-headed stubbornness."

Knox's physical problems—bad eyesight, bad heart, diabetes—finally got the best of him. He had retired at age sixty and died in the Madison VA hospital at sixty-eight. He is buried in the Janesville cemetery.

SGT. MARCUS ARNOLD LAWSON, D/193TB

Arnold Lawson was put aboard a hospital ship in Tokyo harbor, decided it wasn't leaving quickly enough, and volunteered to take an airplane as far as he could. He flew to Okinawa and Luzon and then boarded a ship for San Francisco, which he reached on October 3. Nearly all POWs returned with vision loss owing to pellagra. Diet and time cured some men; the problems of others continued. Arnold Lawson's total night blindness bewildered the Letterman General Hospital staff, who eventually sent him to a VA hospital in Valley Forge, which forwarded him to a hospital for the totally blind in Connecticut. The staff there was totally unprepared to handle a wild bunch of ex-POWs. Conditions were so out of control that one patient attempted to telephone Wainwright, who it was felt would be sympathetic to their drunken behavior, and actually reached General King, who passed the word to Wainwright. "Skinny" and his aide reached the hospital a few days later, and after talking to the men had most of the staff fired or transferred. The new staff could not help Lawson, however, who was discharged as 100 percent disabled. He returned to Kentucky, married, fathered two children, and apparently never worked owing to his blindness. He told one interviewer that he spent most days "on the couch, drinking beer and listening to the stereo." He retained his good spirits but was disappointed that his fellow Company D veterans were never interested in getting together. Lawson died in Florida in 2005 and is buried in the Harrodsburg cemetery.

COL. ERNEST B. MILLER, CO 194TB

Ernest Miller returned to San Francisco from Rokuroshi with a new rank, colonel, but in poor health. The wives of Miller, Russ Swearingen, and Ed Burke traveled to Clinton, Iowa, on October 21 to meet their husbands at the hospital there. The men were given a ten-day leave for a trip to Brainerd, which was time enough for the tank company town to put together a homecoming parade for an audience of 20,000 and a ceremony featuring the state attorney general's award of the Minnesota Medal of Valor to Miller. This was the highest ranking in a set of four Minnesota medals, and was equivalent to the U.S. military's Distinguished Service Cross. Miller was the first man to receive one.

Miller then returned to the hospital for a prolonged stay. Miller told a Brainerd newspaper reporter that he was going to write a book after his hospitalization, including such undocumented gems as the "fact" that the 194th Tank Battalion was responsible only to MacArthur himself and was never attached to any other unit. This was false, since the battalion was part of the PTG from the day the latter unit was established; the claim was indicative of the type of book Miller was planning.

When Miller got out of the hospital in 1946, he put 52,000 miles on the family car traveling to American Legion posts to speak on preparedness and universal military training. On January 10, 1947, he appeared before the retirement board, which was to rule on his continued service. He listed the following medical conditions related to his period as a POW: "malnutrition, beriberi, malaria, dysentery, diarrhea, stomach trouble, left hip ailment, scurvy, pellagra, eye trouble, dengue fever, 'and other POW diseases.'" He was approved to remain in the Guard and was promoted to brigadier general. He served as the assistant director of the Minnesota Department of Aeronautics and for five years as the state director of civilian defense. When he finished his book, *Bataan Uncensored*, it was too toxic for a commercial publisher, and it was released in 1949 by a small Minnesota printer without benefit of editing or proofreading. In the book Miller vented his anger at an apathetic U.S. population, the U.S. government, the U.S. Army, and his own commander in the Philippines, as well as the "tricky and treacherous" Japanese. His fights with Weaver and his open insubordination made this a book that the army kept off its reading lists, and it remained virtually unknown outside Minnesota. The state continued to honor him, and he apparently rarely set foot outside it.

Miller's health continued to deteriorate, although he was never adjudged more than 40 percent disabled. After being hospitalized for more than a year, Miller died of cerebral arteriosclerosis in 1992 and is buried at Fort Snelling.

2ND LT. BEN R. MORIN, B/192TB

Ben Morin returned from Rokuroshi in remarkably good condition. He reached home on October 18 after only five days at Letterman; he had gained sixty-five pounds since leaving the camp, was obviously bloated, and "looked terrible," according to his mother. After a few months of home cooking he was in shape for a long, productive life. He entered a Jesuit seminary in 1946, spent thirty-eight years as a parish priest and a missionary in Peru, and retired to a Jesuit retirement home in Clarkston, Michigan. Morin died in 2015, the last surviving officer of B/192TB.

CPL. GLENN S. OLIVER, A/194TB

Glenn Oliver, the *Arisan Maru* survivor, weighed eighty-five pounds on liberation, and when he reached San Francisco had to be carried off the ship on a stretcher. Glenn's major medical problem proved to be hepatitis, probably the result of his rich initial diet, and it took a year in a VA hospital to cure it. He remained in the reserves, trained recruits during the early days of the Korean War, and was discharged in 1951. He moved from Brainerd to Tacoma, Washington, with his wife Esther, and worked as a locomotive engineer for thirty-six years. He credited a supportive wife and family for a normal civilian life. He avoided discussions of POW matters and did not suffer from the nightmares that bedeviled many of his peers. Oliver died in 2012 and is buried in Lakewood, Washington.

CAPT. ALVIN C. POWELEIT, MD, MED DET/192TB

Dr. Alvin Poweleit was in a Formosa camp at the armistice and was taken to the Philippines for medical treatment. He was in good physical condition—first, he had been in an officers' camp, and second, as we have seen, he took great pains to take care of himself—and was soon put on a ship for Seattle, which he reached on November 1. He returned home to Kentucky and was discharged on September 9, 1946. He went back to medical school, became an eye, ear, and throat specialist, and opened a practice in Covington. He was recognized for aggressive cancer treatment, but it is not known if this owed anything to what he had learned in the Philippines and Formosa. He wrote two books, *USAFFE: The Loyal Americans and Faithful Filipinos* and *Kentucky's Fighting 192nd Light GHQ Tank Battalion: A Saga of Kentucky's Part in the Defense of the Philippines*, which came close to being battalion histories, although the latter was misnamed. Ted Wickord, the 192nd Battalion commander, always referred questioners on the campaign to these books. Poweleit retained an interest in Company D, which seemed to have trouble organizing meetings, and after retirement coordinated a get-together at Northern Kentucky University in 1998 that attracted twenty-five 192nd Tank Battalion veterans and proved to be Company D's last reunion. Dr. Poweleit died in 1997 from injuries received in an automobile accident and is buried in a Fort Thomas, Kentucky, cemetery.

SGT. JOHN E. ROWLAND, C + HQ/192TB

John Rowland reached Darien on the first train out of Mukden. He took a hospital ship to Okinawa, flew to the Philippines, took a troopship to San Francisco, and was put into Letterman General Hospital on September 27. On October 19 he was put on a hospital train for Fletcher General Hospital in Cambridge, Ohio, and reached his home in Westerville, Ohio, on October 27. He was given a 120-day medical leave and then married fiancé Virginia, went to work on the family dairy farm, and fathered two children. He was promoted to staff sergeant on April 8, 1946, and was discharged at the army separation center at Camp Atterbury, Indiana. He had begun college before the war planning to be a veterinarian, had dropped out for lack of funds, and now was too tired to return to school. Building on his six years in the service, he decided on a government career and worked for the VA and a Defense Supply Center, retiring from the U.S. Civil Service in 1973 after thirty-two years of service. Unlike many tankers, he was satisfied with his treatment at the VA. He was national commander of the American Defenders of Bataan and Corregidor in 1982 and died in 2004. He is buried in the Westerville cemetery.

1ST SGT. ERO "BEN" SACCONE, C/194TB

Ero "Ben" Saccone was not liberated from the Aisho copper mine until September 4, 1945, and returned to the United States in poor physical condition. He remained in the hospital until September 1947, after which he married, fathered three children, and rejoined the army in the medical department. He worked at hospitals in Germany and France; spent six years at Walter Reed Hospital in Washington, D.C., where as chief admitting officer he met many famous politicians; and finally worked at the Letterman General Hospital in San Francisco. He retired in 1961 as a chief warrant officer 4th class. Ben moved to San Jose, where he was very active in veterans' affairs. He had been the top sergeant, the senior enlisted man, in the Salinas Tank Company and remained highly respected.

In 1967 Ben, Roy Diaz, and several other C/194TB veterans and their wives made a trip to the Philippines, where they retraced the route of the Death March and were treated as heroes by the Filipinos. Ben and his wife Beatrice then made a side trip to Japan. In 1942 Ben's life had been saved by a Japanese mess sergeant at the Batangas work camp who secretly smuggled him extra food and nursed him to health. Ben remembered his name and traced his address while working in Washington. They began a correspondence, which resulted in an invitation to visit. A meeting was arranged in Tokyo at which the Saccones exchanged gifts with Ben's Japanese friend; their letters then continued for years. Ben Saccone passed away at his grandson's home in Fresno in 2007 and is buried in the Garden of Memories Memorial Park in Salinas.

PFC LESTER I. TENNEY, B/192TB

After liberation from Kyushu, Lester Tenney was taken to the Philippines for debriefing and medical treatment and by ship to San Francisco, where he arrived on October 8, having been given a courtesy promotion to private first class. He was admitted to Letterman General Hospital for an unknown period for additional treatment. He made the newspaper on July 28, 1946, with an engagement announcement (still as Tenenberg), which stated his rank as sergeant and said he planned to return to Northwestern University when released from the army. It is unknown when he graduated from high school; he had dropped out in 1938. On June 8, 1952, Tenney (now his legal name) was in the Chicago newspaper as the first ex-prisoner of the Japanese to be paid for forced labor; this amounted to $1,864.50 for three and one-half years and came from the sale of Japanese property confiscated at the start of the war. He was described as an insurance broker and a "former staff sergeant," with a wife and a three-and-a-half-year-old boy.

By 1957 he was serving as president of Maywood's American Bataan Clan and operating the Bataan Import-Export Company in Chicago with six partners, all buddies from the Maywood Tank Company. Tenney told a reporter from the *Chicago Tribune* that the business had been operating for seven years. It imported hand-carved mahogany art pieces and hand-woven cloth mats to sell to local department stores. Here the timeline gets impossibly fuzzy. Apparently the company's inventory was depleted, and Tenney persuaded the other partners to give him their GI savings so he could buy more stock. He then disappeared. The recent recollections of Bill Hauser's and George Dravo's sons tell identical stories. The partners were embarrassed at being conned by one of their own and decided to do nothing. All had wives and children; the wives were furious but had no vote. At least one woman went back to work to save their house. The children wore hand-me-downs for years and lived on Spam and macaroni and cheese. Tenney wired the partners, supposedly from the Philippines, asking for money to come home. The women threw away the telegram. But Tenney was actually in the United States, continuing his education and selling insurance. According to a reporter's interview of Tenney in 1969, he earned a BA at the University of Miami and taught sales psychology in a Florida high school before going into the insurance business full-time in 1950 and, after fifteen years, becoming president of a statewide insurance agency. He did graduate work at Northwestern, earned a master's from San Diego State, and did doctoral work at the

University of Southern California, all in business administration. He then became a professor of insurance in the Arizona State University's college of business administration, returning to full-time teaching because, as he told the newspaper reporter, he had made a vow in POW camp to serve society.

After Tenney's business collapse in Chicago, he did not make contact with any of the POW organizations until 1993, when he retired from ASU and began traveling the country advocating for a Japanese government apology to POWs and for payment by Japanese firms for POW slave labor. At this time he was a director of the Center for Internee Rights in Florida, a pressure group that probably paid for Tenney's travel for years. The center then vanished, along with its funds. Tenney began appearing at the American Defenders of Bataan and Corregidor (ADBC) conventions to press for his positions. His fellow survivors of Fukuoka Camp #17 noted that he avoided their tables. In 1995 the publication of his book, *My Hitch in Hell*, with self-aggrandizement that was extreme even for memoirs and numerous factual errors, further strained relations between Tenney and those veterans who had known him either in the tank battalion or the camps. He began to be described in his many interviews as a "tank commander," which was not true and further insulted the tankers. Yet there was a faction in the ADBC that liked his activism, and in 2008 he was elected the last president of the organization. He met the Japanese ambassador to the United States in Washington and was invited to visit Japan. Funding was provided by Japan's "Peace, Friendship, and Exchange Initiative." Several veterans and caregivers made the trip in 2010, and these have continued. Tenney's quixotic quest for an apology and reparations had morphed into an effort at reconciliation with Japan, which most of the few remaining POWs and their families found agreeable. Nevertheless, when Tenney was put up for the Presidential Medal of Freedom in late 2011, President Obama was bombarded with letters of protest from Fukuoka Camp #17 POWs, and the nomination was withdrawn. Tenney, the last survivor from B/192TB, died in February 2017 in Carlsbad, California, at age ninety-six, survived by his wife Betty, one son, and two stepsons. The biography in his obituary contains many errors, but describes Lester as he presented himself.

B/GEN. JAMES R. N. WEAVER, CO PTG

While the PTG officers had to endure the same poor food and living conditions as the enlisted men, they were not considered slave labor and did not suffer from beatings and work accidents, and most returned to the states in fairly good health. By September 17, 1945, General Weaver was already back in his hometown of Fremont, Ohio, where he spoke to the Rotary Club before visiting Port Clinton, which was only sixteen miles away, giving a speech there praising the Port Clinton Tank Company's accomplishments and warning against "going soft" on the Japanese. He then went to Washington for debriefing and upon his return thanked Fremont officials for the hospitality they had shown his wife and daughter, who had lived with his parents while he was in the Philippines. In November he sent the women's auxiliaries in each of the four 192nd Tank Battalion cities a "Summary of Service . . . of the PTG" and a plea for any documents and citations in their possession. He warned them that a history of the Bataan campaign (Wainwright's) already appearing as a syndicated newspaper series slighted the tanks. To counter this, he was trying to beef up his own report but had lost all of his records. His report when completed was appended to the USFIP official report and disappeared into the vault. It is not known if he tried to find a commercial publisher, but his turgid, bureaucratic style made it unpublishable as it was, and he did not find a coauthor such as Bob Considine, who made Wainwright's memoir a best seller.

Weaver was a popular attendee and speaker at 192nd Tank Battalion veteran functions for a number of years, but never visited Brainerd. Walt Straka, the last A/194TB survivor, said that he would have been unpopular there. It is not known if he ever came to Salinas, home of the other 194th Tank Battalion company. His career led him in rapid succession to command Fort Benning, Fort Ord, Camp Beale, and the Presidio of San Francisco, but the postwar army had a surfeit of brigadier generals and Weaver retired in the spring of 1948. He and his wife Molly built a house in Menlo Park near other retirees. It was not the house on a hill he had dreamed of, but the couple lived there comfortably, entertaining, starting the "Peninsula 1911" luncheon club for his West Point classmates, and working in community organizations. Weaver kept up his correspondence and succeeded in making some corrections to Louis Morton's official history, *The Fall of the Philippines*, before its 1953 publication. Weaver was anxious to do this because Morton was using inaccurate data from Ernest Miller's newly published book. Weaver died in Menlo Park on August 30, 1967, at age seventy-nine.

COL. THEODORE F. WICKORD, CO 192TB

Ted Wickord was promoted to full colonel on September 2, when MacArthur raised all senior RAMP officers one grade. He had not been one of the healthiest inmates at Rokuroshi and spent time in Philippine hospitals before arriving in San Francisco on October 15, 1945. He was kept at Letterman General Hospital before returning to Maywood and his wife Marie and two sons, and left the army on November 15, 1946. He took part in several veterans' activities. One was the first annual convention of the Zentsujians in Chicago. This group had been organized by Ernest Miller and was open to the 600 officers who had been imprisoned in the Zentsuji camp; six out of the twenty-four area members attended the banquet with their wives. Another notable event was the opening of the Bataan-Corregidor Memorial Bridge over the Chicago River on May 28, 1949. The bridge had been under construction (under a different name) since 1939, and completion had been held up by the war. MacArthur returned from Japan to chair the ceremony, which Wickord attended. Wickord then dropped out of military activities other than public Maywood events. It is not known if he had sustained a memory loss, but he forwarded Morton's request for information on the 192nd Battalion to Weaver, and when Weaver pleaded with him to be more cooperative passed the request down to the surviving battalion officers, Morin, Gentry, and Rue. Wickord and Weaver became friends, and Ted and Marie visited Weaver's house on trips to California. This may seem odd, since the two men had totally dissimilar personalities, but their shared experiences in the Philippines gave them a common bond.

Wickord went back to work at Commonwealth Edison, moved into industrial relations and then safety, and became general chairman of the Public Utilities section of the National Safety Council and president of the Greater Chicago chapter of the American Society of Safety Engineers.

He retired from Commonwealth Edison after forty years, died on October 19, 1967, and is buried at St. Joseph Cemetery in River Grove, Illinois. According to his son he had prolonged physical and psychological problems, for which he got no help, suffered malaria attacks for years, and treated his family badly.

All six tank company towns held ceremonies and built memorials to honor their tankers. Each did this in its own way, but all eventually erected memorial displays containing surplus tanks and tablets with the men's names. Early-model M3s such as the PTG had used were no longer available, and the displays featured M3A1s, M3A3s, or M5s, which were later-model light tanks, or M4 Sherman medium tanks. Salinas eventually added an M3 half-track. Maywood's ceremonies were more elaborate than those of the other cities and continued for far longer. Maywood celebrated their Bataan Day on the second Sunday in September, which did not commemorate any specific historical event, but took place on the anniversary of the earliest program Maywood could put together in 1942. After discontinuing parades from 1947 to 1953, Maywood's American Bataan Clan changed its name in 1957 to the Maywood Veterans Council to include all veterans, and the annual Bataan Day became the largest community event in the western suburbs of Chicago, with a parade, banquet, guest speakers, and a Miss Bataan Day contest. In 1996 the Veterans Council was renamed the Maywood Bataan Day Organization (MBDO), which even today continues sponsoring annual events and tinkering with its memorials. The MBDO marked the 75th anniversary of the town's Bataan Day in 2017 with many special events, including the dedication of a new Veterans Memorial Wall.

Four other tank company towns held annual commemorations that petered out with time, but Janesville's 1947 monument dedication ceremony and parade were especially noteworthy. General Weaver jumped out of the parade's lead car and joined the twenty-two marching A/192TB veterans. The parade also featured a mobile M4 Sherman medium tank borrowed from the Rock Island arsenal and the marching women of the Tank Company Auxiliary. The monument, a tablet of ninety-nine names topped by a bronze model M3 light tank, was unveiled by Weaver and the Wisconsin governor. Weaver was the featured speaker at the banquet, at which Wickord read messages from MacArthur (in Japan) and Wainwright. Weaver's letter of appreciation for the memorial service was published in the local newspaper the following week. No commemoration is known to have topped this one.

Harrodsburg held no parades for its tankers. Most had returned bitter and ill, and it was felt important that they be given time to heal. Also, everyone wanted to forget the war. Ultimately, in 1961 a memorial containing an M4 Sherman tank and a plaque was erected. Eight of the fourteen surviving Mercer County tankers attended the dedication. The managers of the new Hitachi plant, which was located less than a mile down the highway, read the plaque and demanded that the memorial be moved. The Harrodsburg city fathers, in what was probably the last thoughtful gesture they made for the tank company, refused.

Brainerd was the last tank company town to erect a memorial. Brainerd honored Colonel Miller with a new car but did nothing for his men. By 1971 James McComas and Bernard FitzPatrick were tired of waiting and spearheaded a drive that resulted in a memorial being erected in front of the armory featuring an M4 medium tank and Bataan Death March soil that McComas had brought back from a trip to the Philippines. The Minnesota National Guard has taken responsibility for maintaining this and subsequent memorials.

The surviving tankers were glad to see the Japanese war crimes trials get underway. The men provided affidavits in support of the prosecution of their worst POW camp commandants and guards. The trials took place from 1946 to 1950. Those in Tokyo were for Class A crimes, aggressive war, and atrocities, for which 25 were convicted, 7 executed, and 16 sentenced to life in prison. Trials in the countries Japan had occupied were for Class B and Class C atrocities, for which about 5,700 were tried, 3,000 were convicted, and 920 were executed. Those sent to prison were released as quickly as possible to enter Japanese business and government, as Japan was now a key American ally. The last man came out in December 1958. This apparent coddling of their enemies in the interests of the Cold War further embittered the tankers, as did the Treaty of San Francisco in September 1951, which formally ended the Pacific War. Japan was required to pay reparations to the victors, but in forfeited assets and not cash. The tankers were hoping for payment for their labor in the Japanese POW camps. American courts ruled that this was specifically forbidden by the terms of the treaty, as did Japanese courts. In 1988 President Reagan issued a formal apology to the Japanese Americans interned during the war and offered them reparations averaging $20,000 apiece. American ex-POWs felt that they had a good case for equal treatment, but the U.S. government turned a blind eye to their entreaties. In 1999 the State of California passed a law enabling any World War II slave labor victim to bring suit in California State Court. Lester Tenney, who was now living in California, was waiting for this development, and immediately brought suit against the Mitsui Co. and the Mitsui Mining Co. In the next few years hundreds of ex-POWs brought similar suits, but all were opposed by the U.S. government and in 2004 were dismissed by the federal courts for a reason that seems obvious: Foreign policy is made by the national government, not the states, and the 1951 Peace Treaty forbade such payments. Ex-POWs from Britain, Canada, and the Netherlands received small sums from their governments. Only the American POWs collected nothing from theirs but their back pay, disability payments, and in some cases a pittance from forfeited assets.

The ex-POWs' attempts to obtain formal apologies from either the Japanese government or the Japanese conglomerates who had used them for slave labor had no success until the end of the Cold War; they could get no backing from their own government. Japan's attitude seemed to change somewhat in the 2000s. It offered mild apologies in 2009 and 2010, but a speech by the Japanese ambassador to the final ADBC convention, which had been billed as an apology, never used that word, and it was applauded by only half the audience. The accession of Shinzo Abe to prime minister in 2012 closed the door to any stronger apologies while any tankers were alive. Abe, a staunch conservative, questioned Japan's responsibility for the war, and in an April 2014 memorial service honoring 1,800 war criminals, including 130 executed for the abuse of American POWs, Abe referred to them as "martyrs who staked their souls to become the foundation of their nation."

A reconciliation initiative continues despite the attitude of the prime minister. One small Japanese corporation extended an apology in 2014, followed by Mitsubishi Materials in 2015. A senior executive of the latter firm came to California to make a formal apology, but only one POW could be located who was in good enough health to attend the ceremony. A full rapprochement is no longer possible between the National Guard tankers and either their own government or that of Japan.

A quantitative measure of the PTG's sacrifice is of interest. No official PTG roster survived the war. The plaques on the town memorials contain the names of the Guard members who had left in 1940 and 1941, but most did not list the non-Guardsmen who had joined the tank companies later as fillers, primarily at Fort Knox or Fort Lewis, and subsequently shared all of the PTG's horrors. This is an understandable example of civic pride, but frustrating to the historian. After an exhaustive study of the existing data, I conclude that there were a minimum of 1,133 men in the PTG; 617 of them were KIA in the Philippines or died as POWs, for a loss of 54.5 percent. The numerical data are summarized by unit, Guard membership, and type of loss in the table on page 256, which owes a great deal to the alphabetic tables in Jim Opolony's Bataan Project website.

What did the sacrifice of these men accomplish? Despite what they were told, and what many of them believed for the rest of their lives, they did not save Australia from invasion. Japan's rapid advance through Malaya and the East Indies to Australia's doorstep surprised them as much as it did the Allies, and they never had a plan to invade that country. But the psychological value of the delay that the defenders of Bataan and Corregidor imposed on the Japanese was immense, not so much on the Japanese, although it cost General Homma, one of its best field commanders, his job, but on the American people. American morale had to be stiffened to withstand a long war, and the defense of the Philippines provided the first evidence that the Japanese were not invincible and that such a war could ultimately be successful.

But was the loss of the Provisional Tank Group inevitable? No. The National Guardsmen should never have been sent to the Philippines. They were there because the American high commanders underestimated the Japanese and overestimated the capability of the Philippine Army. MacArthur persuaded Marshall that his army needed only a little boost in the form of armor, coastal (antiaircraft) artillery, and field artillery units.

Personnel	HQ PTG		192TB		194TB		17 ORD CO		TOTAL		PTG TOTAL
	ARMY	NGUARD	ARMY	NGUARD	ARMY	NGUARD	ARMY	NGUARD	ARMY	NGUARD	
DIED:											
KIA in campaign	0	0	15	10	0	11	0	0	15	21	
DIED as guerilla	0	0	1	0	0	2	1	0	2	2	
DIED on Death March	0	0	3	3	2	2	2	0	7	5	
DIED in PI POW camp	5	3	87	95	52	84	40	0	184	182	
DIED on Hell Ships	4	2	38	43	15	30	19	0	76	75	
DIED in POW camp north of PI	2	0	16	14	2	8	6	0	26	22	
TOTAL DEATHS	11	5	160	165	71	137	68	0	310	307	617
SURVIVORS:											
EVACUATED during campaign	0	0	0	4	2	2	0	0	2	6	
ESCAPED from PI as guerilla	1	0	1	0	1	2	5	0	8	2	
RESCUED from PI	2	0	15	8	4	7	7	0	28	15	
RELEASED postwar (RAMP)	7	2	130	109	41	96	67	3	245	210	
TOTAL SURVIVORS	10	2	146	121	48	107	79	3	283	233	516
TOTAL PERSONNEL	21	7	306	286	119	244	147	3	593	540	1133
PERCENT FATALITIES	52.4	71.4	52.3	57.7	59.7	56.1	46.3	0.0	52.3	57.2	54.5

Marshall agreed and sent them. The units were all from the recently federalized National Guard, as they happened to be closest to being ready for foreign deployment. (The field artillery battalion was from Texas and got only as far as Java, where it was lost.) Marshall should have known that any Americans he sent to the Philippines would be lost quickly in case of war; he should have known how untrained and underequipped the Philippine Army was, but was either never told, or dismissed the information.

General Arnold sent thirty-five B-17s, half of his sole offensive force, to the Philippines. He believed that this would be an effective deterrent to the Japanese, but this was egregious self-delusion. The loss of half of the B-17s and many P-40s on Clark Field at noon on the first day of the war gave the Japanese air supremacy for the entire campaign, which had no influence on the end result but kept things extremely nasty for the Fil-American forces on the ground. The exact reason for this debacle is still debated, but it reflects poorly on all of the American generals involved.

According to MacArthur scholars, the man suffered a temporary mental breakdown that affected his decision-making the first day of the war and the following week, when firm orders for the inevitable pullback into Bataan should have been issued. Instead, there was a complete breakdown in logistics due to the gross ineptitude of MacArthur's own headquarters. Supplies were destroyed or left to the Japanese instead of being withdrawn to the peninsula. Shortages of everything, especially food, were the result, and the Filipino and American troops suffered unimaginable hardships before their surrender on April 9, all the fault of the theater commander and his staff. MacArthur took most of this staff with him to Australia, where they enjoyed a successful war.

The Provisional Tank Group carried out every mission entrusted to it, despite debilitating shortages, an incredibly hostile environment, a lack of doctrine, and a poor command structure. Its long-term accomplishments were negligible, but the brief campaign did give the Armored Force back home a few lessons it could use. General Weaver radioed Washington on tactics and equipment as often as he could. The surrender cost Washington the further services of an armor general who would have been a good choice to lead an armored division in the favored theaters, Europe and the Mediterranean. The surviving tankers were never given the recognition due them, and found themselves disrespected by the army before they even reached home. They were warned in their debriefings to dissemble rather than tell what they knew about Japanese atrocities. Many of them fought with the Veterans Administration for years for proper treatment and disability ratings. The campaign and its command-level errors embarrassed the army but were forgotten by the general public in light of the war's later successes. The men suffered monetarily from government indifference and in general from a lack of attention by historians. This belated effort is too late for the tankers, but I hope that it will help ensure their legacy.

ACKNOWLEDGMENTS

First I'd like to acknowledge Tony Meldahl, whose desire for a book on the National Guard tank companies and whose extensive files got this book started. Unfortunately, Tony passed away before I could complete the book.

Next, Jim Opolony has been a constant help. Jim, a teacher at Proviso Township High School in Maywood, Illinois, noticed in 1999 a plaque in a little-used hallway listing the Proviso graduates who had died in World War II. The large number of graduates from two years, 1937 and 1938, piqued his curiosity and led him to discover that these men were all from a single National Guard unit that had surrendered on Bataan: Company B of the 192nd Tank Battalion, which was one component of the little-known Provisional Tank Group (PTG). He and two other teachers started a website to record what he was learning; this became a class project and ultimately an award-winning educational site. In 2007 Jim became the sole teacher supervising the site, and the district turned it over to him upon his 2017 retirement. Jim's worldwide correspondence load and ability to get people to open up put my efforts to shame.

Noted historian Iris Chang was planning a book on the 192nd Tank Battalion and had conducted a number of interviews before her unexpected death in 2004. Knowing that this material would be valuable to an author on a similar topic and would thus see the light of day, her husband Brett Douglas supplied me with all of her files, and I acknowledge these here.

Thanks to Leslie Sawyer for the maps, which I can't get him to sign, and Rich Muller for an initial edit of the text.

The following archivists and historians were of great help: Ruth Anderson of the Charles Tallman Archives and Research Center, Janesville, Wisconsin; Douglas Boyd and Judy Sackett of the Louis B. Nunn Center for Oral History, University of Kentucky; Robert Cameron, U.S. Army Armor Branch historian; Charles Conrady, Doug Thompson, and

Ryan Welle of the Minnesota Military Museum; Eleanor Kleiber of the University of Hawaii; Amber Korb of the California State Military Museum; Jason LeMay of the Kentucky Department of Military Affairs; Lauren Lemmon of the Ira Rupp Public Library, Port Clinton, Ohio; Pam Nelson of the Crow Wing County Historical Society Museum; James Perry of the Monterey County Historical Society; Karl Rubis, historian, U.S. Army Ordnance Corps and School; and Natalie Watts of the Mercer County Public Library.

These individuals—many of them descendants of PTG members—supplied documents, photographs, and enlightening correspondence: Kevin Aldred, Ken Ballard, Norm Becker, Karyn Brown, Steven Bull, Mark Cain, Linda Dahl, Lorraine Diaz, Brett Douglas, Micheal Dravo, James Erickson, John Erickson, Merry Evans, Joseph Galloway, Steve Gibson, Shelly Hando, Bill Hauser, Tom Hulihan, Eddie Johnson, Jim Knudsen, Tom Lang, Ann Lee, Sheryl Matejka, Ray Merriam, Sharon Nakamura, Larry Osvold, Ray Peterson, Rodney Preuit, Stephen Ross, Jeff Sauer, Chris Seymour, Wendell Sisson, Brandee Spoor, Pat Spoor, Charlie Taylor, Ted Wickord, and Larry Wuertz.

I apologize to anyone whose name I omitted. I also apologize to anyone who can't find their PTG member in the book. I did read and try to utilize all material submitted, but there were over 1,100 men in the PTG, and I concentrated on the few as representative of the many.

Photographs are from the collections of the Bataan Project, Steven Bull, the Ida Rupp Public Library, Eddie Johnson, Tom Lang, the Mercer County Public Library, the Minnesota Military Museum, Sharon Nakamura, and the author.

Sources

This book would not have been possible without material from three main sources: (1) Tony Meldahl's 192nd Tank Battalion document files, the originals of which now reside in the Ida Rupp (Port Clinton, Ohio) Public Library's Bataan Memorial collection; (2) Iris Chang's files, principally interviews of 192nd Tank Battalion veterans, which her husband Brett Douglas made available after her untimely death; and (3) Jim Opolony and his Bataan Project website. Principal sources for each chapter are listed below.

Chapter 1: The Heartland Mobilizes

The six tank company towns are each the subject of a book in Arcadia Publishing's Images of America series. These form the basis of the town descriptions, supplemented by Wikipedia. Pre-war organization of the National Guard's tank units is well covered in Jacobs, "The Evolution of Tank Units in the Pre-WWII National Guard and the Defense of Bataan." Lingeman, *Don't You Know There's a War On?* is good for the early-war United States. Brief biographies of the men are found in the Bataan Project website.

Janesville: The Janesville Tank Company has two excellent sources: Doherty, "Too Little, Too Late: Janesville's 'Lost Children' of the Armored Force," and Schutt's master's thesis, "Janesville Tankers on Bataan." Interviews of Knox can be found in, for example, Gavin Daws, *Prisoners of the Japanese: POWs of World War II in the Pacific,* and Knox, *Death March: The Survivors of Bataan.*

Maywood: Sources for Morin are his memoir and interview. For Bashleben, his interview; for Bardowski, interviews of his wife and son. Sources for Tenney are his memoir, *My Hitch in Hell: The Bataan Death March* (used with caution) and his interview. The sendoff party can be found in the *Bellwood Star-Progress*, November 27, 1940.

Port Clinton: For additional information on the prewar tank company, see the Ohio National Guard yearbook. The farewell party is described on its fourth anniversary in the *Port Clinton Herald*, November 24, 1944.

Harrodsburg: Articles specifically on Harrodsburg and its tank company are: Peckler, "Heroism at Home: The Struggle of the Women—Harrodsburg during World War II"; Trowbridge, "Commemorating the Sixty-Sixth Anniversary of the Sixty-Six Harrodsburg Tankers"; Harris, "The Harrodsburg Tankers: Bataan, Prison, and the Bonds of Community." Sources for Gentry, Lawson, and Rowland are their interviews.

Brainerd: Kenney, *Minnesota Goes to War* is an excellent resource, with four chapters devoted to Brainerd. Nelson, "Company A 194th Tank Battalion Survivors' Stories" contains submissions of widely different quality from thirteen veterans, plus much general information. Miller's early life is documented in his personal papers; sources for Oliver and Porwall are their interviews.

Salinas: Anderson, "A History of the Salinas National Guard Company 1895–1995" is a good general source. Diaz is discussed by his wife Lorraine in her interview, as is Johnson by his son.

"You had to be dressed in a tux . . . ," Kenney, p. 10.

Chapter 2. The National Guard Tank Companies and the U.S. Armored Force

A good general source on the U.S. Armored Force is Cameron, *Mobility, Shock & Firepower: The Emergence of the U.S. Army's Armor Branch 1917–1945*; another is Gillie, *Forging the Thunderbolt*. For Chaffee, I used M/Gen. Ray Porter, "Adna R. Chaffee, Jr.—Father of U.S. Armored Forces." Schreier, "U.S. Army Tank Development 1925–1940" has a good discussion of early U.S. tank design, as does Ells and Chamberlain, "Light Tanks M1-M5." Zaloga's armor books for Osprey are always good, and those on the M3 light tank and U.S. half-tracks can be recommended.

The 192nd Tank Battalion at Fort Knox: Salecker, *Rolling Thunder against the Rising Sun* is good for the call-up period of both PTG battalions. Fort Knox is described in all of the interviews of 192nd Tank Battalion men stationed there. Information on Allen, Rowland, and Gentry is found in their interviews; on Tenney, in his memoir; on Poweleit, in his two books, *Kentucky's Fighting 192nd Light GHQ Tank Battalion* and *USAFFE: The Loyal Americans and Faithful Filipinos*.

The 194th Tank Battalion at Fort Lewis: Both Miller's book, *Bataan Uncensored*, and his personal papers cover this period. FitzPatrick's *The Hike into the Sun* has material on him from Fort Lewis onward. Tait's *History of the 17th Ordnance Company* covers this unit.

The 192nd Tank Battalion in the Louisiana Maneuvers: Gabel, *The U.S. Army 1941 GHQ Maneuvers* is the standard reference, but it contains little information on the tank units involved. The 192nd Battalion interviews in general are good for color; Morin and Schutt have information on the train convoys and ship loading; the Poweleit, Gentry, and Goldstein interviews are sources for these men.

Chapter 3: The Philippines

Louis Morton's *The Fall of the Philippines*, one of the first books completed for the huge United States Army in World War II series, is still the definitive book on the campaign, over sixty-five years after publication. More than just combat, Morton covers Philippine history, geography, politics, and the military; Japanese war plans; and Douglas MacArthur, all in excellent fashion. He does not do so well with the PTG, but not for lack of trying; he was limited by a lack of material. His book will provide the framework for chapters 3–7 of the present book; I will fill in the missing tank content. Another, more recent (1991), general reference is Edward Miller's *War Plan Orange: The War Plan to Defeat Japan 1897–1945*. Information on Colonel Weaver is from an extensive obituary by a friend and classmate, Harold Nichok. Sources for Wainwright are his memoir, *General Wainwright's Story* and Schultz's biography, *Hero of Bataan: The Story of General Jonathan M. Wainwright*. Poweleit's conversation with

MacArthur and Weaver is found in Poweleit. The "2–3000 brown soldiers" and the young New Mexican lieutenant are in Cave's history of the
200th Coast Artillery Regiment (AA), *Beyond Courage: One Regiment vs.
Japan, 1941–1945*. Miller's book, the PTG memoirs, and interviews are
used throughout.

"Negotiations with Japan appear to be terminated . . . ," Brereton, p. 33.

Chapter 4: December 8

Bartsch's *December 8, 1941: MacArthur's Pearl Harbor* is the definitive history of this fateful day. The MacArthur-Sutherland-Brereton
squabble and the Clark Field debacle have not been covered any better. Manchester, *American Caesar: Douglas MacArthur 1880–1964*, hints
at MacArthur's mental breakdown on this day, and this hypothesis has
been accepted by later historians. Weaver's "Operations of the Provisional
Tank Group," which is the official history of the PTG, albeit existing only
as an addendum to the USFIP Operations Report, begins on this date, as
does Bardowski's hand-written memoir. The Brooks Field dedication is
described in Craft, *Kentucky National Guard History: World War II—Berlin Crisis 1937–1962*. The Morton quote is from page 90 of *The Fall of the
Philippines*. The Stimson quotation is from Young, "Franklin Roosevelt's
Pre-War Intervention Plans." Every PTG member remembered where he
was and what he did on December 8, and Miller and every memoir and
interview have been consulted.

"For the preservation of America . . . ," Craft, p. 31.

Chapter 5. The Lingayen Gulf Landings and the Fil-American Response

MacArthur's comments on "white pilots" and his S-2's on "Germans"
are in Gough, "Failure and Destruction, Clark Field and the Philippines, December 8, 1941." The *Pensacola* convoy is covered in Morton;
the SS *Mactan* evacuation of wounded, in the Gibson newspaper series,
now found online. Bren carriers are described in Chamberlain and Crow,
"Carriers." Weaver and Miller are good sources for the Japanese landings
and the immediate response; Morton is limited by a lack of data. The

conversations between Wainwright and Sutherland are found in Schultz; it is not known to what extent these are reconstructions, but they do cover the actual events well. Morin's battle is covered best in his own memoir, supplemented by Dooley, "The First U.S. Tank Action in World War II," and Woolfe, "Armored Debut on the Road to Damortis." The memoirs and interviews of PTG men mentioned in the text were consulted.

"The strain on the drivers and vehicles . . . ," Miller, *Bataan Uncensored*, p. 82.

Chapter 6. Retreat across the Central Luzon Plain

Weaver and Miller are good sources for this, the PTG's only campaign of movement. Morton and Wainwright are good for the Philippine Army, less so for the PTG. Altman submitted a report on D/192TB's Agno River battle to Chunn for his War Diary. The memoirs and interviews of the tankers who are mentioned in the text were studied.

The Battle of Baliuag: Gentry and Allen are both excellent sources. The Frank Hewlett article that did so much to buck up morale in the United States was published in all United Press newspapers, including the (Phoenix) *Arizona Republic*, on February 14, 1942.

Into Bataan: "Nat Grand" is in James, *South to Bataan, North to Mukden.*

"The area is all open rice paddies . . . ," Gentry, interview with Arthur L. Kelly.

"I was the last tank to leave the area . . . ," Muther memoir, p. 12.

Chapter 7. The Siege of Bataan

Whitman's *Bataan: The Last Ditch* is a huge study of the three-month siege. Weaver and Miller do a good job with PTG coverage. Every tanker knew where he was when he learned of the surrender, and all memoirs and interviews were studied.

"The following message from General MacArthur will be read . . . ," Ortega, *Courage on Bataan and Beyond*, p. 33.

"Tanks will execute maximum delay, . . ." Weaver, paragraph 43.

"Immediately after this war started, . . ." Roosevelt Fireside Chat #20.

"Dugout Doug MacArthur lies ashaking on the Rock, . . ." Miller, *Bataan Uncensored*, p. 193.

"One day our CO got on the radio . . . ," Knox, *Death March*, p. 91.

"Our tanks . . . were sent westward . . . ," Mallonée, *The Naked Flagpole*, p. 122.

Chapter 8. Captives of the Japanese

Weaver's, Whitman's, and Morton's studies end with General King's surrender, although that of Morton picks up again with the siege of Corregidor. The Provisional Tank Group and its attachments were dissolved with the surrender, and the history of the PTG can well be said to end at this point. However, the men's histories certainly did not end. A four-month campaign was followed by three and one-half years of brutal captivity; their time as POWs affected their lives much more than their time as tankers, and their prison experience typically dominates their interviews. I thus found it appropriate to cover the period of captivity in this book, albeit in a condensed fashion. The tankers were split up, and every man's experience was different; I have chosen only a few to follow in detail, but the interviews and memoirs of all were consulted. Books on the POW experience abound, and for readers wanting more, Daws, *Prisoners of the Japanese*, is good, although its anti-American bias may put some off. For sheer literary excellence I recommend Norman and Norman's *Tears in the Darkness*.

The Hike: Falk, *Bataan: The March of Death*, was the first book-length study, and is still good. Knox, *Death March*, contains the stories of many tankers. Colonel Alexander's comments on discipline are found in Caraccilo, *Surviving Bataan and Beyond*.

Camp O'Donnell: The many sources for Tsuneyoshi include Falk and Poweleit.

Corregidor: Miller, *From Shanghai to Corregidor*, is the best source for the Marines. McDonald, "Imperial Japanese Army 3rd Company, 7th Tank Regiment on Route 5, Luzon," is a good, brief discussion of the Japanese tanks.

Camp Cabanatuan: Beckenbaugh, "Casualties in Philippines POW Camps O'Donnell and Cabanatuan," is a good resource for casualties. Sides, *Ghost Soldiers*, is recommended for the Ranger rescue raid.

"I was very fortunate in that I had a buddy . . . ," Knox, p. 129.

"His lard ass was too much to carry . . . ," Knox, p. 124.

"Who had the right to say . . . ," FitzPatrick, p. 114.

"It was the terror vested in the tank . . . ," Wainwright, p. 119.

"When the battle situation becomes urgent . . . ," Mansell POW Resources website.

Chapter 9. The Home Front

The Arcadia series, Wikipedia, Kenney, and Peckler are good sources for the tank company towns during the war. The history of Maywood's American Bataan Clan is in the Bataan Project website; that of the other towns' auxiliaries is found in those towns' newspapers, as are details of communication with the POWs. The California "Jap Scare" is discussed in Yenne, "The General Who Panicked the West Coast." For the *Kanangoora* and *Gripsholm*, see Irtani, "The *Gripsholm* World War II Exchanges." Newspaper articles mentioned in the text are: the first FBI raid on Japanese aliens, the *Salt Lake City Telegram*, February 10, 1942; the June 1942 Harrodsburg ceremony, the *Danville* (Kentucky) *Advocate-Messenger*, June 5, 1942; that town's view of the Death March revelation, the *Louisville Courier–Journal*, January 29, 1944; prediction of the effects of closing the Japanese internment camps, the *Los Angeles Times*, December 16, 1944; the John Steinbeck quote, the *Mercury News*, November 9, 2013; the Blue Network Harrodsburg program, the *Louisville Courier–Journal*, May 30, 1945; Agnes Below's letter on protecting the POWs from the atomic bombs, the *Port Clinton News-Herald*, August 9, 1945; Frances Rue's comments on V-J Day celebrations, the *Louisville Courier–Journal*, August 15, 1945.

"I regret to advise . . . ," *Port Clinton News-Herald*, May 22, 1942.

"We have been crucified anew . . ." *Lafayette* (Indiana) *Journal & Courier*, January 29, 1944.

"We . . . protest the withholding of information . . . ," *Sandusky Register*, February 4, 1944.

Chapter 10. Hell in the North

The Hell Ships: Michno, *Death on the Hellships*, is the standard reference; the quote from Preston Hubbard is in Michno. Daws is also good, as are the tankers' interviews and memoirs.

The Northern Camps: Holmes, *Unjust Enrichment*, covers Japan's slave labor policies. Most of the camps still have an active website; that of Fukuoka's Camp #17, and correspondence with its webmaster, were especially helpful. Adams and Popham, *No Time for Geishas*, was not only useful for Camp #17, but its comparison with other camps was a revelation. Thompson, "History of the Mukden Group," describes the Manchurian camps. James, *South to Bataan, North to Mukden*, discusses the movements of the generals' group.

"Many men lost their minds . . . ," Toland, *The Rising Sun*, p. 749.

"There were five new barracks very flimsily constructed . . . ," Morin, "My Story," p. 12.

"[O]fficers were used to carry food to the enlisted men . . . ," Miller, Personal Papers, p. 78.

"[B]y the time we arrived, half the cash in the camp . . . ," Adams and Popham, p. 162.

Chapter 11. Return Home

Interviews, memoirs, newspaper articles, the Bataan Project website, and correspondence with family members were used for the biographies of the returning men. The Abe speech is in an article by Kirk Spitzer in time.com, which could not be located in 2017. Newspaper articles mentioned in the text are: the Phyllis Wallisch interview, *Janesville Gazette*, November 9, 1997; Forrest Knox's appearance at a school assembly, *Janesville Gazette*, March 13, 1983; Miller's plans for his book, *Brainerd Daily Dispatch*, date unknown (1946); Tenney's engagement announcement, *Chicago Tribune*, July 28, 1946; Tenney's reimbursement for forced labor, *Chicago Tribune*, June 6, 1952; the Bataan Import-Export Company, *Chicago Tribune*, September 5, 1957; Tenney as Arizona State University professor, (Phoenix) *Arizona Republic*, December 15, 1969.

"We came down for a while . . . ," *Brainerd Daily Dispatch*, August 17, 1945.

Permissions

Permission to quote excerpts was received from:

Doubleday, an imprint of the Knopf Doubleday Publishing Group, a division of Penguin Random House LLC, for *General Wainwright's Story* by Jonathon Mayhew Wainwright, copyright 1946 by Jonathon Mayhew Wainwright.

Houghton Mifflin Harcourt Publishing Company, for *Death March: The Survivors of Bataan*, by Donald Knox, copyright 1981 by Donald Knox.

Louis B. Nunn Center for Oral History, University of Kentucky, for Col. Arthur L. Kelly interview with William H. Gentry (2004OH 089 WW330).

Bibliography

Books

Adams, Geoffrey Pharaoh, and Hugh Popham, *No Time for Geishas*, Leo Cooper Ltd., London, England, 1973

Adler, Judith, and Den Adler, *Janesville, Images of America*, Arcadia Publishing, Charleston, SC, 2012

Ancheta, Celedonia, *The Wainwright Papers: Volume IV*, New Day Publishers, Quezon City, Philippines, 1982

Anonymous, *Historical Annual, National Guard and Naval Militia of the State of Ohio 1938*, Ohio National Guard, Columbus, OH, 1939

Anonymous, *The Campaigns of MacArthur, Vol. 1*, http://www.history.army.mil/html/books/013/13-3/CMH_Pub_13-3.pdf

Anonymous, *Philippine Islands—The U.S. Army Campaigns of WWII*, http://www.history.army.mil/html/books/072/CMH_Pub_72-3/index.html

Anonymous, *FM 17-10 Armored Force*, War Department, Washington, DC, 1942

Anonymous, *FM 17-33 Armored Battalion*, War Department, Washington, DC, 1942

Anonymous, *TM 9-710 Basic Half-Track Vehicles*, War Department, Washington, DC, 1944

Anonymous, *TM 9-726 Light Tank M3*, War Department, Washington, DC, 1942

Astor, Gerald, *Crisis in the Pacific: The Battles for the Philippine Islands by the Men Who Fought Them*, Dell Publishing/Random House, New York, 1996

Baldwin, Hanson W., *Battles Lost and Won*, Harper & Row Publishers, New York, 1996

Bartsch, William, *December 8, 1941: MacArthur's Pearl Harbor*, Texas A&M University Press, College Station, TX, 2003

Bartsch, William, *Doomed at the Start: American Fighter Pilots in the Philippine Islands 1941–1942*, Texas A&M University Press, College Station, TX, 1992

Beck, John J., *MacArthur and Wainwright: Sacrifice of the Philippines*, University of New Mexico Press, Albuquerque, NM, 1974

Bergamini, David, *Japan's Imperial Conspiracy—Volume II*, William Morrow & Co., New York, 1971

Brereton, Lewis H., *The Brereton Diaries: The War in the Air in the Pacific, Middle East & Europe*, William Morrow & Co., New York, 1946

Breuer, William B., *The Great Raid: Rescuing the Doomed Ghosts of Bataan and Corregidor*, John Wiley & Sons, New York, 2002

Bull, Stephen, *World War II Jungle Warfare Tactics*, Osprey Elite 151, Osprey Publishing, Oxford, England, 2007

Cameron, Robert S., *Mobility, Shock & Firepower: The Emergence of the U.S. Army's Armor Branch, 1917–1945*, http://www.history.army.mil/html/books/Mobility_Shock_and_Firepower/CMH_30-23-1.pdf

Caraccilo, Dominic J. (ed.), *Surviving Bataan and Beyond: Col. Irvin Alexander's Odyssey as a Japanese POW*, Stackpole Books, Mechanicsburg, PA, 1999

Carroll, Andrew, *War Letters: Extraordinary Correspondence from American Wars*, Simon & Schuster, New York, 2001

Carter, Kit, and R. Mueller, *The Army Air Forces in World War II: Combat Chronology 1941–1945*, Office of Air Force History, Headquarters USAF, Washington, DC, 1973

Cave, Dorothy, *Beyond Courage: One Regiment vs. Japan, 1941–1945*, Yucca Tree Press, Las Cruces, NM, 1992

Chamberlain, Peter, and Chris Ellis, *Light Tank Type 95 Kyu-Go*, Armour in Profile 22, Profile Publications Ltd., Berkshire, England, n.d.

Chamberlain, Peter, and Duncan Crow, *Carriers*, Profile Weapons 14, Profile Publications Ltd., Berkshire, England, n.d.

Chang, Iris, *The Rape of Nanking: The Forgotten Holocaust of World War II*, Penguin Putnam Inc., New York, 1997

Chun, Clayton, *The Fall of the Philippines 1941–1942*, Osprey Campaign 243, Osprey Publishing, Oxford, England, 2012

Cline, Ray H., *Washington Command Post: The Operations Division*, http://www.history.army.mil/html/books/001/1-2/CMH_Pub_1-2.pdf

Connaughton, Richard, *MacArthur and Defeat in the Philippines*, The Overlook Press, Peter Mayer Publishers Inc., Woodstock and New York, 2001

Cox, Jeffrey, *Rising Sun, Falling Skies: The Disastrous Java Sea Campaign of World War II*, Osprey Books, Oxford, England, 2014

Craven, W. V., and J. L. Cate, *The Army Air Forces in World War II—Volume 1: Plans and Early Operations*, University of Chicago Press, Chicago, 1948

Crow, Duncan, *U.S. Armor-Cavalry: A Short History 1917–1967*, Profile Publications Ltd., Berkshire, England, 1973

Crow Wing County Historical Society, *Brainerd*, Images of America, Arcadia Publishing, Charleston, SC, 2013

Daws, Gavin, *Prisoners of the Japanese: POWs of World War II in the Pacific*, William Morrow & Co. Inc., New York, 1994

Deuchler, Douglas, *Maywood*, Images of America, Arcadia Publishing, Charleston, SC, 2004

Dioso, Marconi M., *The Times When Men Must Die: The Story of the Philippine Army during the Early Months of World War II in the Pacific, December 1941–May 1942*, Dorrance Publishing Co. Inc., Pittsburgh, 2010

Domagalski, John J., *Under a Blood Red Sun: The Remarkable Story of PT Boats in the Philippines and the Rescue of General MacArthur*, Casemate Publishers, Philadelphia and Oxford, England, 2016

Doubler, Michael D., *I Am the Guard: A History of the Army National Guard, 1636–2000*, http://www.arng.army.mil/News/publications/Publications/I%20am%20the%20 %20Guard.pdf

Doyle, David, *World War II Jeep in Action*, Squadron/Signal 2042, Squadron/Signal Publications, Carrollton, TX, 2009

Doyle, David, *M3 Gun Motor Carriage*, Squadron/Signal 39002, Squadron/Signal Publications, Carrollton, TX, 2013

Dyess, William E., *The Dyess Story: An Eye-Witness Account of the Death March from Bataan*, G. P. Putnam's Sons, New York, 1944

Edmonds, Walter D., *They Fought With What They Had: The Story of the AAF in the SW Pacific*, Little, Brown & Co., Boston, 1951

Eisenhower, Dwight D., *At Ease: Stories I Tell to Friends*, Doubleday & Co., Garden City, NY, 1967

Ellis, Chris, and Peter Chamberlain, *Light Tanks M1-M5*, Profile AFV Weapons 4, Profile Publications Ltd., Berkshire England, n.d.

Ervin, Rob, and David Doyle, *Stuart Light Tank in Action*, Squadron/Signal in Action 12055, Squadron/Signal Publications, Carrollton, TX, 2014

Esposito, Vincent J., *The West Point Atlas of American Wars, Volume II: 1900–1953*, Praeger Publishers, New York, 1959

Falk, Stanley L., *Bataan: The March of Death*, Jove Publications Inc., New York, 1962

FitzPatrick, Bernard T., *The Hike into the Sun*, McFarland & Co. Inc., Jefferson, NC, 1993

Forty, Jonathan, *M3-M3A1-M3A3 Stuart I to V*, Tanks in Detail 2, Ian Allan Publishing Ltd., Surrey, England, 2002

Gabel, Christopher, *The U.S. Army 1941 GHQ Maneuvers*, http://www.history.army.mil/ html/books/070/70-41-1/CMH_Pub_70-41-1.pdf

Gander, Terry J., *U.S. Half Tracks M2-M3-M5-M9*, Military Vehicles in Detail 3, Ian Allan Publishing Ltd., Surrey, England, 2004

Gillie, M. H., *Forging the Thunderbolt*, Stackpole Books, Mechanicsburg, PA, 2006

Green, Constance McL., *The Ordnance Department: Planning Munitions for War*, http:// www.history.army.mil/html/books/010/CMH_Pub_10-9/index.html

Greenfield, K. R., ed., *Command Decisions*, Office of the Chief of Military History, Department of the Army, Washington, DC, 1960

Greenfield, K. R., Robert Palmer, and Bell Wiley, *Organization of Ground Combat Troops*, http://history.army.mil/html/books/002/2-1/CMH_Pub_2-1.pdf

Hara, Tomio, *Japanese Combat Cars, Light Tanks and Tankettes*, Profile Weapons 54, Profile Publications Ltd., Berkshire, England, 1973

Hara, Tomio, *Japanese Medium Tanks*, Profile Weapons 49, Profile Publications Ltd., Berkshire, England, 1972

Hayashi, Saburo with A. D. Coox, *KŌGUN: The Japanese Army in the Pacific War*, The Marine Corps. Association, Quantico, VA, 1959

Hillenbrand, Laura, *Unbroken: A World War II Story of Survival, Resilience, and Redemption*, Random House, New York, 2010

Holmes, Linda Goetz, *Unjust Enrichment: How Japan's Companies Built Postwar Fortunes Using American POWs*, Stackpole Books, Mechanicsburg, PA, 2001

James, D. Clayton, ed., *South to Bataan, North to Mukden: The Prison Diary of Brigadier General W. E. Brougher*, University of Georgia Press, Athens, 1971

Kelly, Arthur L., *BattleFire! Combat Stories from World War II*, The University Press of Kentucky, Lexington, 1997

Kenney, Dave, *Minnesota Goes to War: The Home Front during World War II*, Minnesota Historical Society Press, St. Paul, 2005

Knox, Donald, *Death March: The Survivors of Bataan*, Harcourt, Brace Jovanovich, New York, 1981

Lajzer, Joseph D., *3.6 Years of Hell: In Japanese Prisoner of War Camps 1942–1945*, The Watercress Press, San Antonio, TX, 2002

Lemons, Charles R., *Organization and Markings of US Armored Units 1918–1941*, Schiffer Military History, Altglen, PA, n.d.

Lingeman, Richard R., *Don't You Know There's a War On?*, G. P. Putnam's Sons, New York, 1970

Lord Russell of Liverpool, *The Knights of Bushido: A History of Japanese War Crimes during World War II*, Skyhorse Publishing, Inc., New York, 2008

MacArthur, Douglas, *Reminiscences*, McGraw-Hill, New York, 1964

Mallonée, Richard C. II, *The Naked Flagpole: Battle for Bataan, from the Diary of Richard C. Mallonée*, Presidio Press, San Rafael, CA, 1980

Manchester, William, *American Caesar: Douglas MacArthur 1880–1964*, Little, Brown & Co., Boston, 1978

Martin, Adrian R., and L.W. Stephenson, *Operation Plum: The Ill-Fated 27th Bombardment Group and the Fight for the Western Pacific*, Texas A&M University Press, College Station, TX, 2008

Mayo, Lida, *The Ordnance Department: On Beachhead and Battlefront*, http://www.history.army.mil/html/books/010/CMH_Pub_10-11/index.html

Merriam, Ray, ed., *War in the Philippines 1941–1945*, Military Monograph 91, Merriam Press, Bennington, VT, 2013

Merriam, Ray, ed., *World War II at Sea*, Military Monograph 131, Merriam Press, Bennington, VT, 2013

Mesko, Jim, *M2/M3 Half-Track Walkaround*, Squadron/Signal Armor No. 4, Squadron/Signal Publications, Carrollton, TX, 2004

Michno, Gregory F., *Death on the Hellships: Prisoners at Sea in the Pacific War*, Naval Institute Press, Annapolis, MD, 2001

Military Intelligence Service, *Japanese Land Operations, from Japanese Sources: 12/8/41 to 6/8/42*, Campaign Study No. 3, War Department, Washington DC, 1942

Miller, Edward S., *War Plan Orange: The War Plan to Defeat Japan, 1897–1945*, Naval Institute Press, Annapolis, MD, 1991

Miller, Ernest B., *Bataan Uncensored*, The Hart Publications, Long Prairie, MN, 1949

Miller, J. Michael, *From Shanghai to Corregidor: Marines in Defense of the Philippines*, Marine Corps Historical Center, Washington, DC, 1997

Monterey County Historical Society, *Salinas*, Postcard History Series, Arcadia Publishing, Charleston, SC, 2013

Moore, Stephen L., *As Good as Dead: The Daring Escape of American POWs from a Japanese Death Camp*, Penguin Putnam Inc., New York, 2016

Morison, Samuel E., *History of US Naval Operations in WW II, Vol. III: The Rising Sun in the Pacific*, Little, Brown & Co., Boston, 1948

Morris, Eric, *Corregidor: The American Alamo of World War II*, Stein and Day, New York, 1981

Morton, Louis, *The Fall of the Philippines*, Center of Military History, US Army, Washington, DC, 1953

Morton, Louis, *Strategy and Command: The First Two Years*, http://history.army.mil/html/books/005/5-1/CMH_Pub_5-1.pdf

Norman, Michael, and Elizabeth M. Norman, *Tears in the Darkness: The Story of the Bataan Death March and Its Aftermath*, Picador/Farrar, Straus & Giroux, New York, 2009

Ortega, Abel Jr., *Courage on Bataan and Beyond*, AuthorHouse, Bloomington, IN, 2005

Perrett, Geoffrey, *There's a War to Be Won: The United States Army in World War II*, Ivy Books, New York, 1991

Poweleit, Alvin C., *Kentucky's Fighting 192nd Light GHQ Tank Battalion*, Quality Lithographing Co., Newport, KY, 1981

Poweleit, Alvin C., *USAFFE: The Loyal Americans and Faithful Filipinos*, privately published, 1975

Rightmyer, Bobbi Dawn, and Anna Armstrong, *Harrodsburg*, Images of America, Arcadia Publishing, Charleston, SC, 2011

Robinson, Claudia, ed., *Heroes from the Heartland: Union County Area WW II Vets Chronicled*, Copy Source, Marysville, OH, 2002

Rottman, Gordon, and A. Takizawa, *World War II Japanese Tank Tactics*, Osprey Elite 169, Osprey Publishing, Oxford, England, 2008

Rutherford, Ward, *Fall of the Philippines*, Ballentine Books Inc., New York, 1971

Salecker, Gene E., *Rolling Thunder Against the Rising Sun: The Combat History of U.S. Army Tank Battalions in the Pacific in World War II*, Stackpole Books, Mechanicsburg, PA, 2008

Schultz, Duane, *Hero of Bataan: The Story of General Jonathan M. Wainwright*, St. Martin's Press, New York, 1981

Sides, Hampton, *Ghost Soldiers: The Epic Account of WW II's Greatest Rescue Mission*, Anchor Books/Random House, New York, 2001

Sloan, Bill, *Undefeated: America's Heroic Fight for Bataan and Corregidor*, Simon & Schuster, New York, 2012

Stauffer, Alvin P., *The Quartermaster Corps: Operations vs. Japan*, http://www.history.army.mil/html/books/010/10-14/CMH_Pub_10-14.pdf

Tenney, Lester I., *My Hitch in Hell: The Bataan Death March*, Potomac Books, Inc., Washington, DC, 1995

Thomson, H. C., and Lida Mayo, *The Ordnance Department: Procurement and Supply*, http://www.history.army.mil/html/books/010/CMH_Pub_10-10/index.html

Toland, John, *But Not in Shame: The Six Months after Pearl Harbor*, Random House, New York, 1961

Toland, John, *The Rising Sun: The Decline & Fall of the Japanese Empire 1936–1945* (Vols. 1 and 2), Random House, New York, 1970

Vanderveen, B. H., *M3 Half-Track APC*, Armour in Profile 17, Profile Publications Ltd., Berkshire, England, n.d.

Wainwight, Jonathan M., *General Wainwright's Story*, Robert Considine, ed., Doubleday & Co., Garden City, NY, 1945

Weintraub, Stanley, *Long Day's Journey into War: December 7, 1941*, Truman Talley Books, Dutton, New York, 1991

Whitman, John W., *Bataan: The Last Ditch—The Bataan Campaign*, 1942, Hippocrene Books, New York, 1990

Williams, Mary H., *US Army Chronology 1941–1945*, http://history.army.mil/html/books/011/11-1/CMH_Pub_11-1.pdf

Witten, Sally Sue, *Port Clinton, The Peninsula, and the Bass Islands*, Images of America, Arcadia Publishing, Charleston, SC, 2000

Yeide, Harry, *The Infantry's Armor: The US Army's Separate Tank Battalions in World War II*, Stackpole Books, Mechanicsburg, PA, 2010

Young, Donald J., *The Battle of Bataan: A Complete History*, McFarland and Co. Inc., Jefferson, NC, 2009

Zaloga, Steve, *Early U.S. Armor 1916–40*, Osprey New Vanguard 245, Osprey Publishing, Oxford, England, 2017

Zaloga, Steve, *Japanese Tanks 1939–45*, Osprey New Vanguard 137, Osprey Publishing, Oxford, England, 2007

Zaloga, Steve, *M3 & M5 Light Tank*, Osprey New Vanguard 33, Osprey Publishing, Oxford, England, 1999

Zaloga, Steve, *M3 Infantry Half-Track 1940–73*, Osprey New Vanguard 11, Osprey Publishing, Oxford, England, 1994

Zaloga, Steve, *Stuart: U.S. Light Tanks in Action*, Squadron/Signal Armor 18, Squadron/Signal Publications, Carrollton, TX, 1979

Zaloga, Steve, *U.S. Armour Camouflage and Markings 1917–45*, Osprey Vanguard 39, Osprey Publishing, Oxford, England, 1984

Zaloga, Steve, *U.S. Half-Tracks of World War II*, Osprey Vanguard 31, Osprey Publishing, Oxford, England, 1983

Articles and Unpublished Documents

200th Coast Artillery Regiment, "200th CA Unit History," NARA Philippine Archive, Box 10, Entry 1054, File 500-4, https://www.mediafire.com/file/cd8cmhf64h07vwc/Hunt.zip

American Red Cross, "Prisoners of War Bulletin," Vols. 1–3 (June 43–June 45) + 1 Far East POW Bulletin (Aug. 45)

Anderson, Burton, "Company C, 194th Tank Battalion in the Philippines, 1941–42," http://ciar.org/ttk/mbt/armor/armor-magazine/armor-mag.1996.mj/3c194th96.pdf

Anderson, Burton, "A History of the Salinas National Guard Company 1895–1995," http://www.mchsmuseum.com/news/0410.pdf

Anonymous, "Allied-Axis: The Photo Journal of the 2nd World War issue 29: M3/M3A1 Light Tank," Ampersand Publishing Group, Delray Beach, FL, 2013

Anonymous, "Hellships," https://www.west-point.org/family/japanese-pow/photos.htm

Anonymous, "Thousands Died on 'Hell Ships,'" *The Quan* 55, No. 4, January 2001

Anonymous, "TO 17-55 Armored Battalion, Tank, Light, GHQ Reserve, 11/15/40," U.S. Army Armor School Library

Anonymous, "The T12 Gun Motor Carriage on Bataan," https://bataancampaign.word press.com2014/03/16/the-t12-gun-motor-carriage-on-bataan/

Armor School, "Armor on Luzon," www.benning.army.mil/library/content/Virtual/Armorpapers/Committee%209%20ArmoronLuzon.pdf

Bardowski, Zenon "Bud," 8-22 December 1941 Memoir, 30 handwritten pp. from Iris Chang files

Barnard, Charles N., "Back to Bataan," *Reader's Digest*, December 1980, 59–68

Bashleben, Jim, "Jim Bashleben's Story," unpublished memoir, 1980

Beckenbaugh, Lisa, "Archival Research Memo: Casualties in Philippines POW Camps O'Donnell and Cabanatuan," Memo from Defense POW Missing Personnel Office, revised 3/2/2010

Bernard, George, "Armor in Defense of the Philippines: 8 December 1941–8 January 1942," http://www.benning.army.mil/library/content/Virtual/Armorpapers/Bernard GeorgeL%20CPT.pdf

Biddle, William E., interview in Mayo General Hospital, July 5, 1945

Blumberg, Arnold, "Tanks of the Rising Sun," *World War II* 19 No. 6, October 2004, 58

Bogart, James H., "Jim Bogart's Stories: Company A, 194th Tank Battalion," unpublished manuscript, 1995

Bowles, George, "Surviving the Death March," *Military History*, February 1986, 42–49

Boyd, James, "Biography," http://www.goordnance.army.mil/hof/1990/1990/boyd.html

Brady, William C., "Corregidor: A Name, A Symbol, A Tradition," *Coast Artillery Journal*, July–August 1947, http://www.airdefenseartillery.com/online/2010/Coast%20 Artillery%20Journal/Extract/CA%201947/Jul-Aug%201947.pdf

Braye, William E., "Oryoku Maru," *The Quan* 56, No. 4, January-February 2002

Brown, Charles M., "The Oryoku Maru Story," https://www.oryokumaruonline.org

BuPers, "The March of Death: Official Army-Navy Report on Jap Torture & Murder of POWs," *ex-PW Bulletin*, October 1997, 26–31

Carlson, Carole, "April 9, 1942: Anderson Doctor's Personal Day of Infamy," *Madison County Monthly*, April 1992, 19–20

Center of Military History, "The War Against Japan: Pictorial Record," http://cgsc.con tentdm.oclc.org/cdm/singleitem/collection/p4013coll8/id/3986/rec/10

Chandler, William E., "26th Cavalry (PS) Battles to Glory," *Armored Cavalry Journal*, March-April 1947, 10–16

Chief of Military History, "U.S. Army Order of Battle in the Pacific Theater of Operations," http://cgsc.contentdm.oclc.org/cdm/singleitem/collection/p4013coll8/ id/2984/rec/42

Chunn, Calvin F., "War Diary Recovered from Cabanatuan," NARA File 999-2-214, https://catalog.archives.gov/search?q=*:*calvin%20chunn&f.ancestorNaIds=1255524&highlight=true

Clay, Steven E., "US Army Order of Battle 1919–1941," part 3, http://cgsc.contentdm.oclc.org/cdm/singleitem/collection/p4013coll11/id/2033/rec/5

Clay, Steven E., "US Army Order of Battle 1919–1941," part 4, http://cgsc.contentdm.oclc.org/cdm/singleitem/collection/p16040coll3/id/200/rec/4

Committee 17, Armor School, "Critical Analysis of the History of Armor in World War II," www.benning.army.mil/library/content/Virtual/Armorpapers/Committee%2017%20of%20the%20History%20of%20Armor.pdf

Craft, Joe, *Kentucky National Guard History: World War II—Berlin Crisis 1937–1962*, http://kynghistory.ky.gov/chp+2+craft+co+d+192nd+wwii.htm

Cranston, John, "German and British Experimentation in the 20s & 30s Inspired the Emergence of the U.S. Armored Force," http://ciar.org/ttk/mbt/armor/armor-magazine/armor-mag.1995.ma/2chaffee95.pdf

Davidson, Donald, "Ask Donald Davidson: The Story of WWII POW Bud Bardowski," http://blog.ims.com/index.php/ask-donald-davidson-the-story-of-world-war-ii-pow-bud-bardowski/

Doherty, Tom, "Too Little, Too Late: Janesville's 'Lost Children' of the Armored Force," *Wisconsin Magazine of History* 75 (4), Summer 1992, 243–83

Dooley, Thomas, "The First U.S. Tank Action in World War II," *Armor*, July-August 1983, 10–15

Dopkins, Dale R., "The Janesville 99: A Story of the Bataan Death March," Janesville Public Library, Janesville, WI, 1981

Dupuy Institute, "The Historical Combat Effectiveness of Lighter-Weight Armored Forces—Final Report," http://www.dupuyinstitute.org/pdf/mwa-2lightarmor.pdf

Edwards, Russell W., "And Nobody Gave a Damn," *The Purple Heart Magazine*, March-April 1998, 13–17

Eisenhower, Dwight D., "War Dept. Operations Division Diary 29 March 1942–31 July 1942," http://cgsc.contentdm.oclc.org/cdm/compoundobject/collection/p4013coll8/id/2296/rec/25

Emerson, K. C., "II Corps on Bataan," http://battlingbastardsbataan.com/IIcorps.pdf

Falk, Stanley L., "The Bataan Death March Remembered," *Armor*, April 1967, 44–53

Flores, M. T., "The Defense of Bataan," http://battlingbastardsbataan.com/defenseofbataan.pdf

Fukubayashi, Toru, "POW Camps in Japan Proper," http://www.powresearch.jp/en/archive/camplist/

GHQ Far East Command, "Philippine Air Operations (Japanese)," http://cgsc.contentdm.oclc.org/cdm/singleitem/collection/p4013coll8/id/2345/rec/4

Gibson, Emmett, "Bataan Was Hell," *Chicago Herald*, American 13-part newspaper series, 1942, http://192nd.com

Gladwyn, Lee A., "American POWs on Japanese Ships Take a Voyage into Hell," *Prologue Magazine* 35, No. 4, Winter 2003

Gordon, John, "The Best Arm We Had," *Field Artillery Journal*, November-December 1984

Gordon, Richard M., "Bataan, Corregidor, and the Death March: In Retrospect," http://home.pacbell.net/fbaldie/In_Retrospect.html

Gough, Michael, "Failure and Destruction, Clark Field, the Philippines, December 8, 1941," http://www.militaryhistoryonline.com/wwii/articles/failureanddestruction.aspx#

Graef, Calvin, "We Prayed to Die (Arisan Maru)," *Cosmopolitan*, April 1945

Graves, William, "Corregidor Revisited: 43 Years after the Siege," *National Geographic*, July 1986, 118–29

Grew, "Report of War Crimes Branch on Atrocities (Palawan)," GHQ U.S. Army Forces, Pacific, Office of the Theater Judge Advocate, War Crimes Branch, 1945

Grimes, Marie, and Hat Miller, "Philippine Postscripts 10/43–12/45" (newsletter by POW wives), http://cgsc.contentdm.oclc.org/cdm/singleitem/collection/p4013coll8/id/3961/rec/1

Harris, J. R., "The Harrodsburg Tankers: Bataan, Prison, and the Bonds of Community," *The Register of the Kentucky Historical Society* 86, No. 3, Summer 1988, 230–77

Hilton, Roy C., "G-4 of Luzon Force Report," http://reta.nmsu.edu/bataan/curriculum/resources/historical%20resources/g_4_report.html

Hopper, Aaron Clyde, "My Most Vivid Experiences as an American POW of the Japanese during WW II," privately printed, 1986

Howard, C. P., "Japanese Centrifugal Offensive," http://battlingbastardsbataan.com/centrifugaloffense.pdf

Hudson, Robert Logan, "Draft Rosters of Army POWs Showing Transfers from Bilibid Prison to Other Camps," http://www.west-point.org/family/japanese-pow/Hudson Fast/BilibidDbf.htm

International Red Cross, "Mukden Red Cross Inspection Report," December 6–8, 1944, Exhibit No. 385, http://www.bataanproject.com

Irtani, Evelyn, "The Gripsholm World War II Exchanges," http://encyclopedia.densho.org/The%20Gripsholm%20WWII%20Exchanges/

Jacobs, Bruce, "The Evolution of Tank Units in the Pre-WWII National Guard and the Defense of Bataan," *Military Collector & Historian* 38 (3), Fall 1986, 125–33

Jacobs, Eugene C., "From Guerilla to POW in the Philippines," *Medical Opinion & Review* 5, No. 8, August 1969, 99–119

Johnson, Harold K., "57th Infantry Regiment (PS)," http://battlingbastardsbataan.com/57thonpoints.pdf

Johnson, Shelby, "The Price of Freedom," Collection #AFC/2001/001/02134, Shelby Johnson Collection, Veterans History Project, American Folklife Center, Library of Congress, 2011

Kentucky National Guard, "Provisional Tank Group: U.S. Army Forces in the Far East," http://kynghistory.ky.gov/NR/rdonlyres/B74F1531-DF3A-4954-8BC0-A152DD82ADCD/0/BookletBataanMemorialDedicationHarrodsburg15Jun1961.pdf

King, Edward P., "Report of Operations of the Luzon Force 22 March–8 April 1942," submitted to General Wainwright January 29, 1946, for USFIP Report

Klimow, Matthew S., "Lying to the Troops: American Leaders and the Defense of Bataan," *Parameters*, December 1990, 48–60

Klimow, Matthew S., "Surrender: A Soldier's Legal . . . Obligations, with Philippine Case Study," http://cgsc.contentdm.oclc.org/cdm/singleitem/collection/p4013coll2/id/1468/rec/29

Lauer, Edward T., "Lineage & History of the 32nd Quartermaster Company of the 32nd Division Wisconsin National Guard," 32nd Division Veterans Association, Wauwatosa, WI, n.d.

Lemons, Charles R., "The Heritage of Armor," http://www.benning.army.mil/armor/historian/content/PDF/THE%20HERITAGE%20OF%20ARMOR.pdf

Mansell, Roger, "Osaka POW Camp #4-B—Tanagawa," http://www.mansell.com/pow_reseources/camplists/osake/tanagawa/tanagawa-main.htm

Martin, Brice J., "51st Infantry Regiment (PA)," http://battlingbastardsbataan.com/samat51st.pdf

Matheny, Joe, "Hold Back the Enemy: Tank Battalion Was Ordered to Delay the Japanese Advance," *The World War II Chronicle* 1, No. 3, September-October 1986, 1–5

McCarthy, William R., "The Angels Came at Seven," *The Quan*, November 1980, 9–11

McDonald, Jason, "Imperial Japanese Army 3rd Company, 7th Tank Regiment on Route 5, Luzon," http://worldwar2database.com/gallery/wwii1452

Mead, Everett, "31st Infantry Regiment (US)," http://battlingbastardsbataan.com/31stbataan.pdf

Mendelson, S. H., "Provisional Air Corps Regiment," http://battlingbastardsbataan.com/aircorps.pdf

Menter, John M., and M. R. Evans, "Remember the Road to Bataan: Training for War in a Resource-Short Environment," http://ciar.org/ttk/mbt/armor/armor-mag1998.nd/6bataan98.pdf

Militia Bureau, Annual Report of the Chief of the Militia Bureau (1921), http://books.google.com

Miller, Ernest B., Personal Papers, Dec 1941–Feb 1945, NARA File 999-2-202, https://catalog.archives.gov/

Miller, Roger G., "A 'Pretty Damn Able Commander': Lewis Hyde Brereton, Part II," *Air Power History*, Spring 2001, 22

Mittenthal, Harry H., "Statement on Oryoku Maru," received from James Perry, Monterey County Historical Society, April 2015, original source unknown

Morin, Ben, "My Story," unpublished manuscript, n.d.

Musselmann, Russel G., "Report from Corregidor," *DAV Magazine*, June 1987, 1–6

Muther, Frank, "The Life of Frank Muther," 2006, courtesy of the Monterey County Historical Society

Nealson, W. R., "41st Infantry Regiment (PA)," http://battlingbastardsbataan.com/41stPA.pdf

Nelson, Glen, "Company A 194th Tank Battalion Survivors' Stories," unpublished manuscript, Minnesota National Guard Armory, Brainerd, MN, 1998

Nichok, Harold, "Obituary—James R. N. Weaver 1911," http://apps.westpointaog.org/ Memorials/ Article/4987/

Parish, Phil, "One Thirteen-Millionth," privately printed, n.d.

Peckler, Danae A., "Heroism at Home: The Struggle of the Women—Harrodsburg during World War II," unpublished manuscript, n.d.

Peterson, Ray, Questionnaires from seven 192nd Tank Battalion veterans, received from Ray Peterson

Philippine Supreme Court, Philippines vs. Fortunato Munōz, G.R. No. L-880, http://www.bataanproject.com

Porter, Ray, Maj. Gen. "Adna R. Chaffee Jr.: Father of U.S. Armored Forces," http://arm chairgeneral.com/maj-gen-adna-r-chaffee-jr-father-of-u-s-armored-forces.htm

Quinlen, Clinton D., "Roster of 194th Tank Battalion Officers and Enlisted Men Who Died or Escaped," Philippines Collection File 1000-1-8-3, 1942, received from Karyn Brown

Reed, George, "The 3rd Field Artillery Battalion in the PI, 1941–42," http://books .google.com/

Roosevelt, Franklin D., "The Fireside Chats of Franklin D. Roosevelt," http://docs.fdr library. marist.edu/firesi90.html

Santos, A. M., "1st Infantry Division (PA)," http://battlingbastardsbataan .com/1stregulars.pdf

Schreier, Konrad, "US Army Tank Development 1925–1940," www.benning.army.mil/ armor/eARMOR/content/Historical/Schreier.html

Schutt, Donald A., "Janesville Tankers on Bataan," MS thesis, University of Wisconsin, 1967

Skarden, B. N., "92nd Infantry Regiment (PA)," http://battlingbastardsbataan .com/92ndbataan.pdf

Skinner, Zoeth, "POW Diary," NARA 999-2-209 from Philippine Archives, https:// catalog. archives.gov/search?q=*:*zoeth%20skinner &f.ancestorNaIds=1255524& highlight=true

Slater, Richard R., "And Then There Were None! The American Army Air Corps' Last Stand in the Philippines," *Airpower* 17, No 6, November 1987, 10–29, 47–51

Smith, Robert Barr, "Justice Under the Sun: Japanese War Crime Trials," *World War II* 11, No. 3, September 1996, 38

Sommers, Stan, "The Japanese Story, American ex-POW Inc.," National Medical Research Council, Marshfield, WI, 1980

Steele, Benjamin C., "Benjamin Charles Steele: Prisoner of War," Eastern Montana College, Billings, MT, 1986

Strobing, Irving, "Corregidor's Last Breath," *Coast Artillery Journal*, July-August 1942, 2–3

Tait, Hal, "History of the 17th Ordnance Company (Armored)," received from Karl Rubis, U.S. Army Ordnance School, April 2014

Taylor, Charlie J., "Private Rogers L. Taylor, Prisoner of the Japanese," term paper by grandson

Taylor, Vince, "The General Who Surrendered Bataan: Major General Edward P. King, Jr., and His Diary," http://www.bataanproject.com—original source unknown

Thompson, William D., "History of the Mukden Group," U.S. War Department, 1946

Trapnell, T. J. H., "26th Cavalry Regiment (PS)," http://battlingbastardsbataan .com/26thcav.pdf

Trowbridge, John M., and J. M. LeMay, "Commemorating the Sixty-Sixth Anniversary of the Sixty-Six Harrodsburg Tankers," http://kynghistory.ky.gov/nr/ rdonlyres/93750f85-9d0e-4372-a4e2-839962d4c893/0/bataancommemorative book66thannivexecsize.pdf

Tupas, Rudolfo G., "World War II in the Philippines: Occupation Years, 1942–1945," *The Sunday Times Magazine*, Manila, PI, April 16, 1967

VandenBergh, William, "Employing an Armor Quick Reaction Force in Area Defense," http://www.militarymuseum.org/Bataan.html

VandenBergh, William, "Executing the Double Retrograde Delay," http://www.196rct .org/Apr%2009%20Foxhole.pdf

Veterans Administration, "POW: Study of Former Prisoners of War," Office of Planning & Program Evaluation, Veterans Administration, Washington, DC, 1980

Wacker, Bob, "The Battling Bastards of Bataan," *The Retired Officer Magazine*, March 1992, 40–45

Wallace, Lew, and J. C. Claypool, "Brief Moments of Glory: Weaver's Warriors—the 192th Tank Battalion in the Philippine Islands," *Armor*, January-February 1989, 26–32

Ward, Geoffrey C., "Douglas MacArthur: An American Soldier," *National Geographic* 181 (3), 54–83

Weaver, James R. N., "Operations of the Provisional Tank Group—USAFFE 1941–1942," Office of the Chief of Military History, Dept. of the Army, Washington, DC, 1957

Whitbeck, Therese, "The Bataan Death March: The Official Press Release," American Legion, April 1992

Woodhall, Jeffrey W., "The 26th Cavalry in the Philippines: A Classic Delaying Action," *Armor*, January-February 1983, 8–16

Woolfe, Raymond, "Armored Debut on the Road to Damortis," *World War II* 21 (2), May 2006, 42

Yenne, Bill, "The General Who Panicked the West Coast," *World War II* 32 (2), August 2017, 30

Young, Donald J., "Franklin Roosevelt's Pre-Pearl Harbor Intervention Plans," network .com/daily/franklin-roosevelts-pre-pearl-harbor-intervention-plans

Zapanta, P. A., "World War II in the Philippines: Bataan, 1942 to the Battle of Manila, 1945," *The Sunday Times Magazine*, Manila, PI, April 9, 1967

Zarate, Michael, "Officer Privilege in POW Camps," http://battlingbastardsbataan.com/ officers.pdf

Zich, Arthur, "Hope and Danger in the Philippines," *National Geographic*, July 1986, 76–117

Websites

American Defenders of Bataan and Corregidor Memorial Society, www.dg-adbc.org
Bataan Project (ex–Proviso High School website, webmaster Jim Opolony), www.bataan project.com
Battling Bastards of Bataan, www.battlingbastardsbataan.com
Encyclopedia Densho, http://encyclopedia.densho.org
Japanese WWII POW Camp Fukuoka #17 – Omuta, www.lindavdahl.com
Mansell POW Resources, www.mansell.com
Military History Online, www.militaryhistoryonline.com
Mukden Prisoner of War Remembrance Society, http://mukdenpows.indiemade.com
Oryoku Maru Online, www.oryokumaruonline.org
POW Research Network—Japan, www.powresearch.jp
Quan: Defenders of the Philippines, http://philippine-defenders.lib.wv.us
Wikipedia, www.wikipedia.org
World War 2 Database, www.worldwar2database.com

Interviews

Interviews by the author (A), Iris Chang (C), William J. Dennis of the Kentucky Historical Society (D), Col. Arthur L. Kelly of the University of Kentucky (K), Tony Meldahl (M), James Perry of the Monterey County Historical Society (P), and Thomas Saylor of Concordia University (S).

The PTG veterans and relatives interviewed included Albert Allen (C, M), Joe Riley Anness (D), Andrew Aquila (C), Rae Bardowski (wife of Zenon Bardowski) (C), Steve Bardowski (son of Zenon Bardowski) (C), James Bashleben (C), Grover Brummett (K), Lorraine Diaz (wife of Roy Diaz) (A), Roy Diaz (P), Earl Fowler (D), Morgan French (C, K), William Gentry (D, K), Frank Goldstein (C), Paul Grassick (C, M), Joseph Hrupcho (C), Charles Jensen (C), Eddie Johnson (son of Lyman E. Johnson) (A), Herbert Kirchhoff (C), Harold Kurvers (S), Joseph Lajzer (C), Arnold Lawson (C, D, M), Carl Maggio (C), Edward Martel (C), Lawrence Martin (D), Ben Morin (C, M), Glenn Oliver (S), Abel Ortega (C), William Peavler (D), Kenneth Porwoll (S), Alvin Poweleit (K), Charles Reed (D), Charles Riedmiller (C, M), John Rowland (C), Edwin Rue (D), John Sadler (C), Ardell Schei (C), Walter Straka (A), Lester Tenney (C), Cecil VanDiver (D), Grover Whittingill (D), Ted Wickord Jr. (son of Theodore Wickord) (A), Maurice Wilson (D), Claude Yeast (D).

Index